Fauvism

Origins and Development

MARCEL GIRY

Fauvism

Origins and Development

ALPINE
FINE ARTS
COLLECTION, LTD

PUBLISHERS OF FINE ART BOOKS, NEW YORK

Acknowledgement

We should like to express our warmest gratitude to Professor René Jullian, whose steadfast, generous friendship and constant advice have been an invaluable encouragement.

Our thanks must go to many others who have helped us: relatives and friends of the painters we are dealing with, collectors, owners and directors of galleries, curators of French and foreign museums, critics and colleagues who have seen us, written and assisted us with unfailing kindness.

Here we should like to thank all those who have helped us in any way.

M. G.

© 1981 by Office du Livre, Fribourg, Switzerland
Published in 1982 by Alpine Fine Arts Collection, Ltd.
164 Madison Avenue, New York, New York 10016

Translated from the French by Helga Harrison
French title *Le Fauvisme: ses origines, son évolution*

ISBN: 0-933516-58-4

This book was produced in Switzerland

NOTE Exceptionally French capitalization rules have been followed on the pre-printed captions to the colour plates.

Table of Contents

Preface

In the complex fabric of nineteenth and early twentieth-century French painting Fauvism stands out as a rather odd phenomenon. It had no lengthy preparatory period, although, naturally, it had antecedents; it did not follow a true evolution nor did it develop in a series of successive phases, although there was a certain distinction between different exponents and different periods; finally, it occupied the forefront of the artistic scene for a moment and then ceased without leading to any further development and without leaving any true succession, even if some artists in a more recent generation echo some of the innovations it introduced. In fact, Fauvism is unlike any other movement, from Romanticism to Surrealism, in the history of French painting; it appeared like a meteor in the firmament of French painting, exploded suddenly, imposed itself forcefully, even violently, for three or four years, and then vanished. But this lightning phenomenon, whose brief impetuous outburst and dynamic colour idiom alone warranted the name it acquired by chance, played a vital role in early twentieth-century French painting because of the outstanding quality of its works and its adherents. In the final analysis, it seems far more complex than its short, concentrated history would suggest.

This is clearly shown in Marcel Giry's study which is the authoritative work on Fauvism we have been waiting for. It is surprising that no systematic and exhaustive study had been undertaken previously, although Fauvism as a whole and some of its representatives have often been discussed and these discussions have thrown some light on this or that aspect. But the very concept of Fauvism had remained uncertain and vague, its place in the history of art at the beginning of this century was ill-defined, and the chronology of events and works far from definitive. It was all too common for Fauvism to be seen and assessed in the light in which the journalists of the time had seen and recorded events; anecdote was resorted to more readily than a critical approach. Even trustworthy publications whose contents might be regarded as sound were not free from ambiguities, even errors, as there was no previous sound analysis to which they could refer. M. Giry's work provides both the analysis and the synthesis.

The author has undertaken an extensive investigative project that was far from easy; indeed, he had to start by defining a *corpus* of Fauve pictures, and the one he has used as a basis for this study is as exhaustive as this kind of body can be. This large volume of works then had to be arranged in some sort of chronological order—without which there can be no history—which was a difficult task. The author undertook it with exemplary scholarship, critically examining the documentary evidence and resorting to the most diverse clues in order to pin down often elusive dates; so, for example, in Vlaminck's case the evolution of the artist's signature provided precise points of reference; in some cases the catalogue of an exhibition helped to establish the chronological place of a work, but this kind of document, as we know, often lacks accuracy and sometimes even contains mistakes; in other cases only a detailed analysis

6

enables us to place a work in its exact chronological context, and this method, the trickiest of all, has been used by the author with precision, subtlety, and a breadth of vision which took into account not only the structure of the picture itself but the way it was affected by the events in the artist's life and the incidents in his psychological development.

Placing the whole Fauve output in an orderly sequence and context has enabled M. Giry to illustrate the mechanism, so to speak, that propelled the movement through its brief history. He has done this by reconstituting the creative activity and artistic evolution of the various painters year by year, and has done so in a masterly fashion. He has closely analysed each work by each painter, examined not in isolation but in relation to other pictures by the same painter and to those of his fellow artists. Thus the author gives us a view of things that is not at all unfocused but shows a constant awareness of the complex interaction at different moments and demonstrates the sequences by which these different moments were linked. Although the author traces the history predominantly of events, this approach is essential if we are to gain a sound, firm knowledge of Fauvism and an overall view.

After reading M. Giry's book we really do know what Fauvism means. The author's deep understanding of Fauve painting has enabled him to define its nature more precisely and with a deeper insight than anyone before him. Previously the entire emphasis was placed, rather superficially, on the arbitrarily violent colour, whereas, in fact, the crux of the matter lay in the relationship between these violent, arbitrary colours and the painter's experience of the world, especially of space. This was the central problem around which the Fauves conducted their pictorial experiments, and it was in this perspective that M. Giry has studied the evolution of each endeavour and of the respective role and importance it assumed. The complex and often subtle tangle of relationships between experiments constitutes the reality of Fauvism, and it is perhaps the nature of its quest which accounts for the concentration and briefness of its history.

But Fauvism must also be seen in a broader context, and the author has realized this fully. He has defined the place of Fauvism—with the necessary reservations—in the currents of its contemporary thought and has linked the Fauve experiments with some of the pictorial experiments of the previous century which the Fauves might have used, for nothing is created in a void. The light he sheds on these points enables us to gain a better understanding of the upsurge, around 1905, of Fauve painting, although this event, perhaps more than other similar happenings, had something unexpected about it. In the conclusion the author widens his study to encompass the broader setting of Fauvism which affected other painters in various ways—some created a softened version of it whereas others saw it as a springboard for further experiments. M. Giry's book finally places Fauvism in its correct context, making it one of the basic works on early twentieth-century painting. It throws light on one of its essential aspects, and for anyone who may want to write about Fauvism in the future it will be a bright beacon by which he will have to steer.

René Jullian

Foreword

From 1904 onward certain painters evolved a new system of artistic expression which, in 1905, was jokingly dubbed "Fauve" (wild beast). We shall try to follow and analyse the creative development of these artists. Our study ends in 1907, because from that time onward most of the Fauve painters ceased to use the figurative method they had perfected until then, and even those who more or less continued to use it did so without adding anything new.

We have concentrated on eight painters: Braque, Derain, Dufy, Friesz, Marquet, Matisse, Van Dongen and Vlaminck. First of all, because their place in the Fauve group is uncontested and unanimously acknowledged by the protagonists themselves. Secondly, we have made our selection on the basis of a precise definition of Fauvism we have formulated. This excludes such artists as Camoin, Manguin and Puy, whose attachment to Fauvism was superficial: all they took from the Fauve manner was a vivid palette without renouncing their fundamentally traditional artistic approach.

We shall be dealing with the Fauve painters in the order commonly adopted by art critics: first, Matisse and Marquet, who can legitimately be placed at the beginning as they were the oldest and were pupils of Moreau at the same time. Then Derain, Vlaminck and Van Dongen, who met at Chatou and Montmartre. Finally, Dufy, Friesz and Braque, who were rather younger, all came from Le Havre, and were all inscribed in Bonnat's studio. But this must not be taken to mean that the Fauves can be divided into groups according to age, studio or hometown. In fact, there was a certain pairing off according to the affinities of the moment in which not only the degree of comradeship but, above all, the interest in certain artistic experiments played a major part.

This is intended to be a critical history of the system of artistic expression called Fauvism, a study of its origins, its development, and its meaning This is vital if we want to understand Fauve works correctly and assess their true place in the history of twentieth-century painting.

Introduction   Fauvism and reality

The historians of Fauvism have very recently[1] been reproached with a lack of precision in their classification, their tendency to regard the nickname "Fauve" (wild beast) coined by Louis Vauxcelles[2] as a concept, which then in its turn is interpreted as something specific so that they have linked Fauvism itself to its given name. Another objection that has been raised is the fact that the content and boundaries of Fauvism have varied according to the ideas of the author.

It is certainly true that Fauvism did not come into being simply because of the name by which Vauxcelles christened it; it sprang from a desire for renewal in painting among young artists who, in 1905, were defining a new figurative system in their works. The use of vivid colours has quite wrongly been singled out as its main feature, whereas the new approach to space has been ignored although it is far more important. What we are actually witnessing is the evolution of a new form of pictorial representation which was shaped progressively and perfected by 1906. The fact that these artists were described in a certain way does not alter the fact that they were the authors of a new system of artistic expression. We also contest the varying interpretations that have been given to the content and boundaries of Fauvism. We shall define the Fauve system in a way that will show why a Valtat, for example, does not belong to it; and we shall also see that the system did not exist before the end of 1904 and that the year 1907 marked its close.

We give the name Fauvism to a set of works produced in France during the period 1904-7 by a group of painters who deliberately and consciously elaborated a specific figurative system which we must clarify before we can discuss its history.

The nickname "Fauve", coined casually by Vauxcelles, has certainly proved a nuisance and bedevilled the fate of this new system of painting by obscuring its true meaning. In fact, the very word used by the critic when he was looking for a strong term to describe the colourful appearance of a painting unconsciously betrays an ideology still current at the time which condemned excessive colouring and gave priority to drawing and composition. This was the ideology at the bottom of the dispute over Caillebotte's legacy and why Delacroix's "drunken brush" had recently been condemned. Colour was still regarded as the "animal part of art", to quote Ingres, to whom, incidentally, the 1905 Salon d'Automne devoted a retrospective homage. When *L'Illustration* ironically drew its readers' attention to the reproduction of some of the canvases noticed by the critics at that Salon, it chose those they had singled out for the brightness of their colouring, thus missing the basic aims of the painters. Above all, to make fun of them, it pointed scornfully to such "colourists" as Matisse, Puy, Rouault, Vuillard, Henri Rousseau, Guérin and Cézanne, whose experiments had very little in common. But *L'Illustration*, the vehicle of the predominant ideology, also had to hold up to ridicule—in the name of Ingres's old precept that "drawing is the probity of art"—those painters who set little store by drawing and composition. Critics hostile to avant-garde art used such words as "spineless" and "incoherent" more often than "Fauve" when passing judgment on the friends of

Matisse, who thought an unfinished form more expressive than a fully defined one. In these circumstances, young painters who sought to change the traditional means of artistic expression clearly could not hope for understanding even from someone like Vauxcelles, the ambiguous champion of modern art. Moreover, his term "Fauve" was considered so inept by those to whom it applied that it was not used inside the group until 1907: the painters themselves felt no need for a label.

It is essential, if we are to know precisely what we are talking about, to define Fauvism, to ask what its distinguishing qualities are.

These distinguishing characteristics do not spring from a pre-defined doctrine: the Fauves could only be hostile to restricting theories. They clearly realized that any predetermined doctrine carries the risk of academism (as is shown by Neo-Impressionism)—the very thing against which they rebelled. The identity of Fauvism was forged through dynamism and action. It was also achieved through consultation. For although we cannot speak of a "school", there nevertheless was a group of artists, and within it special relationships were formed between individuals. These relationships were interchangeable, being formed or strengthened when the artists met, generally during a trip, and compared their different experiments. As a rule, each of the Fauve painters would at one time or other work with one of his fellow artists who had himself worked, or was about to work, with one of the others in the group; thus ideas were exchanged and discussed by "pairs", but these pairs were never the same: for instance, there were Matisse and Marquet in Paris, Matisse and Derain at Collioure, Marquet and Dufy at Le Havre, Derain and Vlaminck at Chatou, Vlaminck and Van Dongen at Montmartre, Friesz and Braque in Antwerp. These periods of collaboration naturally gave the group a great deal of homogeneity, and they quickly developed a common point of view. It seems that they actually discussed theory more frequently than has generally been thought. Valtat, Manguin and Camoin, who associated with the Fauves, tell us that the disquisitions of Matisse and Derain sometimes exhausted them. Friesz mentions discussions at Matisse's, on the Quai Saint-Michel, and numerous meetings with Derain. It would be an exaggeration to say that Matisse was the leader of the group, but it is certainly true that he was a respected elder; we know (all his friends have said so) that his works were widely exhibited and aroused great interest. Derain, although much younger, seems to have played a similar role. The Fauves were thus not without a theory or without exemplars. They had a very clear idea of where they wanted to go.

The Fauve painters did not lay down any preconceived rules on the subjects to be chosen nor did they decide on a scale of values in the subject-matter that differed very much from that of their predecessors. Landscape retained pride of place, to be followed at a great distance by still lifes and portraits. Fauvism defined its original aims and proposed the innovatory relationship between artist and nature through its treatment of problems of landscape. Still lifes and portraits were incidental: they were not central to style. No special problem was ever posed by the portrait that differed in essence from that governing the relationship between artist and nature. For example, it did not challenge ideas on man's position in society. The scope offered by the human figure for the artist's visual and imaginative experimentation is neither more nor less than that of landscape.

The essence of Fauvism lay in a novel way of conceiving the world, of regarding nature not as the subject of art but as a realm in which the painter's own impulses, his emotional and mental tensions, his imagination could find release. Drawing and colour must obviously have the utmost freedom in the way they express reality. The Fauve picture is a lyrical explosion whose brilliant colouring is the most spectacular feature, but—we must reiterate—one that must not be seen out of its context. Fauvism does not consist simply of the use of arbitrary colours but is created by the painter's realization that a harmony of colours unconnected with reality expresses the relationship between his ego and the world.

To the problem of space—so vital in pictorial expression—the Fauves apply a logical solution based on the rejection of objective representation and of naturalism. For illusionary space they substitute space transposed by feeling and imagination, a poetical space, a reinvention of reality. This space is expressed three-dimensionally by means of pure, equally saturated colours. Colour plays the part of a subjective and emotional equivalent of space and of one of its components, light. We can never put too much emphasis on the originality of this theory of space which we find in embryo in the works of Gauguin and Cézanne, but which the Fauves perfected in the summer of 1905.

We can thus see the importance of colour in the Fauve system, but to speak of the primacy of colour, to say—as is so often claimed—that colour reigns supreme is wrong. The imagination reigns supreme. It acts first on the field of chromatic expression, then on that of drawing. This second phase, which is so often misunderstood, is vital: it constitutes the most Dionysiac stage of Fauvism, which for some Fauves came as early as 1906, for others in 1907, and was the ultimate phase, leading to distortion and possibly opening the way to abstract art for those who did not reject it.

We can legitimately speak of a Fauve system composed of a specific set of specific features. But to say that this or that work belongs to the system simply because one of these features is or is not present makes nonsense. We must not think that Fauvism is achieved by the simple addition of certain characteristics. The Fauve picture is created by the relationship between these constituent elements. Thus we might have the contradiction of a work with a naturalist approach, a traditional conception of space without lyricism and yet at the same time with a vivid, somewhat arbitrary palette. This is why a Manguin or a Valtat, for instance, generally remains outside the Fauve system.

Between 1904 and 1907 the Fauves did some original thinking on the problems facing them and found innovatory artistic solutions. They had a rebellious, questing spirit, and a desire to break with the past (especially Impressionism) which has often been neglected. They avoided slavish subservience to any model, however prestigious. But of course this does not mean that they refused to learn from those masters with whom they felt an affinity.

The Fauve system certainly has more than one thing in common with German Expressionist art. Critics have recently tended to associate Fauvism and the *Brücke* in a general movement of European painting towards Expressionism between 1900 and 1910. It is nevertheless admitted that the two are not identical. Some critics, however, have gone so far as to deny that there is any distinction between them,[3] on the grounds that differences were due only to nationalist, racist or competitive considerations, and have suggested that the term Fauve should be applied both to the art of the French Fauves and to that of the painters of the *Brücke*.

Here we shall not attempt to solve this problem. Perhaps it is a legitimate point of view: Fauvism and the *Brücke* might well constitute a single "systematic unit". We do not reject this view out of hand but we would have to see a comparative study in depth to be wholly convinced. Meanwhile, we shall consider Fauvism a specific system separate from the *Brücke*. We shall therefore deal with the history of Fauvism, a coherent, logical figurative system which "came about" in the course of months and years as a result of agreed principles which are clearly demonstrated in the works themselves.

Our approach is mainly chronological. Our chapters constitute so many phases illustrating the dynamic construction of a new method of pictorial expression, the simultaneity of the problems facing different painters, and the coherence of their artistic idiom. We feel that the year-by-year framework we have chosen is in line with reality. Each year marks a definite phase, with its two Salons, the Salon des Indépendants in spring, which exhibited works produced in winter, and the Salon d'Automne, which showed those executed in summer. Each Salon d'Automne played an important part, not only for the public and the critics, but inside the Fauve group itself, where problems were mulled over and concentrated on more intensely through the winter, so that the following Salon des Indépendants often represented the outcome of all their thinking. The Salon d'Automne marks the end of summer, always a period of intensive work for the Fauves. Therefore we place special emphasis on these two annual Salons, and we shall try to identify the works submitted to each by the artists which will give us clear points of reference.

We attach the utmost importance to the problem of dating these works. No serious art-historical study can be undertaken without a prior chronological arrangement of artistic output. We must avoid the absurdity of discoursing on the artistic evolution of such and such a painter on the basis of works whose date is uncertain. We have no intention whatever of following a current fashion in art criticism that consists of pontificating on art with no regard for historical accuracy.

We think it best to consult the works themselves, for we shall find that a critical analysis of them is the most reliable method. We shall use the artists' written or spoken words with the utmost caution. More often than not we are dealing with remarks made long after the event, so that they lose immediacy; we must remember, too, that they lose all meaning if we do not know the context in which they were made. We shall be equally cautious about contemporary judgments expressed in newspapers and specialized periodicals of the time: the fact that they were contemporary with the events treated is no guarantee of their value. We feel it is far wiser to rely on the works themselves.

Chapter I   New ideas, proposals and exemplars

Anarchism

The painters who worked on the renewal of artistic expression and who were between twenty and thirty years old in 1905 had been born, mostly into rather modest families, shortly after the defeat of 1870 and the events of the Commune. They reached their majority at a time when France was shaken and divided by the Dreyfus affair, which challenged all existing ideologies. For a time the Universal Exhibition of 1900 had a reassuring effect and reinforced the myth of the "belle époque"—good times for the middle classes who had grown rich in trade and industry, good times for the conformist artists who catered to them, but not so good for artists like Matisse and Marquet who, in order to make a little money, had to paint patterns on the cornices of the Grand Palais. But the calm was deceptive. The exhibition itself revealed the discrepancy between the display of industrialized European civilization and the so-called primitive civilizations of the Far East, Africa and the South Sea Islands. This discrepancy strengthened the movement—born in the 1890s—that questioned the expanding industrial civilization and the science that promoted it. In fact, protest was widespread. It was a time of challenge to accepted values, of lack of faith in government, justice, the army, the church, and the economic system. It was only natural that the Fauves, like so many young people, were anti-clerical, anti-militarist, anti-conformist, even anarchist. Their artistic ideals went hand in hand with their social ideals. It is revealing that

Derain and Vlaminck used an anarchist vocabulary when speaking of painting: the former said that his colours became sticks of dynamite, the latter wanted to set fire to the Ecole des Beaux-Arts with his cobalts and his vermilions. And perhaps the predilection for red, the colour of fire, of blood, of violence, was the result of an unconscious choice on the part of Ravachol's disciples. Yet by 1900-5 anarchism no longer was an active, violent movement in France; there was no more bomb-throwing—anarchism had become a rather tame tavern affair. Nevertheless it still attracted some young writers and artists. Vlaminck, a fervent supporter of Dreyfus, remained an out-and-out anarchist. During his military service he formed part of a group that followed the "Dreyfus affair" with passionate interest, and subsequently he continued to move in "libertarian" circles. Derain discovered during his military service that many of his fellow-soldiers were anarchists. He was indignant when his regiment was asked to intervene against strikers at Calais. "I am at the strikes," he wrote to Vlaminck. "Can you imagine a Derain, with strap under his chin, holding down the strikers? What an irony!... Regiments are arriving daily, and the officers rouse their men against the strikers. The miners are starving to death and they realize that their lives are at stake. All this is getting very very ugly, although the papers don't talk about it."[4] When Van Dongen arrived in Paris, Félix Fénéon introduced him to anarchist circles, notably the Le Barc de Boutteville gallery popular with Neo-Impressionist painters like Signac, Cross and Luce, all friends of Jean Grave, the director of the paper *Le Révolté*. Dufy was harassed by the police for sheltering Maurice Delcourt. But all this did not really amount to very much. The Fauves, or more precisely some of them, contented themselves with collaborating on such satirical reviews as *Le Rire* and *L'Assiette au beurre*. Those who, around 1906-7, described the Fauves as a "Judeo-Masonic clique"[5] were way behind the times. It is an interesting fact that several Fauves (especially anarchists or their sympathizers) lived in Montmartre, which was represented in the Chamber of Deputies by Marcel Sembat, the Socialist, one of the first to take an interest in Fauve painting and one of the earliest admirers of Matisse.

It was very natural for the Fauves to be close to the anarchists: fighting against conventional bourgeois art leads to fighting the established order that upholds it. This was Courbet's attitude, and also that of Pissarro, precisely the man to whom some of the Fauves went most readily for advice. In *La Rénovation esthétique*, Emile Bernard, who liked killing two birds with one stone, wrote virulent articles against anarchism in politics as well as in art. But the Fauves' anarchist convictions were ephemeral. In 1905 Derain said that it irritated him to meet anarchists everywhere. "I have met yet another anarchist", he wrote to Vlaminck. "Wherever I go, I run into anarchists, who regularly destroy the world in the evening and rebuild it the next morning. It annoys me no end, especially to think that I used to be one of them." Apart from Vlaminck, who continued to sympathize with the anarchists until 1914, all the Fauves were completely integrated into bourgeois society by 1907, i.e. when they had signed contracts with art dealers and Fauvism came to an end. They probably had never really believed, deep down, that art was compatible with revolutionary socialism.

Gide

One of the basic tenets of anarchism is the total championship of the individual. This idea is in some ways similar to that expressed by André Gide in 1897 in *Les Nourritures terrestres*. "Cling only", he said to Nathanael, "to what you feel in yourself that is nowhere but in yourself, and created by yourself, patiently or impatiently, you, the most unique of beings." There are several parallels between the Fauves and Gide's philosophy. Gide exalted the cult of life, that state of ardour in which the individual fulfils himself: he rehabilitated feeling. "It isn't enough for me to read that the sand on the beaches is soft: I must feel it with my bare feet. All knowledge that is not preceded by sensation is useless." *L'Immoraliste*, published in 1902, pursued this egocentric quest with the additional mandatory demolition of traditional moral notions. We might say that Gide's attitude toward literature, striving to renew writing and irritated by its symbolism, is the equivalent of the Fauves' reaction against the sterility of official art, against the excesses of a pictorial symbolism that loses itself in anecdote. Of course, there is no more than a certain similarity between Gide and the Fauves: they never proposed a precise responsibility for the author in the construction of their pictorial system. For his part Gide, far from recognizing an affinity between his writing and Fauve painting, was even unable to discern the Dionysian frenzy in it. As we shall see, his judgment of Matisse reveals a total lack of understanding. A perusal of his *Journal* (Diary) shows that, in 1906, he was interested predominantly in classical art: he was reading *La Méthode des classiques français* by Paul Desjardins, which had been recommended to him by his friend Maurice Denis. At that time the objectives of "Naturism", which had been revived by the poet Saint-Georges de Bouhélier, were not wholly unlike those pursued by Gide. The Naturists wanted to counteract what André Billy called "Symbolist lethargy and Parnassian sterility".[6] They chose to call themselves "barbarians" and proclaimed the return to nature, to simplicity, to a joyful acceptance of the world. In a lecture on Charles-Louis Philippe delivered at the Salon d'Automne on 5 November 1910, André Gide quoted a letter written by the poet during the Naturist period in which we can recognize some echoes of Gauguin, whom the Fauves regarded as one of the masters. "We need barbarians now. We must be able to live very close to God without having read about Him in books, we need a vision of a natural life, we need strength, even fury. The time for gentleness and dilettantism is past. This is the beginning of the age of passion."[7] This rejection of dreamy symbolism in favour of a cult of life is also found in Fernand Gregh, the creator of "Humanism", whose doctrine was close to that of Saint-Georges de Bouhélier. In *Le Figaro* in December 1902, F. Gregh wrote: "We are neither mystics nor sceptics. We are steeped in life: it must be understood and lived." It is interesting to note that Humanism sympathized with anarchist and trade union movements—an attitude, if the truth were told, shared by most intellectual currents of the time.

We do not know if the Fauve painters actually met the writers and poets we have mentioned, but even if they did not, they would probably be familiar with the main lines of their philosophy, for the Fauves certainly read the reviews of the period. Derain read *La Revue Blanche*; Vlaminck was very much in tune with his time when he wrote about love (a trifle vulgarly) and life in his first novels.

The Nietzsche cult

It is certain that some of the Fauves were influenced by the philosophy of Nietzsche. During the last years of the nineteenth century the ideas of the German philosopher began to be widely known. Extracts from his works appeared in *L'Ermitage*, *Le Mercure de France* and *La Revue Blanche* in 1893 and 1894. At that time Henri Albert went to work on the translation of Nietzsche's complete works, and in 1898 published *Thus Spake Zarathustra*, printed by *Le Mercure de France*, which had become the focal point of the growing interest in Nietzsche's philosophy. In January and February 1900 the same magazine, *Le Mercure*, published articles by Jules de Gaultier, who dwelled on the anti-rationalist and individualist basis

of Nietzsche's ideology, and on the lyrical flights of the imagination that abound in *Thus Spake Zarathustra*. It is reasonable to suppose that Nietzsche's exaltation of life and his joyous individualism were regarded at the time as a reaction against *fin-de-siècle* pessimism and morbidity. Another aspect of Nietzsche's thought that was seized on was his defence of paganism, the Dionysian cult, against Christianity, his glorification of the Latin spirit at the expense of the Germanic spirit. This attitude made Nietzsche appear as the prophet of the "Mediterranean cult", the philosopher of the Mediterranean landscape which the Fauves loved so much.

It is obvious that around 1900, young people—not only writers but also painters—could not fail to be attracted by the ideas of Nietzsche, who proposed a new code of conduct and stimulated their search for a fresh artistic approach. A passage from *Thus Spake Zarathustra* quoted by Jules de Gaultier could be taken as a sort of partial manifesto of Fauvism: "It is a taste, a new appetite, a new gift of seeing colours, of hearing sounds, of experiencing emotions that had hitherto been neither seen, heard nor felt."[8] We have proof that Derain and Vlaminck launched on a discussion of Nietzsche in 1900, which was continued in 1901 in the letters Derain, then on military service, wrote to Vlaminck. When Derain quoted Nietzsche he did so in the manner of one who was familiar with the philosopher's ideas. Thus, when he was trying to explain that the unifying factor is the essence of the individual and of his work, the value that remains constant in spite of the passage of time, he said: "According to the language of Nietzsche, a 'value unity'." Indeed, that entire letter is imbued with Nietzsche's thought as well as with a Gide-like feeling for life. Derain wrote: "Any motive for expression must spring from the happiness we first have in feeling, then the passion that compels us to embody our feelings to provide complete proof of the existence of our being. This is the expansion of a lofty egotism." Some years later, no doubt in 1907, Derain again wrote to his friend: "The more I think of Nietzsche, the more he amazes me."[9]

The Bergson cult

During the period of the Fauves, Bergsonian philosophy was a burning contemporary issue, but it is not certain that Bergson's ideas attracted the Fauves as much as Nietzsche's. There can be no doubt that the *Essai sur les données immédiates de la conscience*, published in 1889, *Le Rire*, which appeared in 1900, and various articles by the philosopher in the *Revue de métaphysique et de morale*, in 1903, were far too specialized to be read by the painters, even if they had been sure of finding something relevant in them. However, the case of *L'Evolution créatrice*, which appeared in 1907, was rather different. Not that the Fauves were any more likely to read that work, which was as daunting as the others and which in any case appeared too late, but we know that the course Bergson gave at the Collège de France during the year 1904-5 contained the basic ideas of the later *L'Evolution créatrice*, notably the theory of the *élan vital* (vital impetus). His attentive listeners included Tancrède de Visan, who imparted his enthusiasm for Bergsonian philosophy to his friends in the *Verse and Prose* group at their meeting in the Closerie des Lilas. Did any Fauves attend these meetings? Apparently not. Derain and Vlaminck did not associate with Apollinaire and André Salmon before 1907. Although André Rouveyre was a friend of Marquet, it is highly unlikely that the writer would take the painter along to the Closerie. But, however that may be, powerful and original ideas always circulate and become widely known. We do not have to assume that the Fauves read Bergson's writings or that they argued about them in taverns; they could have known their general content from all sorts of ideas that had gained currency. The Fauves knew perfectly well that Bergson considered artists as visionaries, lyricists able to reveal the true reality that is hidden behind appearances, "to penetrate beneath the surface", as the philosopher said, and that his doctrine clearly justified their faith in an art form that rejected a naturalist representation of the world. There is, for instance, a certain similarity—within limits—between Bergson's quest for a

16

1. Maurice Denis *La petite fille à la robe rouge*, 1899.

2. Odilon Redon *Le Bouddha*, 1905.

3. Gustave Moreau *Jupiter et Sémélé*, 1895.

4. Matisse *La cour du moulin, Corse*, 1898.

deep reality behind outward appearances and Matisse's striving to go beyond the superficial, ephemeral sensations to reach the state he called "condensation of sensations", the stuff of which the picture is made. And, whether consciously or not, the Fauve conception of space leans on a philosophy of space which, in its turn, depends on a philosophy of the relationship between the subject and the world, in this case Nietzsche's and Bergson's.

It would be wrong to believe that the progressive, avant-garde current of thought we have been discussing was the sole predominant one and that it was universally accepted during the whole of the Fauve period. The crisis of the 1890s gave rise to two opposing currents. The first, which we might describe as anarchist and vitalist, agreed with the spirit of Fauvism. But the other, which was conservative and nationalist, extolled the return to traditional and nationalist values in literature and art. The Fauves, as we shall see, were not wholly unaware of this second tendency, which was to some extent responsible for bringing about the end of their movement. In 1891 Jean Moréas created the *Ecole romane* (Romanesque school) which he claimed was not only an aesthetic necessity but a patriotic duty. Fernand Fleuret belonged to the group; he was a friend of Friesz, with whom he spent the winter of 1907 in the South. The Fauvist painter's sudden interest in Poussin may have had something to do with this friendship. Charles Maurras, another distinguished member, extolled the Grand Siècle to vindicate the monarchy: his monarchism was a call for the restoration of French culture through a return to classicism. His dream of a classical renaissance was shared by many, such as Maurice Denis, for whom the Fauves always made more than generous allowance.

We must remember that in art any system is linked to a particularly congenial form of intellectual activity. In the case of Fauvist painting it hinged basically on the anarchist and vitalist trends we have analysed, and at the same time it was a painterly response to the problems that faced the Fauves in their day. It was their way of reacting to the trauma of the emerging industrial society, a way of eliminating science and reason from artistic expression; to replace them with faith in a simple, direct, even frugal art; a need to escape from the life they saw and lived—hence their total recourse to the imagination through which they got away from a disappointing reality; and to assert the existence of a subjective reality that could be communicated by means of suggestion, by equivalents. Nor would it be wrong to see in the concise, quick, rather violent Fauve form of expression the translation of a life-affirming attitude geared to the accelerated rhythm of modern life. Derain and Vlaminck dreamed of owning a car or a motor-cycle; they did not regard speed as an obstacle to the perception of nature, but rather the contrary.

We must use the greatest caution in identifying the artistic sources that might have inspired the Fauves and been used by them.

Most works on Fauvism try to quote as many names as possible of artists who, it is claimed, have some connection with Fauve art. This is not a very satisfactory procedure and is apt to lead to two errors.

The first of these is an excessive faith in the theory that each artistic movement engenders the next. This implies that any artistic movement must be explained in the light of the past. It is rare, especially in art, to find the present dovetailed neatly into the past. Fernand Léger bears this out: "All great artistic movements", he writes, "have always proceeded by revolution, by reaction, and not by evolution."[10] M. Denis, in 1904, noted the existence of this kind of dynamism: "This is the age of temperament, of personalities", he wrote. "Each develops in isolation and tries to re-create, like some Robinson Crusoe on his island, an individual aesthetic and a technique solely through his own experience and by dint of his genius."[11] We must not ignore the fact that artists worthy of that name have often been inspired by a determination to break with past formulae and by an urge for renewal and original creation. We are too apt to forget that a young painter who wants to become a creator and not just to reproduce school formulae does not want to continue in the footsteps of ancient or recent masters, however prestigious. On the contrary, he will want to rebel against them in order to assert himself. To speak of a source of Fauve painting each time we discover a similarity between a certain feature of the Fauve system and a certain feature of an earlier system hardly makes sense. It is equally misleading to enumerate all possible sources, as if the sum total of sources automatically constituted a system of artistic expression. Fauvism can hardly be said to issue from the union of the arts of Signac, van Gogh, Cézanne and Gauguin. Fauvism is not—any more than any other movement—just the sum total of acquired parts.

A second error, which consists of relying on outward appearances, on vague resemblances between works, can lead to a host of misunderstandings. These facile misleading comparisons apply primarily to colour. The so-called sources quoted by critics nearly always consist of painters who have used vivid colours. This comes from the faulty definition of Fauvism we have rejected earlier. To think that Fauvism is no more than a form of art using pure colour would suggest to the naive a whole string of colourist painters who could have been its inspiration. This would not matter so much if critics did not immediately speak of influence whenever one or another similarity has been detected. It is hazardous to assert that a certain artist has exerted an influence on a Fauve painting solely because the works have some features in common.

We will avoid drawing up a supposedly exhaustive catalogue of close or distant sources that might theoretically have contributed to Fauve art; nor will we track down similarities and analogies. But we shall not fail to mention any documented or even probable case where ideas from a past art system or from various artists—mostly older ones, whether still living at the time or recently dead—seem to have helped the Fauves resolve their problems. But these were merely contributory ideas to which we must not attach too much importance.

Just as the Fauves acquired a new state of mind, a new code of human conduct from a certain current of thought, so they acquired a new code of conduct as painters from certain systems of artistic expression, certain artists and certain works. The painters who, around 1905, were striving to elaborate a new artistic idiom were able to find usable material in the work of others. We shall now examine and analyse this material.

Delacroix

We know for certain that the Fauves were interested in the art of Delacroix, which, as we may recall, had been restored to favour by Signac's *D'Eugène Delacroix au néo-impressionisme*, published in 1898 and 1899. In 1903 Derain wrote to Vlaminck: "Delacroix deserves our closest attention and understanding: he has opened the door to our age." At the time of writing this, Derain was copying *The Massacre at Chios* in the Louvre. At that same time, in the Museum of Rouen, Friesz and Dufy were lost in admiration before *La Justice de Trajan* (Justice of Trajan). "It was a revelation", Dufy said, "and certainly made one of the most powerful impressions in my life." What in Delacroix's painting could be of use to the Fauves? Not the historical or literary subjects, nor the romantic approach. The interest the Fauves had in Delacroix was centred entirely on the problem of using colour as a means of expression. Delacroix was perhaps the first painter for whom colour was no longer subjected to a prior drawing. He dissociated it from the contour line, abandoned what we might call "colouring", which means applying colour after the composition has been drawn. In this way he endowed colour with a power of expression, a lyrical strength untapped until then. By giving colour a moral sense Delacroix was able to go beyond narrative, beyond anecdote; the symbolism is no longer strictly dependent on the subject but is also expressed by painterly means. This was the aspect of Delacroix's art that principally aroused van Gogh's admiration. At a time when there was a reaction—of which the Fauve painters naturally approved—against the excess of descriptive symbolism in literature, Delacroix's teaching would obviously seem greatly relevant to them. We must remember, too, that in Delacroix's work colour plays a dynamic part in the rendering of space. This was of great interest to the Fauves although Delacroix did not provide them with a complete solution to the problem of space in the manner in which they posed it. In Delacroix's picture colour never is the sole component of space: it is combined with a traditional system of perspective that Delacroix never queried. There were other boundaries which the romantic painter never crossed. However vivid and warm his colours may be, they were never pure; and they were less arbitrary than van Gogh thought, although Delacroix admittedly made no dogma out of respect for local colour. When we bear in mind, too, that Delacroix liked the unfinished form, we may say that the dismantling of pictorial naturalism really began with him. The Fauves would certainly be well aware of this fact.

Ingres

We might expect that the Fauves would regard Ingres, the anti-Delacroix, with indifference or even hostility. But this was not the case. Indeed, there is no reason why one should not see him as a non-realist capable of daring distortion, stylization, even abstract art. Moreover, Ingres's habit of painting in vivid colours, often a far cry from the local colour, was echoed in the Fauves' own experiments. Matisse thought Ingres was the first to use pure colours and to contain them without adulterating them. In homage to Ingres, the Salon d'Automne of 1905 exhibited sixty-eight of his works, which the Fauves, especially Matisse, examined with great interest. Ingres was certainly instrumental in leading Matisse in 1906—before Islamic art—to the discovery of the lyrical possibilities of the arabesque; this, together with the lyrical power of colour, doubled, so to speak, the expressiveness of a picture. There is no doubt that Matisse's *Le Bonheur de vivre* (Joy of Living; Pl. 69) (Barnes Foundation)

did not simply pick out the iconographic themes from Ingres's composition of the *L'Age d'or* (The Golden Age; Pl. 43) (Fogg Art Museum), of which the Fauve painters had seen a drawing at the Salon d'Automne of 1905.

Impressionism

The relationship between the Impressionists and the Fauves was more complex. The Fauve movement was fundamentally opposed to Impressionism, questioning its naturalist and momentary approach to the physical world, its illusionist concept of space and the passive attitude of the artist. This was the unambiguous position of Derain, who totally rejected any form of Impressionist experiment. When he told Vlaminck that he "adored Claude Monet", he explained that it was "precisely because of his mistakes, which have been a lesson to me"; he himself was looking for something different, "exactly the opposite, whatever is permanent, eternal, complex." Although most of the Fauves went through an Impressionist phase, they were not particularly orthodox and they broke decidedly with it as soon as they awoke to the need for a novel form of artistic expression. The differences between Impressionism and Fauvism are so great that it is difficult to regard the former as an intrinsic source of the latter: logically Impressionism cannot lead to Fauvism.

However, it would seem that the Fauves did at first find the general aesthetic attitude of the Impressionists, their human and artistic conduct, as stimulating and a worthwhile model. The Fauves realized that Impressionism was a movement in violent conflict with its age, a movement of protest, an avant-garde art, which had become respectable, but even then not unreservedly so. Finally, on the artistic level, Impressionism provided some useful hints to the Fauves, such as the rejection of anthropocentricity in favour of landscape, indifference towards composition and finished form, freedom of pictorial expression, and the love of vivid colours.

Of the Impressionists, Manet and Monet seem to have been the two the Fauves consulted most readily. From Manet they could learn a great deal about the art of simplifying, of tackling large areas of contrasting colours; they could learn from his way of outlining forms and applying colour in bold strokes to define shapes. Manet regarded painting as an arrangement of coloured patches broken by discordances that create the illusion of space. This was a particularly interesting lesson for the Fauves. Marquet and Dufy drew on it generously, as did Matisse after 1905 when he used both Manet and Ingres in his new experiments.

Some of the Impressionists posed the problem of colour in new terms. After 1883 Monet and Sisley especially used extremely vivid tones: but they really only overintensified the local colours. Towards 1890 Degas, Renoir and especially Monet went even further. They used not only very brilliant colours but even pure colours far removed from reality, in strong contrast with the delicate naturalist colour values of the preceding periods. In the end it seemed as if colour, which they used to describe the phenomena of nature more fully, actually came to express the feelings of those who were looking at them. It was Monet who pushed that tendency furthest until it became a subjective interpretation of the theme which gave his painting lyrical expression, a trend in which the Fauves would obviously be interested.

The fashion of transposing colour, which became general after 1886-90, affected a younger generation of painters who none the less remained close to Impressionism in their basically naturalist and momentary approach. This applies to Maufra, Moret and Loiseau, who were also to varying degrees affected by the art of Gauguin and van Gogh. It is also true of Guillaumin, whom some authors regard as a precursor of Fauvism. Admittedly, the tendency to transpose led Guillaumin to simplify greatly and to heighten his colours boldly; this is especially noticeable in the canvases he painted at Agay between 1898 and 1905. But we must remember that the famous red rocks at Agay and the intense blue of the Mediterranean tempted the painter's palette (usually less bold

when faced with the landscapes of the Creuse) and brought out all his love of saturated colour. In any case, the representation of space was still based on an illusionist concept: the forms were still moulded by the air.

Guillaumin might be compared with Valtat, whom certain contemporary critics and some galleries try to claim as the first of the Fauves. This is a mistake. The fact that he was a pupil of Gustave Moreau, that he was not far from the *cage aux Fauves* (cage of wild beasts) at the Salon d'Automne of 1905, and that he had the "honour" of being reproduced in *L'Illustration*—all this does not make him a Fauve painter, even if Matisse and Friesz suggested that he was. Admittedly, Valtat expressed himself with a fine lyricism, often combining colour and arabesque, but he did so within the framework of an artistic system that was weakened by contradictions and, above all, did not question illusionist perspective.

We shall see that not all the Fauves reacted alike to Impressionist examples. Generally speaking, in 1905 the question of how much notice the Impressionists merited was still very controversial. Thanks to an enquiry by Charles Morice published in *Le Mercure de France*, we know the opinions of some artists on the place of Impressionism in the contemporary artistic scene. To the question, "Is Impressionism finished? Can it renew itself?" some replied that it was not finished, that it still had a brilliant future, on condition that it was perfected and transformed. The vast majority, though, thought that it was a movement of the past, and they did not regret it. It is not surprising that of the only two Fauves questioned, Dufy and Van Dongen, the former—who was still in his Impressionist period—believed in the painting of Monet and Pissarro, whereas Van Dongen, who was already launched into his pre-Fauve experiments, no longer believed in it.

René Seyssaud

A question that deserves some consideration is whether the painting of René Seyssaud (who has often been classified too readily as a second-generation Impressionist, on the same grounds as Guillaumin and Valtat) was a source of Fauvism. Did it in any way help the Fauves formulate their system of artistic expression?

Some critics have drawn parallels between Seyssaud's painting and that of the Fauves and claimed that he was not only a precursor of Fauvism but a real Fauve-before-the-Fauves. Referring to a work of 1892, Matisse is said to have stated that the Provençal artist (two years his senior) "had been a Fauve thirteen years before him",[12] but this does not amount to acknowledging a debt. It would be mischievous to suggest that the Fauves had a more or less deliberate lapse of memory on the subject.

At first sight it might seem that Seyssaud's artistic preoccupations were similar to those of the Impressionists: effect of seasons, attention to time. But fundamentally there is really little more in common between them than a predominant interest in landscape, in nature and its seasonal variations. Seyssaud's style—his manner of painting, his broad, firm brushstrokes, his way of showing the solidity of form by applying paint thickly—distanced his art from that of Monet and brought it closer to van Gogh's, with whom he also shared a need to take part in the show, a restless lyricism which gives his painting an Expressionist (or romantic) character, a far cry from the passivity of the Impressionist painters. Seyssaud quite often showed an interest in the human figure, whose gestures, attitudes, and sometimes even inner thoughts he conveyed, something most of the Impressionists never sympathized with.

There were some similarities between Seyssaud's art and that of the Fauves: an indifference to the masters of the past, a desire to react against the analytical and momentary approach of the Impressionists, a spontaneous, impetuous, almost frugal treatment, a love of synthesis, the importance attached to colour as a primary means of expression, and finally the use of pure, often violent, tones. In these areas Seyssaud incontestably preceded the Fauves by several years, as is shown in numerous works, particularly of 1895: *Barques au soleil couchant à Cassis* (Boats at Sunset at Cassis) and *Bois de pins au crépuscule* (Pine Wood at Dusk). The forms here are simplified in the extreme, the colours are very intense and apparently transposed (in the first, the yellow-green sky, blue and red soil; in the second, the yellow sea, the orange sky). There is no denying that it is rather surprising to find such works in 1895. A little later, in 1901, during the exhibition at Bernheim's, the critics expressed opinions that were used later, in 1905, when speaking of the Fauves. Roger Marx, Louis Vauxcelles, Gabriel Mourey, Arsène Alexandre—all of them authors who expressed reservations in the case of the Fauves—were unanimous in acknowledging the expressive power of Seyssaud's style and, before there was any talk of Fauve painters, wrote that Seyssaud "yelled", "bawled" and "roared". Even Thiébault-Sisson, the critic of *Le Temps*, was full of admiration for the Provençal painter, from whom the state bought two pictures, one in 1903 and the other in 1904. It is odd that Seyssaud's painting did not shock the critics, whose outlook was very conventional, whereas that of the Fauves did. The reason for this lies in the fact that Seyssaud never ceased to be regarded as a provincial painter (and, moreover, he was from Provence), to whom a measure of flamboyance was allowed. This attitude was common among critics at the time, although they were not prepared to tolerate a similar flamboyance in Parisian painters: what was laudable in a provincial painter was not necessarily so in one from Paris. For while the former only represented the art of his own region, the latter involved the art of the whole country, for Paris, of course, meant the French nation.

In fact, Seyssaud did not go as far as the Fauves. He remained aware of the illusion of the three-dimensional and of the illusion of space. His space perspective was achieved through wide diagonals, through the subtle shading of light, and through variations in his paints, thick and rough in the foreground, smooth and delicate in the background. Thus Seyssaud cannot be compared with a true Fauve painter. Undoubtedly he simplified and synthesized; but his work rarely contained those bold distortions, those extraordinary ellipses found in, say, Derain or Van Dongen as early as 1905. He intensified the colours of his subjects, as many painters had been doing for a long time, but his colour interpretation remained more or less true to the reality he saw. The vividness of his palette owed more to his Provençal nature than to any deep urge to innovate. It is not surprising that the sea in *Barques à Cassis* was yellow and the sky orange since it showed a sunset. The ochre soil in those parts of Vaucluse explains the scarlet streaks we see in *Bois de pins au crépuscule*. The painter's approach remained intrinsically naturalist. But this does not mean that his was an imitative art. Seyssaud's best works are imbued with a lyrical spirit that creates amazing transpositions of form, notably chromatic effects of great poetic value—something we would have expected to interest the Fauves. Although Seyssaud did not live in Paris, he had been taking part in the artistic life of the capital since 1892, the year he first sent work to the Indépendants; in 1897 he exhibited at Le Barc de Boutteville's and in 1899 at Vollard's. His work was shown at the Salon d'Automne of 1903, and from 1901 on he exhibited regularly at Bernheim's each year (he did so until 1911). He also exhibited at Le Havre in 1902, side by side with Friesz, Dufy and Braque, but they do not seem to have noticed him. It is surprising that the Fauves took no interest in Seyssaud, that they did not realize how much they could learn from his art.

Neo-Impressionism

In many ways Neo-Impressionism (or Divisionism) played a role similar to that of Impressionism in the evolution of Fauvism but—one might say—at a higher level. The Fauves found in Divisionism certain ideas for solving the problems they posed themselves, for which Impressionism had had no adequate answer. Thus in 1898-9, on the morrow of his Impressionist experiments, Matisse was faced with the problem of giving structure to a picture. He had been practising painting "without bones" in the manner of

Monet; but then he felt the need for a measure of discipline to give the painted surface a framework and to stiffen the pictorial expression. This was the time when Signac was publishing *D'Eugène Delacroix au néo-impressionisme* (From Delacroix to Neo-Impressionism) and when numerous Divisionist canvases were shown at Durand-Ruel's (March 1899). At that point Matisse alone borrowed from Divisionism: even Marquet was hardly involved.

On the other hand, in 1904 and 1905 all the Fauves, in varying degrees, were affected by Neo-Impressionism, which was more to them than just the most inviting path to colour. The Divisionists had carefully studied the use of colour and drawing as a means of expression. They had notably perfected the means of creating tones with the utmost luminosity and intensity and letting line play a part in creating the expressiveness of a picture. The strict laws they had formulated culminated in an essentially scientific system independent of perceptible reality. Here was abstract material that could be used for the most arbitrary plastic and lyrical creations. However, the approach of the Divisionist painters remained fundamentally naturalist: this was why they retained light-space as one of the constants in the picture, a way of correcting the trend to abstract art which they did not wish to follow. Needless to say, the Fauves had no intention of locking themselves in this naturalist-abstract dilemma, which made many Neo-Impressionist works so inconsistent. They refused to follow the Divisionist doctrine to the letter; none of them adhered strictly to the Divisionist system which, in fact, they used with great freedom. As we shall see later, what they sought (Matisse and Derain made their view on this very clear) was to explore and use Divisionist painting for their personal, original ends, to assimilate the basic ideas in order to go beyond them and use them as the components of a new idiom. In the summer of 1904, at St. Tropez together with Signac and Cross, and again at Collioure at the beginning of the summer of 1905, Matisse looked to the Divisionist system for a measure of discipline—as he had done a few years earlier—which would help create the style of a picture. During the summer of 1905, still at Collioure, Matisse and Derain undertook a detailed study of the Divisionist system, as did Van Dongen. The Fauves had no intention of retaining the naturalist approach to light-space which the Divisionists had inherited from the Impressionists. The Fauves were already aware of the need of expressing a new relationship between the artist and nature, which led them to depict even light and to show it through colour equivalents. This new idea of colour-space was basic: it created the gulf between Divisionism and Fauvism. In 1905, in his picture *Luxe, calme et volupté* (Luxury, Peace, and Sensual Indulgence; Pl. 18) (Private Collection, Paris) Matisse clearly showed the inconsistency between what he called "sculptural plasticity" rendered by light-space and "colour-based plasticity" through which colour-space could be expressed.

What the Fauves actually found most useful and relevant were the technical methods of Divisionism. The rejection of accurately descriptive colours, the systematic use of pure tones (even shrieking ones in the case of Signac and Cross), intensifying colours by breaking them up, using the white of the canvas, the interrelationship of colours themselves—all these the Fauves regarded as so many ways of increasing the expressive power of the painted surface. Although it is certainly true that in the Divisionist scheme colour tended to free itself from any realist bias, it is equally true that it dissociated itself from its content. Thus colour lost its dependency on the subject in order to play a part in the general organization of the picture—a sort of expressive Tachism. This was a lesson—implicit rather than explicit—on which the Fauves meditated: it might lead to the total autonomy of the painting, to creation from the inside, not the outside; it could also lead to the concept of colour-space.

As for Seurat, it is difficult to imagine that the Fauves could have been attracted to his rigidly calculated and rather dogmatic compositions. But it was precisely through these that they realized that the painting had an existence of its own, that the purpose of art was not to show an image of things but to convey them through a special idiom; thus a system of signs, of equivalents, had to be invented. Nevertheless the Fauves seemed to be interested mainly in Seurat's painted studies, which had great stylistic freedom and which expressed the artist's lyricism.

In Signac the Fauves naturally appreciated his new manner of painting shown in his Venetian canvases of 1904. The brush-stroke had become generous, permitting a bolder decorative simplification. Signac simplified, stylized, distorted and transposed with the greatest audacity. "The painter", he said at the time, "has to choose among the different components of beauty and of variety that nature offers him... A picture with linear and chromatic composition will have a better kind of order than the chance result of a direct copy of the subject."[13] Like Maurice Denis, he assigned second place to the subject of a painting. "The subject", he wrote around 1902, "is nothing, or is only part of a work of art, no more important than other parts, colour, drawing, composition." Signac, who liked theorizing and teaching, had always been held in great esteem both by the painters of his own generation and by the younger ones. His hospitality in his property at St. Tropez was open and generous and not confined exclusively to the Divisionists. Between 1903 and 1905 several painters who played a role in the history of Fauvism stayed with him, worked at his side, and had to cope with his fervent attempts to convert them to Divisionism. Valtat stayed with him in February 1903 and at the beginning of 1904; Matisse spent the summer of 1904 there; Marquet, Camoin and Manguin were there in 1905. Signac clearly knew that he was laying the foundation for the painting of the future which, he thought, should give predominance to colour: "The triumphant colourist need only emerge," he wrote in 1899; "his palette has been prepared for him."

To the Fauves, Cross would certainly seem the most lyrical of the Divisionists. Isabella Compin has shown that, from 1903 onward, Cross's art underwent a significant evolution towards lyrical expression. The painter was perfectly aware of this, since he wrote to

Verhaeren at the time that he wanted his art to be not only "the glorification of nature" but "the very glorification of an inner vision", that he wanted to create works that "owe more to the imagination".[14] In the works of Cross between 1903 and 1908 (the latter date marking the peak) we can see an accentuation of subjective distortion. The painter expressed himself arbitrarily, with greatly intensified colours, following a technique that steered away from Divisionist doctrine.

Nabism

It has often been said that there was a connection between the Nabi painters and the Fauves when in fact such similarities are very superficial and there is no really deep affinity. Especial emphasis has been given to a certain likeness in their use of contoured areas. The Fauves, however, did not adopt this method before the end of 1905, a time when the Fauve system had already been formulated in its essentials, that is, when the substitution of colour-space for light-space had been made. The Nabis do not seem to have played any part in this mutation. The Fauves chose to use broad painted areas to express themselves because they were anxious to reject Divisionist methods and not because they wanted to follow the Nabi system. In fact, it was Gauguin's example that led the Fauves, at the end of 1905, to adopt the technique of contoured areas to replace the division of colours, which, Matisse complained, led to not very expressive "jerky surfaces" and, according to Derain, made it difficult to create "deliberate disharmonies". The Fauves were hardly likely to find anything helpful in Nabi painting, for how could they care for an art that had so little lyricism, an art given to such excessive decoration, a sophisticated art bent on technical feats, aiming at the rare, the unusual, the funny? The art of the Nabis was distinguished, discreet, literary and symbolist, whereas the art of the Fauves was immediately violent, direct and non-intellectual. There could be no common ground

5. Marquet *Nu dans l'atelier*, 1903.

6.   Derain *Bords de rivière, Chatou*, 1904.

7.   Vlaminck *Les bords de la Seine à Bougival* ou *Le quai Sganzin*, 1904.

8.   Van Dongen *Le Moulin de la Galette*, 1904.

between an art with a bourgeois cultural bias and a vitalist, provocative art essentially of the people.

The Fauves were unable to glean any useful ideas on expression through colour from the work of the Nabis. It has often been thought that Bonnard might have helped them. But, in fact, if we examine the painter's work we can see that he did not really become a colourist until after 1905 (perhaps prompted by the Fauves); before that date he was primarily interested in values, playing on a range of subdued colours and half-tones.

Vuillard seems to have been more of a colourist than his fellow-artist. Some of the pictures dating from 1890-2, like the *Self-Portrait* (Pl. 9) (Private Collection, Paris), *Le Liseur* (Man Reading) and *L'Actrice dans sa loge* (Actress in her Loge) (Private Collection) have a curious feature: that is, the painter's attempt to represent space not by using values but by the interaction of pure contrasted colours. Colour here seems to be an equivalent of space, light and form. It is perhaps in these works that we have the very earliest version of Fauve painting. Unfortunately these pictures do not seem to have been exhibited in their day, or even a little later. Vuillard hardly exhibited before about 1903, and even then did so mainly at collective exhibitions. Note, too, that these were exceptional among Vuillard's works, and he probably thought of them as a sort of game, even "oddities" that were not worth showing. And even if they had been known at the time the Fauve system was being formulated, it is not sure that they would have been noticed by the Fauves for, strangely enough, their humorous treatment blunted their artistic virulence. In any case Vuillard soon abandoned this kind of experiment.

Drawing presented a different problem from colour. There is no doubt that the Fauves made use of the posters, lithographs and caricatures in which the Nabis, especially Bonnard and Vallotton, demonstrated a new spirit of synthesis, not shrinking from even the most daring simplifications and the most expressive distortions. We know that Derain, during his military service, read *La Revue Blanche* which published several Nabis. Some of them, notably Vallotton and Ibels, collaborated on *L'Assiette au beurre*, which every Fauve read. In April 1904 a series of original lithographs by Bonnard, Denis and Vuillard were shown at Bernheim-Jeune's. Derain's watercolour drawing of the *Maquignon* (Horse-dealer) (c. 1904, Pierre Levy Collection, Troyes) undeniably shows that he learnt from Bonnard. Van Dongen, too, owed something to Bonnard in his lithographs for *L'Assiette au beurre* in 1901, and we can undoubtedly trace the same spirit in the lively silhouettes that run through some of the Fauve landscapes by Marquet, Derain and Dufy.

Every aspect of the work of Toulouse-Lautrec, another artist close to the Nabis, was followed keenly by the Fauves. The extensive exhibition the Galerie Durand-Ruel devoted to Toulouse-Lautrec from 14 to 31 May 1901 (200 pieces) aroused the enthusiasm of Derain who, in a letter to Vlaminck, alluded to one of the pictures that had particularly impressed him. We shall see, too, that Derain's composition of *L'Age d'or* (The Golden Age), undoubtedly finished at the beginning of 1905, owed some of its features to Toulouse-Lautrec, and the Salon d'Automne of 1904 did in fact exhibit twenty-eight works by the latter. Braque and Friesz have said that they were attracted by Toulouse-Lautrec's posters while still in Le Havre; Braque is even said to have peeled one off the wall to keep it—that of Jeanne Avril. Toulouse-Lautrec's art obviously showed the Fauves a way of achieving expressiveness by simplifying drawing and colour.

Maurice Denis

The case of Denis is rather complex. At first sight everything seems to militate against the idea that the Fauves might have learnt anything from that artist. From about 1900 onward, his art veered sharply towards a new classicism; he chose to exhibit at the Salon de la Société Nationale des Beaux-Arts; he was a militant Roman Catholic, an avowed Royalist, a member of the *Action Française*—all of which would

33

make him suspect in the eyes of the Fauves. Yet they were untiring in their affection and esteem for him. They always appreciated his great human qualities, his lofty spirit, the sincerity of his convictions, his understanding for new artistic experiments however much they might differ from his own, and the encouragement and help he gave to young artists in general, from which some of the Fauves had benefited as well. Thus he bought one of Dufy's pictures in 1903; Dufy had the highest regard for his opinions and considered him his godfather. Friesz, too, had a great respect for Denis, in whom he saw "the great father figure with whom one had so many intellectual and artistic ties"; he recalled that Denis "advised and criticized", that he was "as curious and interested in our youthful experiments as he was ready to pass on his own and those of his predecessors with his characteristic clarity and understanding of the past, from the Primitives to Cézanne; this enriched his conversation and made it lofty".[15] It was thanks to Denis that Friesz obtained a contract from Druet in 1907.

The Fauves never forgot that Denis's art owed much to Gauguin and to Cézanne, whom he never ceased to defend and expound. To them he remained the author of the famous definition of a picture that might, to a certain extent, be applied to a Fauve painting: "Remember that a picture, before being a war-horse, a female nude, or some anecdote is essentially a flat surface covered with colours assembled in a certain order." The foundation of his figurative system had been, in varying degrees, the theory of equivalents, of objective and subjective distortion, and of simplification for the sake of expression. Another dictum of his that could not fail to move the Fauves was: "Every work of art was a transposition, a caricature, the impassioned equivalent of an experienced sensation." Although the Fauves had certainly not read any of Denis's writings dating from before 1904, which were not reprinted until 1913 in *Theories*, they knew their main ideas and perhaps some significant dicta. They certainly continued to take an interest in his studies and reviews, which appeared regularly from 1904 to 1907 in various periodicals.

The Fauves read Denis, but we may wonder if they actually looked at his works. It is highly unlikely that they took the least interest in his works of 1900-5. When we examine the works of that period we see that the subject had become primordial, the approach to space was illusionist, an elegant stylization had replaced expressive distortion, and the colour had lost its brilliance. None of this was likely to help the formulation of the Fauve system. But if we consider Denis's paintings of between 1893 and 1899, things are very different. Here we have a case similar to Vuillard's discussed earlier. In some of the works of these years Denis endowed the relatively broad area of colour with an intense power of expression; space was conveyed by the sole confrontation of colours of equal saturation. Denis and Vuillard both strove to demolish the illusionist concept of space. It is also surprising to see how frequently, around 1898-9, Denis made use of the method of breaking up colours, which was in no way a typical Nabi method. This might have been due to a sort of general craze for Neo-Impressionism that affected painting at the time Signac published what was effectively the Divisionist manifesto, *De Delacroix au néo-impressionisme*, and also of the exhibition of March 1899 at Durand-Ruel's which comprised a large proportion of Neo-Impressionists, a fashion to which Matisse more or less conformed. Denis never strictly obeyed the rules of the Divisionist system, but merely gave his pictures a Pointillist appearance. Or rather he superimposed an unusual, bizarre kind of treatment on the Pointillist technique which he introduced into his own artistic system so that the final result never ceased to be fundamentally Nabi. This procedure was very important since it demonstrated the use of a Divisionist system diverted from its original end—an example to the Fauves. In this way Denis may have helped the Fauves to approach the Divisionist experiment in a spirit of total independence. To the question whether the Fauves actually saw Denis's earlier works we can reply in the affirmative. From November to December 1904 Denis exhibited eighty-five studies of Italy at Druet's, some of which dated from 1896 and 1898.

9. Vuillard *Autoportrait*, 1891-2.

Denis may also have contributed in another field—by making the art of the Primitive painters known. Again we must leave aside the example of Denis's own paintings, which borrowed only superficially from them. Direct contact with the works of the Primitives was much more rewarding to the Fauves; for some of them it came during the exhibition of French Primitives at the Pavillon de Marsan in 1904, at the very time when they began to ask themselves a number of questions. Undoubtedly at that moment Denis's writings explaining the art of the Primitives were of help to the Fauves. Thus the lesson the Fauves learnt from the Primitives—poetic invention, the simplicity of artistic methods, the contrast of violent colours to create an equivalent of space—were learnt largely through Denis, who managed to arouse their interest in the subject.

Thus it seems fair to say that Denis played the part of a guide to the Fauves, not so much through his paintings as through his writings. On a number of occasions he showed an astonishing insight. In November 1905 he discerned the beginnings of a new grouping which he called the "school of Matisse", and whose aesthetic he defined rather well: "The young school of painting", he wrote *inter alia* (1906), "obviously seeks to get away from direct copying. The equivalents, the formulae it creates are perhaps too sketchy, but they are on the right lines."

Odilon Redon

Around 1900-5 one painter who, in a way, had been introduced to the young generation by Denis aroused great interest among the Fauves: that was Odilon Redon.

There is proof of the Fauves' interest in Redon's paintings, which they could examine at several important exhibitions: in 1903 at Durand-Ruel's, at the Salon d'Automne of 1904, and again at Durand-Ruel's in 1906. Matisse undoubtedly met Redon in 1900, when the latter was exhibiting at Durand-Ruel's, and he bought two pastels. Later on, he said he was very much interested in Redon. Other painters,

real or part-Fauves, Van Dongen, Valtat, Desvallières and Laprade, have spoken of the impact made on them by the retrospective of 1904. From these accounts it appears that Redon played a role similar to that of Denis, a sort of friendly counsellor whose criticism was appreciated.

The Fauves did not adopt the whole of Redon's figurative system: they rejected the idealist and bizarre aspect, the result of a Symbolist conception of art against which they rebelled. However, Redon's symbolism was not very literary—it was perhaps less literary than Gauguin's. It was more painterly in the sense that Redon invented pictorial equivalents of his fantasies. This showed the Fauves the way to convey sensations through artistic equivalents. More important still, from Redon the Fauves took the fundamentally anti-naturalist approach, the rejection of traditional perspective space and of illusionist space in favour of imaginary space in which colour became the decisive factor. In Redon's case, of course, the juxtaposition of coloured areas aimed at creating a fantastic space, a fitting fabric for the artist's dream. In the case of the Fauves the problem presented itself differently, for they distorted the natural subject-matter to create a lyrical interpretation. But the result is the same in both cases: an invented, poetical space. The Fauves admired Redon's palette: in his work drawing was freed from its descriptive function and colour freed from its naturalist function, so that we might speak of "incredible" colours in the manner of Gauguin. Moreover, Redon's warm, strong, often saturated tones, expressively harmonious without excessive subtlety, and with scant respect for the rules of complementing shades, were bound to attract the Fauves. In their view Redon was certainly one of the masters who most resolutely introduced imagination into art.

Van Gogh

There were some painters whose works the Fauves studied more intently, we might almost say more frenziedly, for their special technical interest than

10. Matisse *La Desserte*, 1897.

those of the artists we have just discussed. Their works contained ideas that helped the Fauves solve their own problems. These painters—van Gogh, Cézanne, and Gauguin—in a way fulfilled the role of mentors: they were models that could be followed.

We cannot agree with the methods of critics who, in the case of van Gogh, find an *a posteriori* doctrinal affinity with the Fauves in the letters he wrote to his brother Theo. The Fauves did not know Vincent's letters, which were published for the first time in Holland in 1914 and in France in 1937. What interested them were the paintings (explicit enough) and they were able to see some of these at Vollard's. The exhibition at the Galerie Bernheim-Jeune from 15 to 31 March 1901 for the first time showed a large selection of his works, comprising seventy-two items. It was at that exhibition that Derain introduced Vlaminck to Matisse. But it was still too early for the future Fauves to benefit fully from van Gogh's art, despite the interest Matisse seemed to evince for his Corsican pictures as early as 1898. Matisse and Derain certainly very soon gave careful consideration to the Dutch painter's art, but this was not true of Vlaminck, in spite of what he said. On the other hand, the retrospective at the Salon des Indépendants in 1905, with forty-five works by van Gogh (including three drawings belonging to Matisse), coincided with the very moment when the Fauve system was being formulated, and it accelerated the process.

It is not difficult to see what it was in van Gogh's painting that could help the Fauves in their quest for a new figurative idiom.

Above all, the Fauves thought that van Gogh had established a new relationship between the artist and nature based not on a naturalist grasp of the perceptible world but on a transposing lyrical approach. To van Gogh the picture was not an imitation of reality: it had to be the artist's creation expressed through it. Thus the painter's imagination intervenes both in line and colour, which are subject to arbitrary distortions. Denis was right when he noted, in May 1905, that van Gogh "fled as fast as he could from nature through his overwrought temperament".

In van Gogh's artistic system colour obviously constituted an essential element; he was neither the first nor the only one to use it as a symbolic idiom, but he was the first to give that idiom such intense, such wild accents achieved through warm harmonies and daring clashes. From van Gogh the Fauves learnt the revived, if not wholly new, function of colour which lost its objective meaning to become a subjective part in a system of equivalents.

Another important aspect for the Fauves was van Gogh's discovery of what Pierre Francastel called "the autonomous spatial quality of colours in their pure state",[16] that a pure tone by itself, in itself, conveyed a certain notion of closeness or distance: blue, for instance, distanced, yellow brought closer. The Fauves made the most of this means of expressing distance simply by the use of pure colour, which took the place of chiaroscuro so that colour-space could be substituted for light-space.

The methods through which van Gogh defined his system of artistic expression served the Fauves as an example. To achieve a personal style, the Dutch painter assimilated certain Divisionist principles and some derived from the school of Pont-Aven. On the one hand, he did not consider them mutually exclusive and, on the other, he interpreted them with the greatest freedom. Like Denis, van Gogh refused to conform to Seurat's orthodox doctrine or to follow Bernard's or Gauguin's teaching blindly. He showed the Fauves unambiguously that an artist was able to remain free and original while making use of the experiences of others.

But it would be wrong to suppose that van Gogh's art supplied all the answers to the Fauves' questions. The Fauves had some reservations. They realized that van Gogh sometimes was poised uneasily between a radically anti-naturalist attitude and a certain attachment to the object; this ambivalence in the artist's psychic distance from the subject meant that van Gogh did not wholly abandon all recourse to illusionist space, especially when it arose from an—even approximate—linear perspective: this sometimes created the effect of a brake applied suddenly to the

11. Matisse *Le Jardin du Luxembourg, c.* 1899.

lyrical flow. Nor were the Fauves able to take over what Georges Duthuit has called van Gogh's "symbolic-humanitarian baggage". We must remember that the Dutch painter shared in the Symbolist trend. His symbolism, though largely based on artistic considerations, is often heavily emphasized. This gives his work an Expressionist character which the Fauves were not prepared to accept. For instance, it is edifying to compare van Gogh's attitude toward the portrait with that of the Fauves. Whereas van Gogh set store by the moral value, the psychological meaning, the illusionist presence of the figure, the Fauves treated the figure in the same way as the landscape, seeing in both cases a mere composition, a vehicle for the imagination, unconnected with any feeling or illusionist rendering of the model.

Cézanne

It is more difficult to see what Cézanne's painting held for the young artists than what they could learn from van Gogh. Around 1900 Cézanne's art was still very little known in spite of the exhibition of over a hundred canvases organized by Vollard in November and December 1895, which actually led to more questions than certainties. The exhibition, which was not seen by the Fauves because they were too young at the time, left the impression of a difficult, even obscure artist. From 1904 onward we can speak of a reopening of the "Cézanne case" which aroused more controversy than van Gogh, long dead, and Gauguin, who had died a long way from France and was hardly remembered.

The retrospective of the Salon d'Automne of 1904, comprising thirty-two works, did not—as far as we can judge—contain any work dated later than 1890: most of them must have been works dating from the interval between the Impressionist period and the so-called constructive period. The same applies to ten works shown at the Salon d'Automne of 1905. It does not seem likely that the Fauves could readily have seen any of Cézanne's post-1890 lyrical landscapes, and we do not know what Vollard exhibited.

On the eve of Fauvism the critics had only an incomplete and superficial understanding of Cézanne's art, and they often exaggerated its impact on the young painters. At the Salon des Indépendants of 1905, Charles Morice commented on Cézanne's presence which was both "hidden and conspicuous". "It is total domination, complete tyranny... The whole school of Gustave Moreau *en bloc* repudiates its master, in practice at least, in order to defect to Cézanne." Morice's criterion was strange: any painter was considered a disciple of Cézanne if he rejected the representation of human beings and seemed to lack sensibility. Admittedly, in the eyes of the critic of *Le Mercure de France*, Carrière was the model artist. Roger Marx, for his part, thought he detected Cézanne's influence in other painters, in this case second-rate ones. François Monod held Cézanne responsible for "that disarray among the artists" he claimed to observe among the majority of exhibitors at the Salon d'Automne of 1905. In his view, Cézanne was "a belated Primitive, a sort of colourist Crainquebille". G. Jean Aubry also commented on Cézanne's impact "on the vast majority of young painters, from Charles Guérin to Marquet, from Henri Matisse to Camoin"; he thought it was a kind of sickness all young people caught, making them victims of what he called "cézannitis". Like so many critics of the time, Aubry reproached Cézanne with painting nothing but "fragmentary" works. However, he admitted that the Aix master might have some worth as a "moral example" for young painters whom he lured away from the "paths of mere virtuosity" and whom he infected with "the sense of perseverance and patience which allows the feelings to create fine works". Camille Mauclair was never so wide of the mark as in his judgment of Cézanne, in whom he saw nothing but "impotence". "Lord," he exclaimed in 1905, "these aren't works that will withstand the onslaught of time." In 1906 he still thought that the name of Cézanne "will always be associated with the most memorable joke in art".

Thus contemporary critics accused Cézanne essentially of being incapable of finishing a work, of contenting himself with sketches and of being clumsy and naïve. As a result, the cry of "Cézanne's influence" went up whenever an artist had unfinished forms, an apparent clumsiness of expression, which would earn the epithets "disorganized" or "invertebrate".

Cézanne did not only have detractors. Some critics attempted to understand him and championed him. This was true of Roger Marx, who introduced three works by Cézanne at the Exposition Centennale de l'Art français in 1900, wrote a very flattering review after the Salon d'Automne of 1904, and even proposed that the state should purchase a picture. Cézanne was also supported by Geffroy, Vauxcelles and Denis, who painted his *Hommage à Cézanne* in 1900 and in 1905 devoted an article to the painter, and by Bernard, who on several occasions devoted a few pages of his review *La Rénovation esthétique* in defense of Cézanne, taking up the pen himself to do so.

If we look at the opinions expressed by the fifty-six painters questioned by Charles Morice for his "Inquest into the present tendencies in the plastic arts" and who replied to the question, "What do you think of Cézanne?" we can see here, too, a great deal of indecision and ambivalence. Most of them, we must admit, thought Cézanne an important artist, even a "pure genius". Victor Binet's judgment that Cézanne's output was "the painting of a drunken tramp" was exceptional. Some appreciated Cézanne's intuitive, ingenuous art; others, however, fiercely accused him of being awkward, coarse, brutal and ungraceful. Some repeated the banal assertion that Cézanne produced nothing but "try-outs". Schuffenecker even wrote that he "had produced neither a picture nor a work". Few ventured to try and evaluate the art of Cézanne: Jean Puy thought that the painter "had restored Impressionism to logical and traditional ways", whereas Denis and Camoin considered Cézanne a classicist. The most perceptive comments came from Rouault, who spoke of Cézanne's "predominant role in the development of a new poetry", and Sérusier, who said that he "was able to strip the art of painting of all the mould that had accumulated in the course of time" and prophesied: "May a tradition be born in our time—and I dare hope it will be born of Cézanne."

We know of only two Fauve painters who replied to Morice's questions—Van Dongen and Dufy. The former said that Cézanne "was the most beautiful painter of his time"; the latter saw in Cézanne only a painter who "wanted above all to assert his exclusive preoccupation with technique".

Some painters went so far as to try and make personal contact with the Aix master. Camoin, who had already met him during his military service between 1899 and 1902, got in touch with him again at the beginning of 1905. Bernard visited Cézanne in February 1904 and from that time on corresponded with him regularly. Hermann-Paul met him in 1904, Denis and Roussel in January 1906. These painters, who admired Cézanne so much that they were eager to cull advice from his own lips, modelled their art on Cézanne's in varying degrees. In this they acted completely unlike the Fauves, especially Matisse and Derain (who had never tried to meet Cézanne). They did not conceal their debt to Cézanne, but used only what they needed to define their own system of artistic expression. They showed the same independence toward Cézanne as they had toward van Gogh and the Divisionists. This does not apply to Camoin, say, who used a manner of painting very close to Cézanne's and followed Fauvism only from a great distance.

What in Cézanne's painting, as they knew it towards 1904-5, could help the Fauves in formulating their figurative system?

To begin with, the Fauves clearly saw that Cézanne was an artist who rejected the naturalist, analytical and momentary approach of the Impressionists, which was precisely what they wanted to do themselves. It was obvious that Cézanne used reality only as a means to an end: reality to him was the artistic fact, that is, the picture. Cézanne realized that it was not possible to reproduce nature in all its space, its colours, its light; on the other hand, it was possible to give a far better equivalent image than any illusionist version. In 1906 Denis quoted a remark by Cézanne, who said he had discovered "that the sun is a thing one cannot reproduce but that one can represent", and we know that the artist represented light by means of colour. Cézanne's system of perspective led the Fauves to the concept of colour-space.

Cézanne's experiments, aiming essentially at expression through colour, were of the greatest interest to the Fauves. He liberated the coloured areas from the contour line. He saturated his tones. "A kilo of green is greener than half a kilo", he is reported to have said—a dictum Matisse discovered at Marie Gloanec's in Pont-Aven. But this did not prevent Cézanne from respecting local colour up to a point; generally he simply exaggerated it. He went no further in this field. He did not even use absolutely pure colours. That was why Duthuit felt authorized to ask Matisse whether he thought Cézanne had influenced his experiments in any way and if he could be associated with the idea of using pure colours. To this Matisse replied: "Not pure colours, not absolutely pure, but Cézanne built with a force-ratio, even in black and white." Thus Cézanne's painting—even though the colours were not very much transposed or exaggerated—attracted the attention of the Fauves because of the hierarchical arrangement of coloured forms. It was mainly Matisse who was attracted by this aspect of Cézanne's art, the result of careful consideration, which provided the very answer to his own problems. In 1899, at the time when he was completing the *Trois Baigneuses* (Three Women Bathing) (which he considered the "starting-point" of his art) at Vollard's, Matisse first became aware of Cézanne's impact. The other Fauves were certainly more concerned with expressing themselves with greater spontaneity than Cézanne. All of them, however, were interested in the new ideas on the relationship between artist and nature they could glean from Cézanne's painting and in the challenge to the traditional methods of expression. Cézanne's art was based on the imagination, even if it did not deprive itself of the chances offered by the concrete. As a result

Cézanne sought a purely pictorial solution to the problem of representing space, which he saw in wholly new terms: he rejected all forms of illusionist space as mere trickery. Thus he introduced an original speculative treatment of space into painting, which permitted unlimited audacity. This the Fauves clearly understood. The system which Cézanne perfected of modulation by means of coloured areas lit by various fictitious sources was the starting-point of the Fauve system of space. For Cézanne's space, although too intellectual for the Fauves, was nevertheless a poetical space, open to the flow of lyricism.

In Cézanne's conception of space, the two-dimensional nature of the picture was respected, and things placed at varying distances were united on the surface of the canvas. Cézanne had given a new importance to the background, which played its part in the three-dimensional organization of the painted surface to the same degree as the other planes of the picture; the background, which no longer had anything in common with the surrounding air of the Impressionists, became an active plane through the saturation of its own tones equal to that of the other planes. This was important for the Fauves.

Cézanne has often been reproached with producing studies and sketches rather than finished work, but the Fauves were far from disapproving that: they saw in it a legitimate attempt to simplify and synthesize. Like Cézanne, the Fauves were determined to express the deep truths of the perceptible world, the intimate structure, the essence of the object rather than the pleasant aspect of the finished form. Neither Cézanne nor the Fauves set out deliberately to paint vague, unrecognizable shapes; rather, the act of painting was halted at the point where feeling and expression coincided, for the perfection of accurate rendering can easily undo the lyrical inspiration.

Nor was Cézanne, any more than van Gogh, a perfect model for the Fauves. They knew Cézanne's painting well enough to recognize in it an intellectual, even abstract approach that might check the flow of lyricism. Vlaminck spoke of Cézanne as "a sad friend". Moreover, unlike van Gogh, Cézanne did not

12. Matisse *Notre-Dame en fin d'après-midi*, 1902.

see in colour itself a way to express spatial distance; his pictorial space grew out of a complex relationship between warm tones and cold tones. We should also add that the sense of local colour, which Cézanne did not abandon completely, fell short of the Fauve experiments.

A very different Cézanne from the one known around 1904-5 engrossed some of the Fauves in 1907 when they wanted to introduce structural aspects into their art. They undertook a reassessment of his paintings, whose meaning became clearest in the latest works. In 1907 numerous exhibitions of his works were held. The Galerie Bernheim-Jeune showed seventy-nine water-colours from 17 to 29 June; from 14 to 30 November six of his canvases were hung on the occasion of an exhibition of "Flowers and Still Lifes" at which artists like Gauguin, Matisse, Redon etc. were also represented. The Salon d'Automne of the same year devoted a retrospective of fifty-six works to Cézanne: art historians generally regard this as the starting-point of the new direction painting took after 1907, which led to Cubism. Added to this were the publication of Cézanne's letters to Bernard and several articles devoted to the great painter. We shall show later that this widespread interest in Cézanne's work, especially at the Salon d'Automne, was not necessarily the sole—or even the chief—cause of the sense of doubt that beset almost all the Fauves. In fact, their anxiety about plasticity dated from before the opening of the Salon. But there is no denying that a deeper familiarity with Cézanne's art, its emphasis on the subjection of feeling to an intellectual order and its resort to geometrical signs must by its nature work against the Fauve system. This was noticeable during the year 1907 in the quest for geometrical starkness by Derain, Braque and Dufy as well as in the return to a sort of classicism for which Friesz is renowned.

Gauguin

Unlike Cézanne and van Gogh, Gauguin did not interest the Fauves very much at the time when the new system of pictorial expression was being formulated. In the scant testimony we possess on their sources, the name of Gauguin is rarely mentioned. In his letters to Vlaminck, Derain never alluded to Gauguin, which also means that Vlaminck had never initiated a discussion on the subject with his friend. Vlaminck regarded Gauguin's painting (he said so later) as too intellectual, too stylized, lacking in feeling, the very opposite of his views on van Gogh. Matisse, too, was very reserved on the subject until around the end of 1905, no doubt for the same reason (although in 1898 he had bought a work by Gauguin, *Jeune homme à la fleur* (Young Man with Flower) from Vollard). For the Fauves, of course, as for van Gogh and Cézanne, a picture always emanated from a confrontation with nature, whereas Gauguin was separated from nature by a decorative element; as he himself said, "Art is an abstraction, wrest it away from nature by dreaming over it and give more thought to the created work that will come of it." Charles Morice's 1905 opinion poll among fifty-six artists is only of relative interest because of the scantiness of replies about Gauguin. Whereas Morice's fourth question was solely on Cézanne, the third introduced the name of Gauguin in combination with that of Whistler and Fantin-Latour in the form of: "Whistler, Gauguin, Fantin-Latour... what did they take with them at their death? What have they bequeathed us?" Several of those who did not evade the question replied that Gauguin was the heir of the Primitives. There were some who said they specially appreciated his sense of balance in the forms and the harmony of colours; some added a pejorative note, regarding Gauguin as no more than a "scene-painter". Victor Binet, whose opinion of Cézanne we have discussed earlier, saw in Gauguin a "canoe decorator in the land of the Red Indians". The majority expressed their admiration for the painter. Some of the replies expressed serious reservations; some came from painters who considered Gauguin inferior to Cézanne. For Rouault, "with time Gauguin will be of lesser stature than Cézanne", and for Sérusier, "Gauguin is not the initiator of today's world... it is Cézanne, whom Gauguin revealed to us." Of the only two Fauve painters to be questioned, Dufy and Van Dongen, the former said "I do not know enough of Gauguin's work to talk about it" and the latter regarded him as "the precursor of a new religion of art".

On the whole, the reticence of the Fauves was logical enough. There is a great deal of incompatibility between their painting and Gauguin's. Gauguin's painting irritated them because of its appeal to thought, its retention of a certain kind of symbolism that did not wholly exclude literature, its occasionally sophisticated technical skill and perhaps also because it had a sort of exotic classicism seen as a substitute for Graeco-Roman classicism. We must remember that many people regard Gauguin's art as an adaptation of Puvis de Chavannes'. Nor must we forget that the Fauve system started from a way of considering Divisionist painting which was bound to reject any serious reference to Gauguin's art. But reservation does not mean hostility. From the time of the pre-Fauve experiments Gauguin's painting must, in its essential components, have appeared propitious for the new artistic movement. Gauguin's teaching tended towards an anti-naturalist art, an art of the imagination, in which the arbitrary use of colour conveyed the artist's emotions. This was explained at length by Denis in articles which the Fauves knew of even if they had not actually read them.

But the essence of Fauvism, to which all the experiments of 1904 were leading, was something that was lacking in Gauguin's painting. Matisse has made this clear: "Gauguin cannot be put with the Fauves," he remarked, "because he does not use colour to construct space, he uses it to express feeling." Gauguin did not unequivocally solve the problem of representing space in a picture; his space was no longer perspective space, but it was not yet colour-space. His solution consisted of a kind of non-space or a rather vague undifferentiated space with a more or less fictitious light, and/or the contour line to distinguish the different planes, and/or the relationship of more or less contrasted tones.

During 1904 and 1905, the vital years in the formation of Fauvism, the Fauves had little opportunity to see many of Gauguin's works. In 1903, the year of the painter's death, A. Vollard, who had a large proportion of his works, organized an exhibition of fifty pictures and twenty-seven drawings while, at the same time, the Salon d'Automne was showing eight canvases. But it was too early for the Fauves to gain much from these events. In 1904 there was not a single exhibition of Gauguin in Paris; in 1905 there was one—undoubtedly a small one—in July at Vollard's.

Towards the end of 1905 the attitude of the Fauves to Gauguin changed completely. This change was the work of Matisse and Derain, who at the end of the summer of that year, which they spent at Collioure, applied the lesson learnt from Gauguin to help them substitute more expressive areas for the excessive breaking up of forms—what Matisse called "jerky areas"—into which their Divisionist experiments had led them. Both of them realized that the fragmentation of form is more or less connected with the idea of light-space as part of a naturalist approach, whereas the synthesized area is connected with the idea of colour-space in the framework of a transposing approach. They were given the opportunity to get to know Gauguin's painting better: thanks to Maillol they visited Daniel de Monfreid, who had most of Gauguin's South Sea canvases at Corneilla-de-Conflent (not far from Collioure). Thus Matisse and Derain began to take an interest in Gauguin when they felt the need to break with Neo-Impressionism. This was also true of Van Dongen, who had the opportunity to discuss Gauguin's art with his friends of the Bateau-Lavoir, where the memory lingered on of the master spreading the good word from one studio to another at the time when Maufra was living in what was then still the Maison du Trappeur. There was something more definite: Paco Durio, a friend of Picasso and Van Dongen, owned several canvases by his old friend, Gauguin, whom he still admired. We shall see that Van Dongen's manner evolved very quickly once he had made contact with Gauguin's work: he chose expressive areas and harmonies of kindred tones instead of harmonies of complementary tones. The other Fauves, too, began to examine Gauguin's work, so much so that we might say that the year 1906 was placed under the shadow of the master, whom they were able to study at the great retrospective devoted to him by the Salon d'Automne of 1906. They now realized that he was an artist who had tried to simplify the idiom of painting to make it more expressive, who thought that a picture was not a technical *tour de force* and that all the scientific, analytical and barren aesthetic of the Neo-Impressionists had to be rejected in favour of a style of linear rhythms and freer chromatic combinations which were better adapted to the artist's subjectivity.

For Matisse, who was thinking increasingly of the organization of coloured areas, of their relationship to each other, and of linear expression combined with chromatic expression, the impact of Gauguin was added to that of Ingres and to that of Islamic art. For Derain, Gauguin's example opened the door to all manner of fantastic harmonies and to a riotous lyricism. The quest for total Fauvism led Derain to impose on drawing distortions as arbitrary as those he imposed on colour. Derain seems to have reached that position as the result of a personal thought process explained, as we shall see, in his correspondence with Vlaminck. But this quest may well have proceeded by way of an examination of Gauguin's wood sculptures. In fact Derain himself did some very fine wood sculptures in the manner of Gauguin. This development is particularly interesting as it soon led Derain to an interest in African art, which he was able to satisfy thanks to Gauguin.

Among the incontestable sources of Fauvism—incontestable either because they have been acknowledged by the Fauve painters themselves or because they can be seen clearly in the works—there are a few rather exceptional ones, for they did not make their mark at the moment when the Fauve system was being formulated but during its evolution, and they generally did not affect all the Fauves. These were the painting of the Primitives (we have mentioned them

13. Marquet *Nu dit Nu fauve*, 1898. p. 47

46

in connection with Denis), Romanesque, Islamic and African art, and some of the arts of the Far East. They became sources of inspiration at given moments in the artistic evolution of certain Fauves: we shall look at them as seems logical in the chapters devoted to the development of Fauve art.

Above we have examined the sources we can in general regard as positive, that is, as having undoubtedly been used in varying degrees by the Fauve painters at the time when they were seeking to create a new artistic idiom. We shall now examine the less certain and perhaps even negative sources.

Gustave Moreau

Here we have to decide whether Gustave Moreau had some responsibility for the advent of Fauvism. Most art historians (of the Fauves and of Moreau) reiterate that Moreau's teaching influenced the Fauves; some even venture to find early Fauve traces in his work. Should we agree with this?

Moreau's personality is not too difficult to understand, in spite of his reserve, thanks to numerous testimonies and to his own surviving writings.[17] His view of art was noble, idealistic and elitist. He was convinced that "art should elevate, ennoble, moralize"; that reality was vulgar and thus it could not be the aim of art to reproduce it. Henri Evenepoel reports that he said: "Yes, positively, the paintings that will survive are those which have been dreamed up, thought out, contemplated, come from the head."[18] He seems to have regarded art as a kind of grace that came to some privileged beings, that had something mysterious of which it was unbecoming to speak. "We feel, we love art," he said, "we don't talk about it, we don't explain it." However, he could talk about it, even enthusiastically; he was highly cultivated, and his conversation was said to be "unfailingly fascinating and pleasing". He believed in God, and his approach to Him is interesting because it was exactly like his approach to art. His God was felt in the heart, not by the mind. He wrote: "Do you believe in God? I

believe in Him alone. I don't believe in what I touch or in what I see. I believe only in what I can't see and solely in what I feel. My brain, my mind seem ephemeral and their reality doubtful; my inner feelings alone seem eternal and incontrovertibly certain." In the same way, for Moreau the aim of art was "the expression of inner feelings", which could not mean copying reality, which was only an illusion.

Moreau taught at the Ecole des Beaux-Arts from 1891 to 1898. We know his educational principles from some of his pupils who described them at the time or subsequently. By nature he respected every human being. Thus he respected the personalities of his students and believed that the intrinsic aim of his teaching was to arouse and develop them. Far from imposing his idea of art and his manner of painting, he encouraged individual experiment. "Go on, let yourselves go", he advised his pupils. In this he evinced a measure of courage, for when his pupils showed works outside the studio that did not conform to the academic teaching of the Ecole des Beaux-Arts, they unwittingly brought the reprobation of his colleagues on their master. Thus he told Evenepoel: "You can't show this... you'll have me killed... and yet I definitely want it."

Moreau told his pupils to study the Old Masters. He himself led them round the Louvre, commenting on some of the pictures, encouraging them to make copies, not just faithful copies but copies that brought out their spirit. According to Evenepoel he set great store by correcting his pupils in the Louvre itself. The Old Masters he held up as examples were the Italian and Flemish Primitives, Rembrandt and Chardin; he did not go beyond the eighteenth century. He thought that the Louvre was all a painter needed for his education. When he said to his pupils, "Don't content yourselves with going to the museum, go down into the street," he meant they should add an inspection of nature to the lesson of the masters, as Poussin had done: it did not mean they had to work in the open air, direct from the subject which, he claimed, did not enrich "the depth of the imagination, the heart, or the vision".

In his teaching Moreau gave at least as important a place to colour as to drawing. He often spoke of the need to introduce the imagination into colour. Evenepoel quotes him as saying: "Remember one thing: you must think colour, you must carry it in your imagination: that's what makes the artist. Colour must be thought, dreamed, imagined." For Moreau, of course, this did not mean preaching a systematic arbitrary use of colour but endowing colour with a beauty beyond common reality.

Although the examples he held up to his pupils did not go beyond the eighteenth century (there is some doubt as to what he thought of Delacroix), Moreau must have spoken to them of contemporary painting. He is known to have rejected the Realists and the Impressionists; he disparaged Manet. Evenepoel tells us that he himself showed a study to his master in which the latter discovered "tones in the manner of Manet", and that this became the pretext for "a sharp, but very just, criticism of the whole modern young school, not because they were saying what should not be attempted but because the young people in general were taking the wrong direction." We know, too, that he condemned Seurat's Divisionist theories in which he saw the death of the imagination. He did not approve at all of the use of complementary colours. "This system of complements is nonsense", he said. "Where are our Flemings and our good Italian Primitives?" However, this lack of sympathy for contemporary art did not stop him from accepting innovations. "I am old," he said, "but I assure you that I am open to all young ventures." He is said to have told his pupils of his admiration for a work by Toulouse-Lautrec he had seen in the window of a newspaper stall. On the other hand, it is more than doubtful that he really praised the art of Van Dongen.

We must admit that Moreau's teaching was truly innovative when we compare it with that meted out by Bonnat, Bouguereau and Gérôme, his colleagues at the Beaux-Arts. They perpetuated a restrictive academic type of teaching founded on objective drawing to which the local colour is added, on technical precepts, on eclectic copies of past masters or a servile pastiche of fashionable artists of the day. Moreau's educational principles, however, were liberal and did not exclude the pupils' personal experiments; they recommended frequent direct contact with the works of some of the great creators of the past and did not censure colour. Moreau's studio could perfectly reasonably be considered rather revolutionary. R. Marx judged it thus in 1896: "In the heart of the Ecole des Beaux-Arts a spark of revolt has been kindled; all those who rebel against routine, all who want to develop according their own individuality have gathered under the aegis of M. Gustave Moreau." But we may wonder whether Moreau's teaching, despite its obvious qualities, was really an apt preparation for a pupil to create a modern artistic idiom appropriate for his time. We would reply in the affirmative if it had been followed up by the presentation of an œuvre of his own that might have stimulated the young painters. But what was this œuvre?

For the duration of his professorship Moreau did not show his pupils what he himself had painted. He did not allow a single one of them to see his pictures in private collections nor did he let them into his studio. This he never explained. P.-L. Mathieu thinks that he was afraid of disappointing his pupils. We know that he did not like confiding in anyone. He exhibited very little; his submissions to the Salons were few and far between (the last one seems to have been in 1880); in 1886 the Galerie Goupil had shown a large number of watercolours based on La Fontaine's *Fables*; there were also a few pictures at the Expositions Universelles, for the last time in 1889. It was perfectly reasonable therefore to regard Moreau's œuvre as mysterious, one which "overheated young imaginations", as Marquet said, and—as Evenepoel remarked—made plagiarism impossible.

Although it was practically impossible between 1891 and 1898 for a pupil of Moreau's to see a work by his master, the situation changed after the latter's death when several of his friends attempted to make him better known. At the Exposition Universelle of 1900 five major pictures were exhibited. What is more, the artist's studio, which had become a museum, was opened to the public in January 1903. Rouault was its curator. Did he encourage his friends to visit the studio? Did he open the door a crack before 1903? It seems not. At that time he himself was engaged on a work that was far removed from Moreau's art and it is difficult to imagine him advertising a form of expression in which he no longer believed. We know that J. Flandrin visited the studio at the end of 1898, but the Fauves do not seem to have rushed to the Gustave Moreau Museum. It is more than likely that not one of them set foot in it, not even Matisse. Nor did the Fauves use the opportunity offered them in 1906 to examine Moreau's work during the large exhibition devoted to him at the Galerie Georges Petit. This exhibition left them completely indifferent.

To give a concise definition of Moreau's painting, we might say that it was primarily history painting. The subject of the picture—mythological, religious or literary—constituted the main feature, for it was the vehicle for the symbol embodying the author's thinking. This thinking expressed itself in a "past-oriented", backward-looking kind of figurative system: perspective space, accuracy of modelling, a predilection for description going into the minutest—even excessive—detail, a technique of glazing which continued to the end in spite of the frequent use of impasto whose jewel effect has often been commented on. Moreau's work was plastically weak. His artistic expression was undeniably unequal to his intentions. We are aware of the inadequacy of the plastic equivalents of his fantasies when we compare his pictures with those of Gauguin or Redon.

We cannot say that Moreau's teaching and his work must inevitably lead to Fauvism or would even smooth its path. It may be surprising that a Prix de Rome winner (Jérôme Sabatte) was produced by his studio. Admittedly, Moreau's pupils may have learnt sound principles from his teaching, which scorned academism and naturalism and which postulated the premise that art must not copy reality but express inner feelings. Moreau, however, was not gifted enough to illustrate this himself in strong, convincing works.

If we exclude the pseudo-Fauves, Rouault, Camoin, Manguin, Flandrin etc., only two true Fauves actually graduated from Moreau's studio: Matisse and Marquet. On the other hand, we can cite a large number of pupils whose art, though not without interest, was unconnected with Fauvism: Guérin, Hoffbauer, Piot, Séguin, Tissot etc. It was simply (but this is a great deal) that Moreau's teaching was apt to produce a sensitive and honest artist, capable of questioning, refusing to be restricted by conventional methods; his teaching broadened the mind and taste and created an independent spirit. Thus it produced artists who were able to take any direction whatever, but not particularly the direction of Fauvism.

The world of the Fauves was diametrically opposed to the world of Moreau. The Fauves were not intellectual painters, they did not live in a fantasy world; their introspection was expressed on direct contact with nature. Their relationship with nature functioned differently from Moreau's. Moreau excluded nature or called it in as a corrective to his fantasy, whereas the Fauves blended with it, threw themselves into it, turned it upside down to express themselves better—whence the lyricism of the often Dionysian Fauve picture—while Moreau's paintings seem to lack resonance. How could the Fauves have learnt from Moreau's skilful, moral art steeped in bourgeois ideology, in which excess kills expressiveness? If we speak of imagination in Moreau's art, we must first define it: his imagination was a quest for idealism, an illustration of ideas, it clothed the idea, it was no more than the discovery of an allegory. The imagination of the Fauves was a transposing vision, an exaltation of the senses, the faculty of going beyond reality. Moreau's imagination in the use of colour has also been greatly exaggerated. Admittedly, it was not wholly imitative, but it was not really very far from the local colour: the sky was blue, flesh was ochre, flora and fauna almost invariably had their true colouring, and even the fantasy beasts had obvious similarities with existing animals. His arbitrariness was limited to clothes, jewels and accessories—in fact, it amounted to very little. And it would be a mistake to think that the Fauves, had they visited the Gustave Moreau Museum, would have been able to find in some of the incomplete works, in certain oil or watercolour studies, an answer to their questions or some helpful ideas. The fact that there were some very free sketches with saturated colours has no importance, for there was never a hint of colour-space.

There can be no serious comparison between Moreau's painting and that of the Fauves. Yet some critics have claimed to see a likeness between some of their works. These similarities, however, are based on outward appearances, seen subjectively, which makes the arguments unconvincing. Vlaminck, referring to one of Matisse's paintings, claims that he was influenced by Moreau. "Moreau's art", he wrote, "was only an art of accessories, of attributes, which overloaded the model with trinkets, pearls, crosses, diadems and lustrous fabrics. Although Matisse believed that this spirit was completely alien to him, he was imbued with it against his will; it is in his mind, for ornaments and accessories have the chief place in his canvases. He does not smother his subjects with jewels, but he composes his canvas solely with the blue patterns of the table-cloth, the red stripes of the curtains, the yellow floral design of the wallpaper, the flowers of the tapestries, the check pattern of the tiles, the stripes on the trousers of his odalisque." Nothing could be further from the truth. Vlaminck did not understand that Moreau's art consisted of adding in order to accentuate the desired effect while that of Matisse asserted itself through restraint in order to achieve greater expressiveness. We shall show later that there is no superfluous accessory in Matisse's picture, that everything is necessary, nothing could be modified without upsetting the equilibrium of the painted surface. Who could say that a Moreau painting would be changed if we took out any of the jewels?

Matisse entered Moreau's studio in March 1895 as a free pupil and stayed there until the master's death. The fact that Moreau accepted a pupil who had failed in the competitive examination suggests that he had a high opinion of him; Matisse's considered choice, on the other hand, suggests that he too had a high regard for Moreau. We hardly dare add another of Matisse's reasons for attending the studio—to have models at disposal.

Matisse had nothing but praise for Moreau's teaching. "There, with Moreau, I found intelligent encouragement... What a charming teacher he was. He, at least, was capable of enthusiasm and even rapture. One day he would express his admiration for Raphael, the next for Veronese. One morning he arrived proclaiming that Chardin was the greatest master of all. Moreau knew how to select the greatest painters and how to make us see them, whereas Bouguereau just told us to admire Giulio Romano." Matisse appreciated the fact that Moreau encouraged visits to the museums. "By doing this," he said, "he saved us from the prevalent trend of the Ecole, where no one had eyes for anything but the Salon. Teaching us to go to the Louvre was almost a revolutionary attitude at a time when official art, confined to the worst imitation, and contemporary art, ensnared by the cult of the open air, seemed to conspire to divert us from the right path." Even Matisse was moved to ask the master's advice on what he should submit to the Salon de la Société Nationale des Beaux-Arts in 1896. It has sometimes been said that Matisse inherited his love of Persian and Hindu miniatures from Moreau. This is not at all certain. Moreau does not seem to have shown such works to his pupils: none of them referred to them. Matisse made the acquaintance of Islamic art several years after Moreau's death. In any case Moreau and Matisse would not have seen these illuminations in the same way.

Did Matisse only appreciate Moreau the teacher? A sibylline remark made by Matisse suggested that he may have seen more in Moreau. Questioned by André Masson, he replied: "There has been too much emphasis on the teaching alone, the freedom of the pupil which he respected even when giving advice, there was more."[19] What did he mean by "there was more"? Could he be alluding to Moreau's work? That would be extremely surprising. It just seems possible that Masson had pressed him with too many leading questions until he made Matisse say what he himself wanted to hear.

From the summer of 1896 the incompatibility between Moreau's teaching and Matisse's artistic experiments became obvious. From that time onward he began to make a habit of working outdoors; he painted at Belle-Ile-en-Mer in Brittany and returned there in the summer of 1897. J. Flandrin tells us of Moreau's reaction to the works Matisse showed him at the end of 1897: "Good old Moreau has changed a lot and wilted a lot. However, this does not prevent him from remonstrating vigorously or worse with pupils who have indulged in some daring brush-play. First and foremost with Matisse, who brought him a huge bulk of holiday work all permeated with the countryside and the open air."

It is not surprising that Matisse finally replied to the question "Has Moreau taught you a lot?" with "Nothing, no one ever teaches us anything, and Moreau was too literary."

Marquet, who, like Matisse, was Moreau's student from March 1895 to April 1898, also appreciated Moreau, the man and the teacher. But Marquet's attitude toward the master seems to have been tinged with irony. Moreau called him his "intimate enemy", perhaps because he sensed a certain opposition in his pupil to all that was indisputably traditionalist in his teaching and also a certain disapproval of the condemnation Moreau heaped on contemporary young painters.

Thus only two Fauves came through Moreau's studio and it is noteworthy that they founded their figurative system on precisely those examples Moreau condemned. It is out of the question that any of the other Fauves might owe anything to him. Friesz, Dufy and Braque attended (very rarely, to tell the truth) Bonnat's studio. Derain, Vlaminck and Van Dongen never set foot in the Ecole des Beaux-Arts. When Fauvism was taking shape, well after 1898, Moreau's painting had lost its mystery, and its faults had become only too obvious to young artists anxious to renew the means of artistic expression. The Fauves could not fail to see that the flaws in his painting had no redeeming qualities that might be even remotely useful to them. In this respect Redon came off better than Moreau, whom he resembled in some ways. Unlike Redon, Moreau never was cited by the Fauves as a mentor; they soon forgot him, whether they had been his pupils or not. We can confidently assert that Fauvism owes nothing to Moreau's teaching and even less to his work.

Other sources

Sometimes, usually on the occasion of an exhibition, a footnote in a catalogue will cite the names of some foreign painters from whom the Fauves might have borrowed. These assertions are never backed by any valid arguments. The painters thus cited are Ensor, Munch, Kandinsky and Jawlensky.

It is hard to see why Ensor's brightly coloured Impressionism should be of any interest to the Fauves, who could draw on numerous French examples in this field. There were very few occasions when the works of the Belgian painter could be seen, and then they were greeted with indifference. The small exhibition organized in December 1898 in Paris by *La Plume* passed unnoticed, and the artist's submission to the Salon des Indépendants in 1901 fared no better. The fantastic, even macabre content of Ensor's art was hardly likely to enthral the Fauves.

Munch was better known in France than Ensor. During his third stay in Paris in 1896 he met Gauguin, Denis, Bernard and van Gogh. He exhibited at the Salons des Indépendants of 1903, 1904 and 1905. At the time when Fauvism was being formulated, Munch's art was already fully developed, but in a direction that could be of no help to the Fauves. Admittedly, Munch and the Fauves drew upon common sources, but Munch saw in them primarily a means of establishing an Expressionist idiom which the Fauves discarded. Thus Munch used saturated colours not as a space equivalent but as an equivalent of emotion, as a means of expressing feeling. This

14. Marquet *L'Abside de Notre-Dame de Paris*, 1901.

Symbolist attitude, which does not wholly exclude literature, aroused the Fauves' suspicion (as we have seen in the case of Gauguin); and the whole anxious, pessimistic, sick side of Munch's art was hardly congenial to them either.

Kandinsky's painting did not serve the Fauves as a model, even remotely. There are two reasons for this. First of all, Kandinsky exhibited in Paris for the first time at the Salon d'Automne of 1904: that is, at a time when Matisse, Marquet, Derain and Van Dongen were already well into Fauve experiments. Thereafter the works Kandinsky exhibited each year at the Salon d'Automne were far from possessing that assertiveness and stylistic cohesion that might arouse interest; nothing in them revealed any precise orientation—this did not really appear before 1908. Nor would the Fauves be attracted by the subjects Kandinsky dealt with: they were mainly medieval scenes, compositions showing some kinship with Symbolist and *Jugendstil* iconography; landscapes were rare. However, it is an interesting fact that Kandinsky's experiments, which are reflected in his works from 1904 to 1906 (whether or not they were shown in Paris) were comparable with those of the Fauves: that is, they freely borrowed and used the style of Monet, Signac and Denis, whose canvases Kandinsky had seen in Munich, especially in the gallery of the Phalanx. But there is a certain lack of boldness and a slight time-lag on the part of Kandinsky as compared with the Fauves. For instance, in 1906 Kandinsky was still using the Divisionist technique, which the Fauves had already abandoned. We might say that Kandinsky examined more or less the same sources as the Fauves, but lagged behind, and that he tried to find a personal solution in them. He achieved this aim at Murnau in 1908, and the Fauves undoubtedly had made his task easier for him.

As for Jawlensky, he was in Brittany in 1905, and no doubt also stayed in Paris, but he does not seem to have had any contacts there with Fauve painters. In that year, too, he exhibited six works at the Salon d'Automne. Thus he made his appearance in Paris later than Kandinsky and that is why it is difficult to

see how he could have interested the Fauves. The works he painted at that time were little known. As far as one can judge, they owed a great deal to the school of Pont-Aven and to Gauguin; their colours were very intense, even violent (in this Jawlensky went further than Kandinsky). But on the subject of space, Jawlensky was less innovatory than the Fauves.

Oddly enough, the Fauves were basically very nationalist in their sources and hesitated to look at examples that were not French. Yet this is not really surprising: their mentality was that of their era. It was not until 1906-7 that we come across the first serious attempts to internationalize art and have regular artistic exchanges. Until then French artists in general took very little interest in the art of other countries.

At a particular moment in the stylistic evolution of some Fauve painters the arts of the East, the Far East and Africa came to play a part. This phenomenon, however, had no general application and did not affect the essence of the Fauve figurative system.

Japanese art had only a negligible bearing on Fauvism. No Fauve painter studied Japanese art directly or in any depth. When Matisse and Derain painted Madame Matisse dressed in her Japanese *peignoir* they were far from invoking Japanese art. Marquet was the only one to study Japanese drawing and to use it in his own. Admittedly, we can find some Japanese features in Fauve painting, technical processes whose origins were unquestionably Japanese: plunging perspective, forms cut by the frame, the play of opposing diagonal lines, the contrast between broken-up and unified areas, patches of colour, contour lines etc. These were not really features taken directly from Japanese art but were methods that had long been in use, fashionable from the time of the Impressionists, popularized by their successors, the Divisionists and Nabis, and so fully integrated in the artistic vocabulary of the time that their Japanese origin had been forgotten. Their presence in Fauve works was derived more from the direct study (in varying degrees) of Divisionist and Nabi painting, especially that of Gauguin, Denis and also Toulouse-

15. Marquet *La Porte de Saint-Cloud*, 1902.

Lautrec. These are only details in no way fundamental to the Fauve system of expression, and we should not see them as important components of it. There is nevertheless a not altogether negligible hint of Japanese prints in the work of Matisse, who found in them the expressive power of transposed colours which descriptive colours lacked. Essentially, Japanese art and Fauve art have nothing very basic in common. The Fauves sought neither unusual, surprising or humorous effects nor elegance of expression; technical virtuosity left them cold; they had nothing but suspicion for anything more or less decorative. Above all, they knew that Japanese painters could not supply any useful solutions to the problem of space in the picture. The age when Japanese art could renew the vision and idiom of Western painting had passed.

In considering the formulation of the Fauve figurative system we must take into account a whole series of facts, from the socio-cultural climate in which it was happening to the various close or distant artistic sources that affected the system as a whole or only one or other individual painter. It is impossible to say which of the sources explored or used by the Fauves was the most important. One source might predominate at a given moment, another at a different time; it depended on the questions the painters asked themselves as their quest progressed. Divisionism, however, seems to have played a decisive role. In any case, the Fauves questioned extensively and deeply. We are sometimes surprised by the keenness of their critical eye: probably no artists before them had been so fiercely determined to achieve a complete renewal of artistic expression. Their experiments very soon turned to two basic aims (which were linked with each other): on the one hand, to define a new relationship between the artist and nature and thus to find a new definition of figurative space; on the other, to find the means to express lyrical impulses.

Interestingly enough, the choices the Fauves made were very much along the lines hoped for by the majority of artists questioned by Charles Morice in 1905. Besides the questions we have analysed above, he asked: "Do you feel that art today tends to take a new direction?" and "Do you think the artist should expect to get everything from nature or should he only ask for the artistic means to express what he is thinking?" Some thought that art was not taking a new direction and did not want it to, but these were few; most of them had a sense of artistic renewal which they defined in contradictory ways. Few artists were prepared to submit wholly to nature. Many of those questioned said that the artist, though not dispensing with nature entirely, should strive to express his inner self and draw on his imagination. Note, though, that Signac was enigmatic ("Art is unchangeable... Let's be painters"), that Denis, Camoin, Dufy and Van Dongen avoided the questions. Of course, we cannot attach too much importance to this opinion poll, for we know nothing about the conditions in which it was held. Nevertheless, it seems to suggest that the Fauves gave a positive response to the hopes expressed in 1905 by a number of artists. There is no doubt that we can take this as proof that Fauve painting was firmly rooted in its period.

16. Matisse *Notre-Dame*, 1901-1902.

17. Matisse *Vue de Saint-Tropez*, 1904.

18. Matisse *Luxe, calme et volupté*, 1904.

19. Matisse *Arbres à Collioure*, 1905.

20.   Marquet *Le sergent de la coloniale*, 1904.

21. Derain *Bougival*, 1905.

22.   Vlaminck *Bords de Seine à Nanterre*, 1905.

23.   Dufy *Les bains du Casino Marie-Christine à Sainte-Adresse*, 1904.

Chapter II Prior to 1905—pre-Fauve experiments

Obviously Fauvism did not suddenly burst upon the scene in 1905. The requisite influences were present much earlier; in fact, as we have just seen, they came from certain older artists of diverse inclinations, whose ideas ultimately converged to provide a theoretical basis for the next generation of painters in their attempts to create a new artistic idiom. Prior to 1905 only a few basic concepts had been established, but these were enough to suggest—vaguely at first, then with increasing clarity—that a specific system of pictorial expression was coming into being. It is the pre-Fauve experiments of the future Fauves themselves that we shall examine here.

Matisse

It can be said that, in general, quite a lot is known about the work of Matisse. Even as regards the Fauve period, there are no really important gaps; most of the works are well documented and dating raises no major problem. However, the period prior to 1905 still presents some difficulties. Not that there is any lack of pictures—unlike some other Fauve painters, Matisse did not destroy his early works. It should be borne in mind that he was the oldest of the Fauves: to take 1898, the date of Moreau's death, as a point of reference, Matisse was then twenty-nine years of age and, although still feeling his way, already an artist worthy of consideration in his own right.

Although there have been a number of studies of Matisse, some of them very thorough, strangely enough there is still no descriptive catalogue of his paintings: the one undertaken by the artist's daughter, Marguerite Duthuit, has not yet appeared. There is, however, the excellent, though incomplete, catalogue prepared by Pierre Schneider and Tamara Préaud for the exhibition "Centenaire de Matisse" (Paris, Grand Palais, April-September 1970).

Matisse himself had occasion to speak about his art and always did so clearly and sincerely, making no attempt to divert criticism.[20] The relevant document closest to the Fauve period is the interview of the artist by Apollinaire, which appeared in December 1907. In December of the following year Matisse contributed "A painter's notes" to *La Grande Revue*; these are valid not only for the work he was doing at the time but also for his Fauve paintings of the years 1906 and 1907. In later years he often harked back to his Fauve period.

Up to 1896 Matisse painted mainly "intimist" subjects—still lifes in which he was particularly concerned with tone values, using muted lighting to produce silvery tones. Evenepoel, his fellow-student at Moreau's studio, described him as "a delicate painter, skilled at handling greys". His favourite masters, whose works he copied at the Louvre, were Rembrandt, Jan Davidsz de Heem and—in particular—Chardin; of more recent painters, he particularly valued Corot. Clearly, at this stage Matisse could hardly have been less concerned with vivid colour and the part it could play in organizing a picture. Nevertheless, as we have seen, the period was not lacking in examples of colourful painting. At

Durand-Ruel's he discovered Manet, but what he mainly appreciated was the virtuosity of the brushwork and the feeling for tone values. The few landscapes he painted at the time show a desire to render perceptible reality objectively. It is not surprising that the Société Nationale des Beaux-Arts should have elected him to associate membership in 1896, after his success at the Salon: one of the pictures he exhibited there—*La Liseuse* ("Woman Reading")—was even purchased by the state for the Château de Rambouillet (it is now in the Musée National d'Art Moderne, Paris).

A transformation took place, however, in the summer of 1896. Through Emile Wéry (a pupil of Bonnat's at the Ecole des Beaux-Arts), who took him to Belle-Ile, Matisse made the acquaintance of the amateur painter John Russell. An Australian and rather an odd character, Russell had settled in Belle-Ile and was married to an Italian model who had posed for Rodin. He had known and corresponded with van Gogh; he was on friendly terms with Rodin and Monet; his collection included works by Guillaumin, Bernard and van Gogh (two of whose drawings he generously gave to Matisse). It is certain that Russell, as well as Wéry (who, according to Matisse, had an "Impressionist palette"), encouraged Matisse to use brighter, warmer tones. In fact, he said that he had returned to Paris "with a passion for the colours of the rainbow". The seascapes painted at Belle-Ile in the summer of 1896 are indeed much brighter in colour than his earlier works, though his exceptional feeling for tone values is still very much in evidence.

Matisse's initiation into Impressionism by Russell and Wéry was an important stage in his reaction against the traditional type of painting he had practised initially, although his approach was still based on direct perception of reality. A much more important step was taken when he discovered the Japanese print, which demonstrated that it was possible "to work with expressive colours quite apart from descriptive colours". In this way, he became aware that painting need not aim at a faithful reproduction of reality. Round about the same time he was advised to

heighten his colours by Georges Linaret, another of his fellow-students at Moreau's studio, who was in the habit of making highly transposed copies at the Louvre. However, in the year 1897 Matisse was even more attracted by Impressionism than before. He studied the canvases in the Caillebotte bequest to the Luxembourg Museum and consulted Pissarro, whom he visited several times on Russell's recommendation and who advised him to go and see the Turners in London. Just when Moreau was affirming that "bitumen is the atmosphere", Evenepoel observed with some distress that Matisse "now thinks only according to Monet". *La Desserte* (The Dinner Table; Pl. 10) (Private Collection, London), painted during the winter of 1896-7 and exhibited in April 1897 at the Salon of the Société Nationale des Beaux-Arts, certainly showed that the painter had not yet lost all his old habits. On the other hand, it introduced some new features: luminosity rendered by whites, coloured shadows, and—most notably—vivid tones. Although it may reflect no more than a timid attempt at Impressionism, scarcely venturing beyond the traditional context of spatial perspective and naturalistic vision, the picture nevertheless had a certain novelty that was enough to impel Carolus-Duran to try to have it rejected by the jury. Impressionism was much more successfully assimilated in the landscapes painted at Belle-Ile in the summer of 1897.

After admiring Turner's paintings in London in January 1898, Matisse spent the next five months in Corsica. This was an important visit since it brought him the revelation of southern landscape and, in particular, of southern light, which inevitably hastened the evolution of his painting as a means of expression through colour (see Pl. 4).

An examination of the series of canvases painted in Corsica reveals the creative path followed by Matisse over a period of several months when he was left to his own devices, seeking by means of self-imposed solitude to solve his problems as an artist independently. It is clear that he went to increasing lengths to avoid "finish"; some of the paintings even have a sketch-like quality, accentuated by dynamic splashes of colour in

66

which the forms explode. The palette is not only vivid, but made up of arbitrary tones. Here we can see the painter distancing himself from reality; henceforth what was important to him was to interpret the impact of nature rather than the objects producing this impact. In our opinion the novelty of Matisse's art resided in his need to express himself forcefully, using elementary means and daring simplifications. We find it difficult to agree that such works were—as is often asserted—inspired by, say, Delacroix, Turner or Signac. We feel, rather, that the artistic idiom evolved by Matisse in Corsica sprang from a determination to assimilate Impressionist techniques freely for his own purposes. This led him to break down forms in a violent, unsystematic manner recalling that of Seyssaud, who had exhibited his work at Le Barc de Boutteville earlier that year (1897). But there was an even greater affinity with the art of van Gogh.

Matisse had no hesitation in saying that his Corsican paintings contained "glimmers of Fauvism", and indeed this cannot be denied if one thinks of their heightened colours, stylistic freedom, refusal to imitate nature, and lyrical inspiration. On the other hand they lacked one feature that was essential to true Fauvism: a new concept of space, based on the relationship of equally saturated colours. Matisse had certainly discovered the function of colour as a means of expression, but not its space-defining properties.

In Corsica, Matisse let himself be carried away by his lyrical sense, his need to convey the emotion he felt on discovering how nature was enhanced by the intensity of light, and this led him to neglect form, to attach less importance to the anatomy of a picture. In our view, this is why the canvases painted in 1899 are, by contrast, especially noteworthy for their experiments with structure: the drawing is strongly emphasized by contour lines, which at the same time give the surface rhythm and harmony, while the planes can be distinguished with no possibility of confusion. It will be noted that here Matisse attached particular importance to richness of colour: the tones are manifestly purer than in the canvases painted in Corsica, but less untidy since they are kept under strict control in order

to achieve the pictorial unity and cohesion he sought. In his search for discipline he toyed with Neo-Impressionism, but only in the form of some very free Pointillist experiments, in which he was content to achieve a certain degree of order in the composition and colour harmonies without following Divisionist precepts to the letter. He was also attracted by the art of Cézanne (doubtless for the same reasons that drew him to that of Seurat), so much so that he bought the *Trois Baigneuses* (Musée du Petit Palais, Paris) from Vollard and said his whole art was based on it.

Tradition has it that Matisse and Marquet worked together at Arcueil and in the Luxembourg Gardens about 1899-1900. But, although Marquet certainly painted some twenty views of Arcueil and the Luxembourg Gardens, Matisse painted extremely few.[21] Those he did paint, however, show a definite reaction against the free, energetic style of the Corsican landscapes, for the picture surface is strictly organized. From the standpoint of Matisse's budding Fauvism these are important works, in which he is especially concerned with making his colours as expressive as possible through their interplay, and with defining space without recourse to naturalistic lighting: just as he creates arbitrary colours, so he imagines a non-illusionist space.

Throughout the various, apparently contradictory experiments of the period 1900-3 a spirit of inquiry prevails, both when Matisse bases his pictorial system on colour and when he bases it on value: the structural study of forms, what Matisse called *dessin compris* (drawing that expresses the essence of an object) combined with *dessin d'aplomb* (drawing that expresses the object's stability). Henceforth Matisse's mastery of his art was such that he wielded an enormous influence, particularly over the group from the Académie Carrière set up in 1898, on Moreau's death, and consisting of Derain, Chabaud, Puy and Laprade. Derain admitted that Matisse "was to some extent the master of our little group and had a great deal of authority".

It was a further encounter with Neo-Impressionism, a little less superficial than the vaguely Pointillist experiments of 1899, that led Matisse to Fauvism. After a one-man exhibition at Vollard's in June 1904, he spent the summer at St. Tropez, where he painted with Signac and Cross. What were his real motives for going there? Was it simply, as some have said, to save money? We think, less flippantly, that it was in response to an invitation from Signac—and even if there was no such invitation, Matisse was well aware that he could not avoid meeting Signac and painting with him, that it would be difficult for him to resist the elder man's proselytizing zeal. In other words it is possible that, consciously or unconsciously, Matisse wanted to experiment with Divisionism rather more seriously than he had done a few years earlier.

After painting *La Terrasse de Signac à Saint-Tropez* ("Signac's Terrace at St. Tropez") (Isabella Stewart Gardner Museum, Boston) with generous brush-strokes that Signac deplored, Matisse finally gave in to the arguments of Signac and Cross and strove to apply the rules of Neo-Impressionist painting. But he had great difficulty in doing so. "I couldn't bring it off at all", he reported. "Once I had put my dominant tone in place, I could not resist adding its rather violent opposite. I was trying to paint a small landscape in patches, and I couldn't manage to harmonize my lighting according to the prescribed rules, so that I had constantly to begin the whole thing over again. As I was starting from white light, this had a lowering effect and I could not avoid bruising all my colours. That was the last straw! For even when I was working at the Louvre, I worked in a colour range that was sombre but not bruised. In particular, I couldn't succeed in containing my drawing and I was tempted to put in too much. Cross, watching my vain efforts, observed that in my paintings I finished off with the contrasts as strong as the dominants and declared that I wouldn't be able to stay with Neo-Impressionism for long." These comments refer to the *Etude pour Luxe, calme et volupté* (Study for Luxury, Peace and Sensual Indulgence) which is indeed far from being a pure product of Divisionism. The rules of contrast, gradation and luminosity of colour are faultily applied; there are tired colours as a result of mixing pigments, white patches giving light, broad brush-strokes side by side with narrow ones, and heavily outlined forms—all serious blunders for a would-be follower of Signac. However, the final composition *Luxe, calme et volupté* (Pl. 18) (Private Collection, Paris), finished in Paris a few months later, follows Signac's principles more closely, although there are still certain heresies: for example, Matisse could not restrain himself from drawing, from marking contours with a continuous line, and from suggesting bodily curves by the direction of the brush-strokes. Was Matisse eventually "carried away" by Neo-Impressionism, as Puy suggests, to the extent of applying its precepts with greater conviction? We do not think so. In our opinion Matisse—as he had already done in the case of Impressionism—simply sought to assimilate Divisionist principles in order to go beyond them and discover those components he still needed in order to perfect a personal style. It must also be recognized that his interest in Neo-Impressionist principles was justified, since they dealt with matters of particular concern to him, such as synthesis, composition, rhythm and harmony. In other words, by assimilating the teachings of Neo-Impressionism, Matisse gained the ability to organize a picture intellectually, while giving free rein to his imagination. But it would be a mistake to think that he was completely satisfied with his composition. We know, from a letter addressed to Signac on 14 July 1905, that he considered there was a disharmony "between the character of drawing and the character of painting". "As I see it," he wrote, "they appear to be totally different from one another, and even contradictory. One—drawing—depends on line and modelling, and the other—painting—on colour." Matisse's aberration, in fact, proved beneficial. By thinking now in terms of drawing, now in terms of colour, he stopped himself from subjugating colour to drawing, as had been his custom. We believe that in this way he came to realize that colour could be given a power of expression that had nothing to do with drawing. This was demonstrated in the *Vue de Saint-Tropez* (View of St. Tropez; Pl. 17) (Musée de Bagnols-sur-Cèze), which was exhibited at the Salon

24. Marquet *Notre-Dame (soleil)*, 1903.

des Indépendants in 1905. We believe it to be later than *Luxe, calme et volupté* since it would otherwise be inexplicable. Here the drawing is obviously secondary, even though there is the same type of Neo-Impressionist composition as in *Luxe, calme et volupté*. Matisse's emotion is conveyed mainly by means of colour used without any attempt at an orthodox application of Divisionist rules. Pure colours are applied, not too thickly, and enhanced by means of elementary contrasts and the white priming that provides the transitions between them. Line and outline are rare; where there is no white, the colours confront one another directly, for the first time in Matisse's work. The saturation of colours is uniform throughout, ignoring the position of the planes in space, but unfortunately spatial lighting is not done away with entirely, since, for example, the distances are indicated in melting strokes that suggest the existence of a real light and its dissolving effect. The painter has also respected local colour, simply heightening it, whereas there was a much greater degree of transposition in *Luxe, calme et volupté*. Nevertheless Matisse had never come closer to a Fauve rendering of space. This work, we think, must be considered as the product of the artist's reflections on Divisionist theories. But we also think that a more thorough examination of the works exhibited by Cézanne at the Salon d'Automne in 1904 made it possible for the budding Fauve to solve his own problems by showing him how conflicting approaches could be reconciled. Henceforth Matisse knew how to avoid the bondage of "linear plasticity", to liberate colour from the tyranny of the contour line, and to structure space in terms of the relationship between contrasting colour planes. *Vue de Saint-Tropez* was Matisse's real introduction to Fauvism; it fits in with the two or three paintings executed by Derain in late 1904 or early 1905, which display more boldness but less confidence.

Marquet

We still know relatively little about Marquet. Although some of his close friends, as well as his wife,

have given us excellent accounts of him, there has not yet been any critical study of his work, apart from a few articles. This is carrying the painter's own discretion too far. The descriptive catalogue of his work, announced as long ago as 1969, has not yet appeared.[22] The retrospective exhibition at Bordeaux and Paris in 1975, though interesting in many ways, failed to throw any light on Marquet's earliest Fauve paintings, since it showed only one of the views of the Luxembourg Gardens and none of the Arcueil landscapes. We do know that Marquet did not like to talk about himself and his art; he published no memoirs and, to the best of our knowledge, only once ventured any information about his early work.

Between 1895 and 1898 Marquet studied under Moreau at the Ecole des Beaux-Arts, but before that he had gone to evening classes where he became acquainted with Matisse, six years his senior. On Moreau's advice he copied the works of various painters at the Louvre, including Veronese, Chardin and Poussin. But he also drew an admirable series of street scenes, which Matisse compared to those of Hokusai. After Moreau's death he attended the Académie Carrière with Matisse.

Marquet naturally went through an experimental phase, like all the other Fauves, but it is difficult to follow it with any degree of accuracy since the dates of the relevant works are uncertain. We shall nevertheless try, though with some caution, to retrace the probable development of Marquet's art from 1895 to 1904.

Marquet's first works seem to show affinities with the art of the Nabis, which was scarcely the case with Matisse. They are portraits of his parents, mainly his mother, in cold but rather bright tones and have something of the intimist poetic quality of Vuillard's portraits.

After devoting himself exclusively to portraits, Marquet started to paint outdoor scenes. An example, dating from 1897, is *Banlieue parisienne* (Parisian Suburb) (Musée des Beaux-Arts, Besançon), which demonstrates his interest in Impressionism. Although this landscape is more or less contemporary with the

25. Marquet *Portrait d'André Rouveyre*, 1904.

portraits, it has less detailed forms and a greater element of suggestion, as well as direct light and rather vivid colours, whose brilliance is accentuated by areas of unpainted canvas. On the other hand, it may be observed that the painter breaks with Impressionism in his refusal to indulge in too much analysis of the effects of light on form; this is demonstrated more particularly by his use of unbroken brush-strokes.

In 1899 Marquet began painting at Arcueil and in the Luxembourg Gardens. It is not certain whether Matisse often joined him there, but this need not stop us from surmising that he encouraged Marquet to use purer colours, as he himself had done since his visit to Corsica in 1898.

We have already mentioned that Marquet said little about his own work; all the more attention is due, therefore, to what he did say about it. He told Duthuit: "Before the Exhibition, as early as 1898, Matisse and I were working in what would later be called the Fauve manner. The first of the Salons des Indépendants at which we were, I believe, the only painters to express ourselves in pure colours was back in 1901. I have never painted in this style except at Arcueil and in the Luxembourg Gardens." Thus Marquet considered the paintings he did at those two places were his only true Fauve pieces. This raises a problem meriting closer investigation, for unfortunately we know very few of the works in this series, even though it probably comprised some twenty paintings.[23]

Often works by Marquet exhibited at the Salon des Indépendants in 1901, five were views of the Luxembourg Gardens and four were landscapes painted at Arcueil. At the same Salon in 1902, again out of ten paintings, only two had to do with the Luxembourg Gardens and one with Arcueil. In 1903 no pictures of this series were listed either in the catalogue of the Salon des Indépendants or in that of the Salon d'Automne. It can thus be concluded that Marquet's "Fauve manner", as he himself understood it, ended late in 1901 or early in 1902. One work in the series is well known: *Le Réverbère à Arcueil* (Street Lamp at Arcueil). In it Marquet has clearly detached himself

from reality, which he simplifies in terms both of drawing and colour, and is swept along by an irresistible lyrical impulse, employing a style rather like van Gogh's with very violent, even arbitrary colours. It may be considered as a pre-Fauve work but nothing more, since the artist does not offer any new solution to the problem of representing space on a surface. It is true that line intervenes only rarely as a means of suggesting space but, by modifying the intensity of the colours according to the distance of the planes from the spectator, light is assigned the space-defining function. The retrospective exhibition in 1975 unfortunately included only one canvas from the Arcueil—Luxembourg series: *Jardin du Luxembourg* (Luxembourg Gardens), which, with its facile twilight effect, seems to us rather less inspired than *Le Réverbère à Arcueil*. The spirit of transposition seems to have been more apparent in the pastels of the same period, to judge from those we know. It would be extremely useful if one day there could be an exhibition of the greater part of the œuvre, both oils and pastels, executed by Marquet at Arcueil and the Luxembourg Gardens, perhaps along with the works—as yet undiscovered—that Matisse must have painted in the same spots. In that way it might be possible to gain some insight into a phase of pre-Fauvism that is in many ways obscure. What is the explanation for this series of Marquet's? In our opinion these works should be considered as a systematic exploitation of Impressionist procedures, experiments with a view to assimilating Impressionist principles in order to go beyond them and arrive at a personal solution. Marquet was of course wrong to consider his Arcueil landscapes and views of the Luxembourg Gardens as Fauvist. But it must be borne in mind that the Fauve painters attached little importance to the word "Fauve", which they did not in fact use among themselves or interpret very strictly.

Like Matisse, Marquet was led to examine the possibilities for colour offered by Neo-Impressionism, but it must be admitted that he did so without much conviction. The *Nu dit Nu fauve* (Nude known as Fauve Nude; Pl. 13) (Musée des Beaux-Arts, Bordeaux), dated 1898, is a little later than the Arcueil—Luxembourg series and has nothing of the latter's novelty. This painting was wrongly called "Fauve Nude" because the colours were fairly bright and applied directly on the canvas, but this did not take into account the fact that the lighting was utterly naturalistic, and the handling of space and relief traditional. Nor can it be said to be a product of Divisionism, being far removed from Seurat's principles—Marquet has simply put a few Pointillist dabs in the background to enliven the colours. In the *Portrait de Mme Matisse* (Portrait of Mrs. Matisse) (Musée Masséna, Nice), painted around 1900, Pointillist technique is extended to the whole picture, even the face, which was not the case in the preceding painting, where solid modelling of the human form and continuity of contour were preserved. The work does not, however, follow the strict rules of Neo-Impressionism either; nor is it any more "Fauve" than the previous one. Although the colour planes are handled in a less traditional way, space is still defined in terms of light.

It was certainly during 1901 that Marquet adopted a new style. Unfortunately the list of the works he exhibited at the Salon des Indépendants in 1902 is not very helpful, since the rather vague titles make it difficult for even one of them to be identified with certainty. We have better luck with those exhibited at the Salon des Indépendants in 1903, which must have included *L'Abside de Notre-Dame de Paris* (The Apse of Notre Dame de Paris; Pl. 14) (Musée des Beaux-Arts, Besançon). The striking thing about this view, painted in 1901, is the synthetic treatment. The artist sought to express only what was essential; the picture is based on an overall vision, so that the forms are rendered in a kind of shorthand as regards drawing, volume and colour. Marquet's intention in revising and correcting that which is perceptible to the senses was not to produce an arbitrary image of some fabulous dream-world but to convey the essence of the emotion aroused by the scene. The colours are pure, but not violent, and only slightly heightened by comparison with reality. Light is treated in a very

special way. It is present in the picture and even active, since it creates reflections in the Seine and shadows at the foot of the trees. It modifies the volumes, which are clear in the foreground and blurred in the background. It does not, however, affect the colours; thus the tones of the trees and buildings in the background are as intense as those of the trees in the foreground and those of the quay and street. By this procedure Marquet not only brings recessive planes to the surface of the canvas but seeks, in particular, to achieve autonomy of colour. The artist thus juggles cunningly with the representation of space, sometimes in terms of light, sometimes in terms of colour, suggesting depth by oblique strokes and at the same time restoring a sense of flatness. This new idiom of Marquet's was at once simple and complex, traditional and innovative. He was drawn instinctively towards a kind of fresh and lyrical naturalism, which has sometimes led to his being considered a sort of Impressionist. This is not a very accurate classification, however, since Marquet is not concerned with the objective and instantaneous analysis of light, nor has his space the fluidity or dimensionality of Impressionist space. Taking quite the opposite path, Marquet made a choice among the different planes offered to him by reality, selecting some and discarding others; what he creates is a subjective, poetic space, the product of deep lyrical feeling. It is difficult not to see in this a further pre-Fauve tendency developing on a more complex and less spontaneous basis than before.

While we know little about Marquet's output during the year 1903, the same cannot be said for 1904, although we can identify none of the canvases exhibited at the Salon des Indépendants and only two of those shown at the Salon d'Automne: *Porte de Saint-Cloud* and *Les Arbres à Billancourt* (Trees at Billancourt) (Musée des Beaux-Arts, Bordeaux). Two works are even more reliable points of reference as they both bear the date 1904: *Balcon, vue sur le mont Valérien* (Balcony, view of Mount Valérien) (Edouard Senn Collection, Paris) and *Portrait d'André Rouveyre* (Portrait of André Rouveyre; Pl. 25) (Musée

National d'Art Moderne, Paris). These confirm that in 1904 Marquet was moving away from pre-Fauvism by studying a master with whom he had more than one affinity: Manet. Like Manet, Marquet had no imagination as regards subject and composition. His landscapes hardly vary in type, and he repeated the same types of composition. But his purely painterly imagination, like Manet's, was inexhaustible, and his often unexpected colour harmonies are remarkably varied, going from extreme richness to extreme simplicity. Again like Manet, Marquet refused to confine himself within a system. Just as Manet maintained quite an independent attitude towards Impressionism, frequently taking his distance from it, Marquet did not limit his work to pre-Fauve experiments. Thus, in neither *Vue sur le mont Valérien* nor *Portrait d'André Rouveyre* are pre-Fauve criteria respected, and one might well suspect such models as Manet's *Le Balcon* (The Balcony) and *Le Fifre* (The Fife-player). From the latter Marquet borrows Manet's way of setting a figure starkly against a clear background, as in a silhouette, and applying the colour in flat, slightly modulated brush-strokes.

But it would be wrong to take such technical comparisons too far, since the work of the two artists is radically different when it comes to representing space. Whereas Manet creates an impalpable, weightless, immeasurable space, Marquet does not stray nearly so far from tradition. He plants his model firmly on the ground, closes the space behind him, and heavily emphasizes the meeting of the horizontal and vertical planes. Another special characteristic of Marquet's work is the quality of the drawing, which gives the figure its comical air and its appearance of arrested movement, and which derives so much humour from the wavy outline of the sleeves. This sort of thing surely points to masters other than Manet, namely the Japanese.

The period up to 1905 seems to have been a rich and active one for Marquet. This was probably attributable to his age, for he was the oldest of the Fauve painters, apart from Matisse—with whom, moreover, he kept in close and constant contact. It is thus hardly surprising that, in certain respects, his art developed along the same lines as that of Matisse. In both cases their pre-Fauve experiments around 1899 were followed by a lull during which they explored the uses of colour, though toward different ends. Matisse considered colours as a means of heightening expressiveness and handling space, whereas Marquet simply saw them as offering an infinite number of harmonic possibilities.

Derain

There is no school of Chatou any more than there is a school of Le Havre. Following a chance meeting, Derain and Vlaminck became friends and rented a studio at Chatou, but in working there they had no intention of cutting themselves off from their contemporaries in Paris. On the contrary, they kept in touch with the artistic circles of the capital. They simply lived in Chatou because they found it convenient—one had a wife and family there, the other lived there with his parents.

Apart from Braque (who did not join the movement until 1906), Derain was the youngest of the Fauve painters, and also the most precocious if one omits Matisse, eleven years his senior. Even taking into account the influence of Matisse on Derain (an influence that the latter never denied), the precocity of the painter from Chatou was astonishing. In fact, it seems that Picasso did not hesitate to call him the "father of Fauvism".[24] It is all the more remarkable that he should have spent the years 1901-4—years of particular importance for the history of Fauvism—on military service. But he soon made up for lost time, so much so that by 1905 he was considered, on the same level as Matisse, as a model for newcomers to the movement.[25]

Certainly, Derain's first really significant works, from the standpoint of Fauvism, were painted after his return from military service in September 1904. Yet the preceding period is extremely interesting with regard to his training as an artist, a number of his

26. Derain *La Rivière*, autumn 1904.

personal pronouncements, the masters he chose to study, and the promise shown by certain pictures.

An irresistible desire to paint led Derain to enter Carrière's studio in 1898, a few months earlier than Matisse. At the same time he was paying daily visits to the Louvre to study the masters; he made copies of the Primitives, whom he greatly admired, and even produced a highly colourful version of Ghirlandaio's *Carrying the Cross*. In this he was encouraged by Linaret, a former schoolfellow at the Lycée Chaptal, who studied under Moreau with Matisse.

Derain and Vlaminck met by chance in 1900 and, in September of that year, as soon as Vlaminck finished his military service, they rented a makeshift studio in the old Levanneur hotel and restaurant in Chatou. No painting of Derain's seems to have survived from this period, which ended with his departure for the army in September 1901, because he had been concentrating on drawings. There are frequent allusions to them in the letters he wrote to Vlaminck soon after his departure.[26] Throughout his stint in the army, drawing continued to be his main interest. "One thing that bothers me", he wrote, "is drawing. I'd like to make a study of children's drawings. The truth is surely to be found there." In this domain, his master was always Toulouse-Lautrec. "Have you seen", he asked Vlaminck, "Lautrec's *Race-course* with the unsaddled horse trotting about on the grass and the jockeys in the distance?" On another occasion he expressed surprise that anyone should think his drawings resembled Lautrec's, but added: "I do dream, though, of a synthesized type of illustration, of crazy lines and values."

While Toulouse-Lautrec and probably, in a more general way, the Nabis were Derain's models in the area of drawing, in that of painting he concentrated his attention on van Gogh and especially Cézanne. He was very enthusiastic about the van Gogh exhibition at Bernheim-Jeune's in 1901. But the evidence—especially in his letters—is clear: unlike Vlaminck, Derain took less interest in van Gogh than in Cézanne. Considering the former "too theoretical", he preferred Cézanne whom he saw as a more integrated and coherent artist. One name, however, never appeared in his letters—that of Gauguin. This is, at first sight, all the more surprising since Derain seems to have been obsessed by the problem of synthesis. In this respect, however, Toulouse-Lautrec and the Nabis could fill the place of Gauguin to a certain extent. At the end of 1904 Derain began to take a greater interest in Gauguin's art, but it was not until later that he felt impelled to examine it more closely, when he was working with Matisse at Collioure and felt it necessary to find an antidote to Divisionism.

As for Impressionism, no trace of it can be found in Derain's early works. This seems remarkable since all the other Fauve painters, without exception, started off by going through a more or less extended Impressionist phase. Derain deliberately spurned the Impressionist approach for its naturalism and concern for immediacy. He was very definite about this in his letters to Vlaminck. At one point he took exception to his friend's attitude: "Your letter saddens and wearies me. You always go on about the immediate sensation." A little later he told him: "The great mistake of all painters is, in my opinion, to have tried to render the momentary effect of nature without realizing that this effect and the artistic rendering of it upon our impressions did not originate from the same source, and without thinking that a simple luminous arrangement would have the same effect on the mind as a landscape actually seen. On the whole, isn't this the result we should aim at?" In other words, the aim of the painter was to substitute his inner vision for his perception of the world about him and a figurative light for that of reality.

Certain aspects of Derain's artistic orientation, as shown in his writings at the time, are illustrated by *Le Bal à Suresnes* (Dance at Suresnes) (City Art Museum, St. Louis), which he must have painted while on leave in 1903. The draughtsmanship reflects a thorough knowledge of the art of the Nabis. We are reminded specifically of Vallotton by the dry humour of the scene, the comical appropriateness of the attitudes, the equivocal gesture of the enormous white-gloved hand placed on the hip of the rigid

27. Derain *La Seine à Chatou*, autumn 1904.

dancer. The colour is no less masterly, being reminiscent of Manet in its subtle harmonies and the way the brush-work models the forms.

On completing his military service in September 1904, Derain immediately set to work again, studying (against Vlaminck's advice) at the Académie Julian and painting a great many pictures. His experiments soon took a new turn. They seem to have been centred at first on the theme of "the old tree", of which the earliest sketch, probably executed in the late summer of 1904, is to be found in an album of drawings.[27] The first painting relating to this theme may be *Bords de rivière, Chatou* (River Bank, Chatou; Pl. 6) (Private Collection, New York). Here the artist's vision seems to be essentially a naturalistic one. Yet the striving for formal synthesis, the careful organization of the surface, the drawing of the tree with its excessively long and rectilinear branches, the uniform brilliance of the greens (due to their not being subject to normal light)—all these features show that the picture is not intended to represent reality but to suggest an equivalent for it. Hardly less naturalistic are *La Rivière* (The River; Pl. 26) (Musée d'Art Moderne de la Ville de Paris) and *La Seine à Chatou* (The Seine at Chatou; Pl. 27) (Kimbell Art Museum, Fort Worth, Texas), both probably painted in the autumn of 1904. A much more decisive breakthrough was *Le Vieil Arbre* (The Old Tree; Pl. 40) (Musée National d'Art Moderne, Paris), probably painted shortly afterwards, in winter, which offers a new treatment of the left-hand part of the preceding work. Here reality is so transposed that one can already speak of this as a Fauve work, even though the colour effects are rather subdued. The artist is attempting to create a new kind of pictorial space, not on the basis of light (a constituent of reality) but on that of the colour dreamed up by the artist.

From now on Derain's concept of the work of art would be based on the imagination or on a lyrical view of nature. There is certainly no lack of imagination in *Le Pont du Pecq* (Bridge at Le Pecq) (Private Collection, Paris), which was probably exhibited at the Salon des Indépendants in 1905. This picture could only have been painted during the period between Derain's return from military service and the opening of the Salon des Indépendants, that is, between September 1904 and March 1905. We would place it at the end of the summer, or at least not later than October, because of the brightness of the light and the accentuation of the shadows. This is a work of capital importance. It shows a total disdain for naturalism, with an expressive transposition of drawing and colour taking the place of external imitation. The blue shadows and broken brush-strokes should not deceive us—they are simply borrowings from the technical repertoire of the Post-Impressionists. Their Impressionist origin is forgotten and Derain has put them at the service of a new kind of vision. For the painter the important thing is the organization of the picture surface, which is remarkably dynamic in the manner of van Gogh, an obvious inspiration here. The colours are perhaps still a little understated and their space-

defining function may not yet be exploited to the full—space is still created by curved lines (at times absolutely vertiginous, as in van Gogh) as well as horizontals and verticals. But Derain has also adopted Cézanne's technique of unrealistic perspective, plunging in the foreground and soaring in the background.

With regard to *L'Age d'or* (The Golden Age) (Museum of Modern Art, Teheran), whose date varies according to the critic, we think that it cannot have been painted much later than 1904. There are two studies in the album already mentioned, one of which contains the broad outline of the final composition. These studies are at the very beginning of the album, before those for *Le Bal à Suresnes* of 1903. But the chronological order of the drawings is not necessarily the same as that of the paintings, and it is arguable that *L'Age d'or* was painted a few months later than *Le Bal à Suresnes*, towards the end of 1904 or at the very beginning of 1905. This hypothesis is supported by certain stylistic feaures.

L'Age d'or may be linked with the taste for the pastoral and idyllic that had been brought back into fashion by poets, musicians and painters. It may also be considered part of a long unbroken tradition exemplified in Poussin's Arcadian vision, Watteau's *fêtes galantes*, the compositions of Ingres and Puvis de Chavannes and, more recently, Gauguin's Tahitian canvases. However, it is difficult to imagine Derain indulging like his predecessors in vain regrets for some mythical age. Rather, we think he should be placed among those who considered the golden age an ideal to be attained, a model of justice and brotherhood for humanity. This school of thought, an offshoot of Fourier's utopianism, inspired such works as Dominique Papety's *Le Rêve de bonheur* (Dream of Happiness) (Musée de Compiègne) during the nineteenth century; later on, its influence was still apparent in certain works by Neo-Impressionist painters more or less attracted by anarchist or Rosicrucian ideas. Cross's fine landscapes peopled with happy figures offer us the image of a free, flourishing and harmonious society. The same type of inspiration is found in

Signac's *Au temps d'harmonie. L'Age d'or n'est pas dans le passé, il est dans l'avenir* (In the Age of Harmony. The Golden Age is not in the Past, it is in the Future; Pl. 42) (Town Hall, Montreuil-sous-Bois).[28] We find a similar subject and composition in Derain's painting, which has even borrowed from Signac's title, although its ideological message is relatively muted.

The exhibition of 123 works by Signac at the Galerie de l'Art Nouveau in June 1902 probably made Derain aware of the new possibilities for painting offered by Divisionism. The surface arrangement adopted in his *Age d'or* is completely Neo-Impressionist, with a foreground consisting of reclining or kneeling figures arranged diagonally and painted in cold colours, in contrast to a background peopled with dancers and bathers, painted in warm colours. Here the type of composition found in Seurat's *Le Chahut* (Rijksmuseum Kröller-Müller, Otterlo) and *Le Cirque* (The Circus) (Musée du Jeu de Paume, Paris) is faithfully followed by Signac. But it should not be forgotten that it was also a type of composition favoured by the Nabis, such as Bonnard, and by Toulouse-Lautrec, whom Derain greatly admired. One need only think of the *Moulin-Rouge/La Goulue* poster, in which the dark purple silhouette of Valentin le Désossé stands out in the foreground, while the dancer herself occupies the lighted area. Derain also resembled the Neo-Impressionists in favouring very broken brush-strokes, though he used them in a somewhat unorthodox way since he applied his colours irregularly in short streaks, small squares or dots, sometimes spacing them out, sometimes crowding them together. His capriciousness in this respect was enough to make Signac shudder. Even more illogical, from the standpoint of Divisionist principles, was the way in which he broke up forms and at the same time maintained continuity in the form of contour lines. Contour lines did not, of course, have any place in the work of the Neo-Impressionists, who used discontinuous colour contrasts to define forms. Derain's apparently contradictory attitude can be explained by his determination to get the best out of current doctrines without being enslaved by any of them, to create a pictorial idiom free from the constraints of the two key artistic movements of the time. However, *L'Age d'or* was primarily an exploratory venture into the realm of Divisionist painting. Derain's position was similar to that of Matisse after his visit to Signac and Cross in the summer of 1904. In fact it is possible that Matisse showed his composition *Luxe, calme et volupté* to his friend at the end of 1904 before it was exhibited publicly. Had Derain completed his own canvas by then? We think so. At any rate, Matisse's work can hardly have been a revelation to Derain; it would have done no more than reassure him about his own experiments, which already included *Le Pont du Pecq*. We are convinced that Derain's *Age d'or* must have been painted at a time of intensive Divisionist experimentation, when his contacts with the circle of the Indépendants and particularly with Signac were closest—that is, at the end of 1904 or the beginning of 1905.

Thus, even before the end of 1904, Derain—after rejecting Impressionist naturalism as obsolete and experimenting with other approaches, notably Divisionism—had evolved a new kind of art which, if it had not yet resorted to pure colour, proposed a new vision and a new handling of space. In fact, more than any other Fauve painter, Derain subordinated technique to poetry.

Vlaminck

Few things could be more difficult than a study of Vlaminck's beginnings as a painter and his Fauve period, because of the lack of information on relevant events and dates. This situation is largely due to Vlaminck himself who, although he had a compulsive need to unburden himself and produced a great deal of autobiographical material, kept on adding so much that was contradictory and confusing that his memoirs must be approached with considerable caution. Nevertheless, his writings are far from negligible.[29] It is true that their historical interest is considerably diminished because there are far too many details that would need to be checked against more reliable sources. It is also true that their artistic interest is slight since Vlaminck's views on the painting of the period and on his own art are sketchy compared with the subtle and penetrating analyses by his friend Derain. On the other hand, from a psychological standpoint his writings let us get to know Vlaminck the man, who is indistinguishable from Vlaminck the painter, so much so that one seeks to give forceful expression to the other: "As the man is, so is his painting", was Vlaminck's own view. For their part, writers such as André Salmon, Francis Carco, Georges Duhamel, Maurice Genevoix and Pierre Mac Orlan, who were drawn to Vlaminck by his colourful personality, his gift as a raconteur, and his childlike spontaneity, have not helped to clarify matters. In fact, their affection for the painter (in contrast to their dislike of Matisse) led them astray to the point of spreading the myth of Vlaminck as the one true and original Fauve. The confusion thus created by Vlaminck and his friends has discouraged art historians, and there have been few real studies of the painter. No scientific or remotely serious treatment of his work has appeared, and no critical catalogue is available. Marcel Sauvage's book[30] is the only one, for the moment, that is of the slightest value, thanks to its attempt at a catalogue, although incomplete and often wrong. In addition, of all the Fauve painters, Vlaminck has benefited least from large-scale exhibitions; there have, for example, been only two retrospectives, both of them in Paris: one at the Petit Palais in 1933 and the other at the Galerie Charpentier in 1956.

In our study of the development of Vlaminck's art we have taken into account a factor that has been wrongly neglected: the painter's signature. We have been able to reconstruct the history of the various forms of Vlaminck's signature and this has, in many cases, enabled us to date particular paintings. Up to the end of 1905 the painter showed the greatest eccentricity in the way he signed his works. Successively we find: "VLAminck" in capitals followed by lower-case letters, "VLAMINCK" in capitals only, "FLAMENC", "Vlaminck" in rough, uneven lettering, "M. Vlaminck", "M. de V.", then "de Vlaminck" and "Vlaminck" in neat lower-case letters and not underlined. In 1906 the signature became *"Vlaminck"* painted in separate lower-case letters and always underlined—this lasted until 1908. After that, it was written in thicker letters, lower-case but linked, was rarely underlined and assumed an elliptical character.

It is absolutely certain that Vlaminck exhibited no works either at the Salon des Indépendants or at the Salon d'Automne before 1905. Nor did he exhibit at Berthe Weill's; in particular, it is wrong to claim that he did so in 1904. However, his absence from exhibitions does not mean that he did not paint at all before 1905.

When did Vlaminck actually start to paint? When he was quite young he was taught painting by Robichon, a member of the Society of French Artists and a neighbour of his parents at Le Vésinet. Some time later he received instruction from Henri Rigal, the saddler at Le Vésinet, a kind of quasi-Primitive painter whose efforts included paintings on glass. But these early studies cannot be taken seriously. In any case the young Vlaminck did not feel that he had any particular vocation for painting and was more interested in playing the violin with his father. During his military service at Vitré from 1897 to 1900, he was more attracted by music and had no reason to make himself known among his friends as a painter.

It is certain, however, that he was active as a painter (though in a limited way to start with) from the time of his meeting with Derain—a meeting that, according to Vlaminck himself, took place in July 1900. The two young men first met one day on the train from Chatou to Paris. On the return journey they had more time for conversation, for the train was derailed and they had to walk. This meeting, the date of which has been more or less confirmed (perhaps June rather than July), was extremely important for Vlaminck, since it gave him the idea of becoming a painter. "In fact, it is certain", he wrote, "that without that meeting, with-

28. Vlaminck *Paysage près de Chatou*, 1905.

out that providential railway accident, it would never have occurred to me to take up painting as a profession, to make a living from it." Shortly afterwards he and Derain jointly rented a studio at Chatou, though they had to leave it after fifteen months, not only because the landlord put them out, but, more particularly, because Derain had to start his military service in September 1901. We have seen that Derain painted very little during this period. As for Vlaminck's output, we know of only two canvases—not very many for someone who asserted that Fauvism was born from his brush at that particular time.

L'Homme à la pipe (Man with a Pipe) and *Le Père Bouju* (Old Bouju) (Musée National d'Art Moderne, Paris) and *Sur le zinc* (On the Counter) (Musée Calvet, Avignon), all dating from 1900, cannot really be considered as precursors of Fauvism. They are energetic efforts—energetic in brush-work rather than colour—by an amateur painter eager to shock, if not provoke, his friend Derain.

We readily admit that Vlaminck may have been bowled over by the works of van Gogh exhibited at Bernheim-Jeune's in March 1901. He certainly said so: "In him I found some of my own aspirations. Probably from similar Nordic affinities? And, as well as a revolutionary fervour, an almost religious feeling for the interpretation of nature. I came out of this retrospective exhibition shaken to the core." "I felt like crying", he wrote on another occasion. "My soul was overwhelmed by joy and despair. On that day I loved van Gogh more than my own father." In actual fact there is no trace of van Gogh's influence in Vlaminck's work earlier than 1905, which was the date of the second retrospective exhibition of the Dutch painter's work at the Salon des Indépendants. It is possible that Vlaminck got the two exhibitions mixed up when recalling the impact made on him by the revelation of van Gogh's work.

When Derain returned from military service in September 1904, Vlaminck had painted only a few canvases. It is true that he had a family (a wife and two children) to support and was busy giving music lessons, playing the violin in bars or theatre orches-

tras, and writing a novel. How could he have found time to paint? It should also be remembered that he did not have enough money to buy canvases and paints, and that the studio at Chatou was no longer available to him. Even more important, his friend and adviser Derain was absent. In the latter's letters to his friend, it is surprising to observe that there is not very much about art but a great deal about literary projects, novels, plays. It can be gathered from them that there was little curiosity about painting on Vlaminck's part. One feels that when Derain expressed a few ideas on the subject, he was calling the tune and was far ahead of his friend. As mentioned previously, his reply, dated 18 October 1902, to a letter from Vlaminck is revealing: "Your letter saddens and wearies me. You always go on about the immediate sensation." Vlaminck seems to have been taking an interest in Impressionist painting at the time. "I took advantage of every visit I paid to Paris to stroll for a few minutes down rue Laffitte, where the art dealers were. I was happy whenever I saw, in one of their windows, a Jongkind, a Monticelli, or a Monet... I missed none of the exhibitions at Durand-Ruel's and, after looking at the Manets, Monets and Sisleys, I remained full of confidence and enthusiasm."

It is impossible for us to make a judgement on the basis of actual works since paintings from this period are very rare, either because some have been lost or because Vlaminck (and this, we believe, is the most likely explanation) had painted practically nothing. We have been able to examine one of the three works that have come down to us: *La Maison de mon père* (My Father's House) (Gérard Collection).[31] It is wholly naturalistic in conception, and may have been influenced by contact with certain Impressionist works closer in style to Pissarro than to Monet.

When Derain returned from military service and enthusiastically resumed his painting, Vlaminck was able to find more time for art and they worked together on studies from life. Then Derain decided to go and work at the Académie Julian with Matisse and his friends. This decision greatly displeased Vlaminck, who reproached him for "seeking more academic certainties" and was also afraid that he might reveal something of their experiments to the others. "Together," he wrote, "for a year, we have examined and attacked the problem of expression by colour from every angle. Together we have worked in the same direction, towards the same goal. The result was not a gamble or a joke, but a serious, valid and new form of interpretation and, although the public at large might consider it as a student's hoax, more sensitive people might see it as a new and original path." It is hard to believe that Vlaminck and Derain, after a year's work together in the Chatou studio between 1900 and 1901, could have succeeded in defining a "form of interpretation" that would practically pass for Fauvism. At the end of 1904 the situation was different—we have seen that by then Derain had almost achieved genuine Fauvism, but the same cannot be said of Vlaminck.

There is one painting from which we can judge Vlaminck's artistic development in 1904: *Les Bords de la Seine à Bougival* (Banks of the Seine at Bougival), also known as *Le Quai Sganzin* (Pl. 7) (Private Collection, Geneva). Here the painter's approach is perhaps more naturalistic than in the preceding works; in fact he barely avoids an objective rendering of form. He is striving to convey the impact of reality directly without any intervening transposition. Faced with a work like this, one can well understand Derain's complaint that his friend would "always go on about the immediate sensation". The muted colour arrangement consists mainly of drab tones, barely relieved by a few dirty whites. The brush-work has neither the expressive vigour nor the dynamic sweep evident in the earlier canvases. What the artist has gained in discipline he has lost in spontaneity. There is no doubt that observation plays a greater part than imagination in the picture. This canvas, then, offers nothing revolutionary and certainly no new approach to the handling of space. To come to the painter's rescue by dating it to 1902 does not solve the problem, for the work was exhibited at the Salon des Indépendants in 1905, showing that Vlaminck did not consider it anachronistic at that time and that he was

unable to replace it by a more imaginative work since he had not yet painted any. It may be added that the signature—"M. Vlaminck", using the initial of the first name—is a form not found earlier than 1904.

In the summer of 1904 Vlaminck decided to add "de" to his signature; this continued until the following summer. The canvas entitled *Femme dans la campagne* (Woman in the Country) (Private Collection), signed "M. de V.", is later than *Bords de la Seine à Bougival*. It does not have the same sense of realism, but the colours are still fairly faithful to nature. The interest of the picture lies in the vitality of the thick expressive brush-strokes.

In short, it is unnecessary to go very far into Vlaminck's work in 1904 to discover that there was no justification for his assertions and those of his friends concerning his beginnings as a Fauve.

Van Dongen

Van Dongen's malicious pleasure in confusing the record, his indifference as to whether he was the first of the Fauves or the last, and the absence of any critical study of his work—all these factors have combined to give us an incomplete, not to say false, image of the artist. There is no descriptive catalogue of his paintings. An attempt to provide one was made by Louis Chaumeil[32] with the help of the painter, who wanted a "serious" catalogue at last, but unfortunately both men died before it was finished. It was thus left to the editor of the work to clear up doubtful points and decide on questions of dating; as a result many of the dates given are unacceptable. Hence the risk that the chronology of Van Dongen's work for the years preceding Fauvism, and in particular for the Fauve period itself, will always remain uncertain. The years 1905-7 have proved to be a particular trap for the unwary. Yet, while it may not be feasible to establish an absolutely accurate catalogue of all Van Dongen's output up to 1907, we think that agreement can be reached on the dates of a certain number of works, providing us with the only points of reference that will enable us to follow the development of his style—something that has too often eluded the critics. A particularly striking feature of this development is that a tendency towards Fauvism was apparent at a very early stage, and accordingly the theory that Van Dongen was a latecomer to the movement is wrong.

Van Dongen's early landscapes, painted in a dark range of colours, reflect a realistic vision of nature probably derived from certain Dutch painters popular at the time: Anton Mauve and the Maris and Mesdag brothers, who were closer to the tradition of the Barbizon school than to Impressionism in the style of Monet. However, other works of the same period—*Autoportrait en bleu* (Self-portrait in Blue) (1895, Private Collection) and *La Chimère pie* (Pious Illusion) (1895, Private Collection, Monaco)—show in their daring composition and expressive draughtsmanship an artist who was already a non-conformist.

After a first brief stay in Paris in 1897-8, Van Dongen took up residence there in March 1900, although for several years he returned to Holland for holidays. His output from 1900 to 1903 is of the greatest interest; it has two sources of inspiration—one Dutch, the other Parisian—neither of which conflicts. The Dutch source is not the same as before, for Mesdag and Mauve have been succeeded by a much more exciting fellow-countryman, namely Breitner. Van Dongen must have been attracted by Breitner's personal brand of Impressionism, his uncluttered compositions, his bright colours sometimes applied with the knife, and his tendency towards Expressionistic lyricism. Otherwise there is no explanation for some of the landscapes he painted in Holland between 1900 and 1903. We refer particularly to *Péniches à Delfshaven* (Barges at Delfshaven) and *L'Eglise de Dordrecht* (Dordrecht Church) (Private Collection), both of which are remarkable for their direct instinctive apprehension of the perceptible world, the schematization and dynamism of their forms, and their use of pure colour enhanced by passages left white. At first sight they seem to be akin to the pictures painted by Matisse and Marquet at

Arcueil and in the Luxembourg Gardens at practically the same time (1899-1900). In fact, it can be said that all three painters were motivated by a desire to rearrange the perceptible world, adding their own lyrical note, and that their technique was the same in each case, consisting of the vigorous application of pure colours. But Van Dongen's style has not quite the same significance as that of Matisse or Marquet, for he expresses space in terms of light rather than colour. Matisse and Marquet use violent, even discordant colour contrasts to create space without the intervention of light. Van Dongen, however, breaks down some of his colours under the influence of light in order to suggest the enveloping atmosphere.

During the same period (1900-3) Van Dongen produced some works of a very different kind: drawings for humorous magazines in the style of Forain, Steinlen or Toulouse-Lautrec. Derain was doing the same sort of thing at the time. Van Dongen contributed mainly to *L'Assiette au beurre*. He even did a whole issue himself, that of 26 October 1901, entitled "Petite histoire pour petits et grands nenfants *(sic)*" ("A little story for little and big children"), which related the life of a prostitute. It is partly on the basis of these drawings, heightened with watercolours, that Van Dongen has been considered a pioneer of Fauvism. This is a rather exaggerated claim, even if the drawings did reveal him to be a remarkable draughtsman, capable of suggesting the dramatic content of a scene with a few lines.

It was probably at the end of 1903 or, at the latest, the beginning of 1904 that Van Dongen met Fénéon; this was a major event in the painter's life and certainly led to a transformation in his art. The two men definitely did not meet any earlier, as is often maintained. It was through Fénéon that Van Dongen entered the circle of the Société Nationale des Artistes Indépendants, and his work was first exhibited at its Salon in 1904. Until 1903 Van Dongen showed his work only at the Salon of the Société Nationale des Beaux-Arts, and he did not take part in the Salon d'Automne in 1903. His sudden appearance at the Salon des Indépendants in 1904 can only be explained

29. Van Dongen *La Tour Eiffel*, 1904.

by the encouragement he received from Fénéon and the possibility that he was presented by his fellow-countryman Siebe Ten Cate, who had introduced him into anarchist circles. This is how he must have met Signac and also Luce, who covered the young painter's exhibition fees. His growing friendship with Fénéon also gained him an introduction to the group associated with *La Revue Blanche*, which asked him for some illustrations. He thus had an increasing number of friends in the artistic world, and the circle was extended still further in the course of 1904 when he met Picasso, Derain and Vlaminck at Azon's bistro in Place Ravignan.

Van Dongen showed six canvases at the Salon des Indépendants in 1904. They probably included *Le Moulin "Le Muet"* (The "Le Muet" Mill) (Private Collection), which can be placed among the works inspired by Breitner, and certainly *Le Zandstraat* (Private Collection) which lacks the originality of the 1907 version. For the moment realistic observation and narrative prevailed.

During the summer of 1904 Van Dongen was busy preparing for a one-man show to be held at Vollard's that autumn. He painted in Paris (mainly in Montmartre), on the outskirts of Paris and in Normandy. He does not seem to have gone to Holland since no recent canvas (in fact, none later than 1902) inspired by his native land was shown at Vollard's. Before his own exhibition opened, Van Dongen took part in the Salon d'Automne with two paintings: *Portrait de Mlle M. K. du Théâtre Antoine* (Portrait of Miss M. K. from the Antoine Theatre) and *Chevaux* (Horses). The first, which has unfortunately vanished, was a portrait of Marie Kall. The second has been preserved (Private Collection, Lausanne); the horses were almost certainly observed by Van Dongen at the Médrano Circus, to which he often went, perhaps already accompanied by Picasso. Here Van Dongen's art is akin to that of the Nabis in a number of ways: the absence of realism, the daring stylization, the respect of the surface, the flat forms, the indeterminate space, and the minor colour harmonies, consisting here of whites, greys and blacks producing an almost mono-chrome effect, relieved by small touches of red and blue.

On the very day the Salon d'Automne ended, Van Dongen's one-man show opened at the Galerie Vollard; the catalogue had a preface by Fénéon. The exhibits included fifty-three canvases painted in Holland between 1892 and 1902, fifty-three canvases painted in or near Paris or on the Normandy coast between 1902 and 1904, and twenty drawings of the same period, ten of them on the subject of mountebanks. L. Chaumeil, basing himself on the preface and the critics of the period, asserts that most of the works exhibited were not only "pre-Fauve" in style but even "wholly Fauve". Naturally, he chooses quotations favouring such a view, but even these fail to indicate any real Fauve tendency. It would have been just as easy to choose other quotations to show that the painter was anything but a Fauve. Unfortunately, very few of the paintings shown can be identified today; either their titles have been changed, confusing the issue, or their actual whereabouts is unknown. In the 1904 group there are two paintings on the subject of the Moulin de la Galette, one of which is perhaps the picture in the Lévy Collection at Troyes (Pl. 45). Here the syncopated rhythm of the drawing and the heightened colours suggest the frenetic joy of the dancers. The rapid, lively brush-strokes, a little more broken than in earlier works, stress the spirit of reckless gaiety possessing men and women alike. In no instance does the brush-work have a space-defining effect; it is closer to the brush-work of the Impressionists than that of the Fauves, even though it is endowed with a kinetic quality at which Van Dongen excelled. The painting certainly combines dynamic subject-matter, liveliness of drawing and form, and delight in colour, but none of these are specifically Fauve qualities. In the case of a landscape like, say, *La Tour Eiffel* (The Eiffel Tower; Pl. 29) (Private Collection, France), which must have been shown at Vollard's, the link with Impressionism seems even greater; however, a kind of chromatic lyricism relegates the rendering of forms in space to a position of secondary importance.

Among the drawings shown by Van Dongen at Vollard's were two entitled *Sur les cochons* (On the Pigs), which depict the merry-go-rounds in Boulevard Clichy or Place Pigalle with their wooden horses and pigs. It can be surmised that the canvases entitled either *Manèges* (Merry-go-rounds) or *Carrousels* were done during the same period as the drawings, which are studies for them, and that they must therefore date from the end of 1904. Their style differs very little from that of the previous works showing dancers performing the *maxixe* at the Moulin de la Galette. These *Carrousels* reflect the same wish to convey the direct, immediate sensation of the cheerful sight of merry-makers being swept along in a whirl of light and colour (see Pl. 44). Such works undoubtedly owe more to Impressionism than to Fauvism. Yet if we compare them with the preceding canvases we find something new, namely the destruction of three-dimensional space as the Impressionists knew it. Van Dongen covers the surface of his pictures with little dabs of pure colour which do away with form; the subject disappears, dissolving as it were into the painted surface to the point of illegibility, undergoing a sort of disfiguration or process of abstraction, in such a way that only the sensation of the fair is expressed and not the fair itself. This seems to have been the point at which Van Dongen came to consider a picture as primarily a painted surface whose ultimate aim is to offer an equivalent of the perceptible world. A good illustration of this new creative approach, which was to lead the artist to Fauvism, is a version of *Le Moulin de la Galette* (Pl. 8) (Private Collection, Switzerland) that must have been painted at the end of 1904. Van Dongen renders the subject abstract by simplifying it, schematizing it to an extreme. At the same time he gets rid of all spatial illusionism by placing patches of equally saturated colours on the picture surface in a very free-and-easy way. For the idea of spatial relief inherited from the Impressionists, he came to substitute that of space-colour by discovering the space-defining property of patches of colour.

Thus the year 1904 saw Van Dongen making rapid strides in the direction of Fauvism. To do this he had to suppress the capacity for naturalistic observation that he owed to his Dutch background and had cultivated in a number of drawings, for the true Fauve had to break away from the faithful representation of reality. However, he did show a great deal of imagination in his drawing and liked to use bright colours. In other words, before 1905 Van Dongen already showed tendencies in his work that logically led him to Fauvism. The circles he frequented—those of the Société des Artistes Indépendants and *La Revue Blanche*—helped to hasten his development so that, while it is true that he came to Fauvism later than Matisse, Marquet or Derain, he did not come to it as late in the day as some would have us believe.

It has often been concluded, somewhat hastily, that Friesz was the leader of the group of painters from Le Havre, and it is frequently asserted that he introduced Braque to Fauvism. As long ago as 1907 Apollinaire was referring to him as the chief of a "School of Le Havre"—even though such a school never existed outside the poet's imagination. There is no evidence whatsoever that Friesz acted as the leader of his fellow artists in Le Havre. In fact, the eldest of the three was Dufy (born in 1877) and, although he arrived in Paris in 1900 (at the same time as Braque, but two years later than Friesz), he was also the first to join the movement. The fact that he could have initiated the others is generally ignored. He very soon made friends with Marquet, with whom he felt an affinity, and with Matisse, who at first resented his rapid intrusion into the Fauve group.

The three painters from Le Havre all received the same training. After studying at the Municipal Art School in Le Havre under Charles Lhullier, who knew little about the Impressionists but unreservedly admired Boudin, they came together again in Paris at Bonnat's studio. They were all aware of the inadequacy of their academic training and tried to escape from it, either by contemplating the windows of the art galleries in Rue Laffitte—Durand-Ruel's, Vollard's or Sagot's—or by going off, mainly to Normandy, to paint from life.

Dufy

Dufy's output prior to 1905 is well known, much more so than that of Braque or Friesz. He is the only one of the trio from Le Havre for whom there is a descriptive catalogue.[33]

From 1900 to 1904 Dufy's painting remained true to a naturalistic vision of things. Over the years this vision grew more subtle: rather heavy, static representations of reality gave way to lighter, freer ones.

Le Port du Havre au crépuscule (Port of Le Havre at Twilight) and *L'Eglise Saint-Gervais* (St. Gervais Church), both of them executed about 1900 and now in the Musée Calvet, Avignon, are painted in thick, dark colours, though in the latter there are delicate harmonies of white and pink. The spirit and technique of Boudin are echoed in the series of canvases representing the beach at St. Adresse, but there is a greater attempt at rhythmic treatment of the picture surface and, as the brush-strokes are not so broken, the forms are left more or less intact. Dufy was already coming round to the idea that a picture should not just convey a passing sensation but should also satisfy formal requirements.

For Dufy it was not a question of repeating the Impressionism of the 1880s; no Fauve painter, whatever his interest in that movement, thought of doing this. Dufy's Impressionism was that of the close of the nineteenth century—that is, colourful, assertively painted, and giving due importance to linear rhythm—like, say, Guillaumin's Impressionism. Examples include *Carnaval sur les grands boulevards* (Carnival on the Grands Boulevards; Pl. 30) (Private Collection, Paris), which may have been shown by Dufy at the 1903 Salon des Indépendants, and, in particular, certain canvases painted in the South of France in 1903 or 1904, such as *Le Quai à Marseille* (Quay at Marseilles) (Kunsthaus, Zurich) and *Les Martigues* (Musée Cantini, Marseilles), in which the application of colour in parallel hatchings gives the forms considerable density. But Dufy did not limit himself to breaking up his brush-work in this way; at the same time he used an entirely contrary

technique whereby colours were, so to speak, blended over quite extensive areas which were generally outlined. Canvases illustrating this approach include *Un Canal aux Martigues* (Canal at Les Martigues) and *Quai à Rouen* (Quay in Rouen). This apparent contradiction in Dufy's work need not surprise us; it was common to all the Fauve painters. As regards Dufy, however, whatever technique is used, he always aims at a markedly rhythmic treatment of the picture surface, thereby making it possible to analyse direct sensation, bending it to the demands of transposition and synthesis.

Thus, although Dufy's vision is predominantly an Impressionist one, he avoids breaking up form and gives his pictures consistency through their solid structure; and, while he tends to favour heightened, almost pure colour, his harmonies are always subtle.

Friesz

On leaving Le Havre, where he was born in 1879, Friesz studied under Bonnat at the Ecole Nationale des Beaux-Arts from 1899 to 1904, though not very assiduously. This was not because he was wildly hostile to his elderly teacher (he always refused to speak ill of him); in fact, he objected less than most art students to the academic side of his apprenticeship and quite naturally showed his work at the Salon des Artistes Français up to 1903. Then, rather suddenly, he was attracted by Impressionism and began to paint out of doors. It was not just personal taste that drew him to Impressionism, but also a desire to be part of a movement that at the time was still considered as modern, if not avant-garde. "For painters like myself," he wrote, "who came to painting around 1900, armed with their basic training, their developing talent, and their unspoilt responses, the example of Monet, Renoir, Pissarro and Sisley was the only contemporary truth." He often went along to study the Impressionist paintings in Durand-Ruel's gallery in rue Laffitte. He was also captivated by the

30. Dufy *Carnaval sur les grands boulevards, c.* 1903.

changing skies of Normandy and frequently went on painting expeditions to Falaise and Guibray. In 1901 he went painting with Guillaumin in the valley of the Creuse, at Crozant and Gargilesse; he returned there in 1902. He frequently met Pissarro, who advised him on his work. The result was that Friesz's Impressionism was not the insubstantial Impressionism of Monet but the solid Impressionism of Guillamin and Pissarro. In addition Pissarro often spoke to him of Cézanne. No wonder then that Friesz sought to reconcile, as he would say later, "direct sensation and intellectual order". He related how this aspi-

that of Seurat, whose work was being honoured at the Salon des Indépendants. He had reached a point in his thinking that permitted him to find confirmation in the art of both these masters. Van Gogh inspired him to aim at a lyrical interpretation of reality, a free and spontaneous technique that did not exclude a certain degree of discipline, and intense, expressive colour harmonies. He was attracted to Seurat by the latter's sketches and studies from life, of which there was a lavish display at the Salon, and which demonstrated greater sensitivity and a less restrictive and more dynamic composition than were to be found in his cold, over-deliberate full-scale works.

Thus it was through a continuing thought process, a series of questionings (very typical of his character), that Matisse was led to the path of Fauvism—not so much a Fauvism that expressed itself in pure colour as one that offered a lyrical view of the physical world and a non-illusionist definition of space.

Here the problem arises as to how we should take Vlaminck's assertions (echoed by several critics) that Matisse's Fauvist vocation was aroused by the experiments of Derain and Vlaminck himself. In fact, Matisse and Derain had been acquainted since 1898 or 1899 and neither held any secrets for the other. "I knew Derain", Matisse said, "from having met him at Carrière's where he was working, and I was well aware of the very serious and painstaking work of this highly gifted young artist." According to Vlaminck, Derain may have invited Matisse to Chatou. "This visit", he wrote, "was decisive for him. Moved by a vague sense of uneasiness, as well as a need for affirmation, Matisse returned the next day. 'I couldn't sleep all night,' he told us. 'I want to see it all again.' He strongly urged us to show our work at the Salon des Indépendants that would open in April." It is difficult to endorse these statements of Vlaminck's wholeheartedly. We think that the two visits did take place, but at a much longer interval than Vlaminck asserted and under different circumstances. It is known that in February 1905 Derain obtained a contract with Vollard on Matisse's recommendation. We may deduce from this that Matisse was familiar with Derain's recent work,

31.   Matisse *La sieste* ou *Intérieur à Collioure*, 1904.

32. Marquet *Le port de Saint-Tropez*, 1905.

33.   Derain *La femme au châle*, 1905.

34. Derain *Portrait de Matisse*, 1905.

35. Derain *Portrait de Vlaminck*, 1905.

36. Dufy *Bateau pavoisé*, 1905.

37.   Dufy *Le yacht pavoisé*, 1904.

38. Vlaminck *Les régates à Bougival*, 1905.

so that he must have been to Chatou before that date. The only picture mentioned by Vlaminck in connection with this visit is *Le Quai Sganzin* (Pl. 7) (Private Collection, Geneva), which, as we have seen, he painted at the end of 1904. How could a work like this have impressed Matisse? Vlaminck himself did not consider it very original, since he asked: "Don't you find it a bit like Sisley?", to which Matisse is reported to have replied: "I find it much more powerful"—an answer that (if he actually made it) confirms his well-known politeness.

We know, too, that Matisse and his wife went to Chatou to meet Derain's parents, to convince them that painting was a respectable profession, and to ask them to let their son go to Collioure (where Matisse himself was going) in the summer. This would have been about April or May, and Matisse took the opportunity to go back to Vlaminck's and see canvases marking a further stage in his progress towards Fauvism. It must have been on the occasion of this second visit to Chatou when his wife was with him (they may have gone on to Rueil), and not the first one, when he was on his own, that Matisse observed: "To tell the truth, I was not at all surprised by the painting of Derain and Vlaminck, as it was very close to the experimental work I was doing myself. But I was touched to see that these youngsters had certain convictions similar to my own."

Vlaminck's account of Matisse prying into the discoveries of the mythical "school of Chatou" is a travesty of the truth. In this respect Vlaminck had a one-track mind: he imagined himself to be the guardian of a secret—that of expression through pure colour—and was convinced that Matisse had wrested it from him.

In May Matisse set out for Roussillon, his wife's birthplace. On 13 May he was at Perpignan[36] and shortly afterwards he moved to Collioure, where he stayed until he had to be back in Paris to take part in the Salon d'Automne (i.e., until about September or October). It is possible that he chose Collioure not only because of his wife's links with the region, but also because Signac (who had stayed there in 1886)

may have advised him to go there and may even have put him in touch with a painter in Elne named Etienne Terrus, who was a friend of Maillol's (Maillol himself lived at Banyuls).

It is important to follow the various stages of Matisse's creative development during his stay in Collioure.

First of all, he continued his Divisionist experiments. *Le Port d'Avall, Collioure* (Avall Harbour, Collioure; Pl. 54) (Private Collection, France) was probably painted shortly after his arrival. It is a work of perfect harmony embodying the essentials of Seurat's teaching, but, like Seurat's compositions, it looks rather constrained. The same theme is handled (a little later, in our opinion) in *Vue de Collioure* (View of Collioure; Pl. 55) (Museum of Fine Arts, Houston) in a style that could be termed "Anti-Divisionist". A comparison between these two completely dissimilar interpretations will show that the differences are a matter of pictorial technique rather than artistic vision, the relationship of the artist to nature. Despite its decorative side, *Le Port d'Avall, Collioure* is still tinged with naturalism; this is certainly not the case with *Vue de Collioure*, in which objective reality is completely shattered by a transposition imposing a wholly arbitrary "colour-based plasticity" in both the strictly chromatic and spatial spheres. Here Matisse embarks on a reappraisal of his painting that will enable him to shake off the yoke of Divisionism. The canvas in Houston illustrates his determination to get away from the systematic breaking-up of form and replace it with a Tachist procedure better adapted to the lyrical interpretation of emotion. In this way he gained the means needed to make a picture a poetic creation.

Derain came to Collioure in July, and it was probably under his influence that Matisse increasingly came to interpret Divisionism with such freedom that it could hardly be called Divisionism any longer. We shall see that Derain went to considerable lengths in exploiting techniques based on the division of tones; he certainly did so in a less disciplined and less backward-looking spirit than Matisse and, according to himself, he even dropped Pointillism before Matisse did. As a result of his contact with Derain, Matisse eventually gave himself up to a more spontaneous kind of expression, a freer lyricism. "At that time", he said of his friend and himself, "we were like children before nature and gave our temperaments free rein, painting from imagination when we did not make use of nature itself. I spoilt everything on principle and worked as I felt, by colour alone." This was the starting-point for a series of very freely painted canvases, inspired by an exuberant lyricism that transposed the world of reality into one of almost abstract structures, so great was the painter's determination not to copy.

In this series (in which the Houston picture may be included) the brush-strokes grow progressively broader, forming patches, then coloured planes that play a part in the construction of space. The stretches of colour are not yet set directly side by side—the sizing of the canvas provides intervening areas of white.

Derain and Matisse came to the same conclusion about the division of tones. It results, observed Derain, in "a self-destructive world". Matisse's analysis is similar: "The breaking-up of colour leads to the breaking-up of forms and contours. Result: a jerky surface. The sensation is purely retinal, but it destroys tranquillity of line and surface. The objects are distinguishable only by the degree of luminosity they are given. Everything is treated in the same way. All things considered, there is only a kind of tactile animation comparable to the *vibrato* of the violin or the voice." Here, it would seem, is the key to the crisis Matisse was experiencing. We know for certain that there was such a crisis that July, since Derain mentioned it in a letter to Vlaminck, without, however, going into details. It is nevertheless possible to reconstruct it, since Derain has left us a clear account of a parallel crisis in his own development. Basically, it consisted of a critical reassessment of Divisionism as regards both content and form. The fundamentally naturalistic Neo-Impressionist approach ran counter to the new relationship between man and nature established by Matisse, a relationship based on lyrical feeling. In the same way, the Divisionist idiom was scarcely designed to convey the impact of nature on the artist in a direct and comprehensive way. "I tried", Matisse said later, speaking of this period, "to replace the *vibrato* by an accord whose very simplicity and sincerity would produce a less troubled surface." No doubt he realized, like Derain, that broken brushstrokes were suitable for "luminous and harmonious pictures" (Derain's phrase) but less so for arbitrary transitions—what Derain called "deliberate disharmonies". Another of Matisse's worries (shared by Derain) was the difficulty of reconciling lyricism with style. This difficulty is still apparent in the earlier works painted at Collioure, particularly *Le Port d'Avall, Collioure*, in which it can be seen that, for every gain in style, there was a loss in lyrical feeling. Matisse thus had to replace the concept of style with a different concept, namely that of the organization of colour, which was perfectly compatible with lyrical inspiration. At Collioure, Matisse very soon began to liberate his colours from their slavery to illusionism—to the rendering of local colour, light. "Everything, even colour", he said, speaking of this period, "can only be a creation... Colour contributes to the expression of light, not the physical phenomenon which is the only light existing in reality, but the light in the artist's mind... Called forth and stimulated materially, recreated mentally, colour can interpret the essence of each object and, at the same time, reflect the intensity of the emotional impact... When I use green, it doesn't mean grass; when I use blue, it doesn't mean the sky." In other words, a picture is an artistic fact interpreting a lyrical feeling—which is basically a definition of Fauvist art.

Matisse recognized that this new concept of the work of art had been prompted to some extent by a closer acquaintance with Gauguin's painting. We know that, thanks to Maillol (to whom they had been introduced by Etienne Terrus), Matisse and Derain paid a visit to Daniel de Monfreid who lived at Corneilla-de-Conflent, a short distance from Collioure, and who was looking after the greater part of

Gauguin's last paintings, pending the settlement of the artist's estate. Perhaps they also went to Béziers to see Gustave Fayet, another collector of Gauguin's works. "What I wanted", Matisse said, "was an art of expression and equivalence; basically Gauguin was better qualified than the Neo-Impressionists to help me take a step in that direction." He even considered Gauguin the only one who could "save" him. In other words, Matisse began to take an interest in Gauguin's work (for which he had earlier felt some aversion) when he thought it might provide him with an answer to his own problems, "when"—as he said—"my studies permitted me to see where Gauguin's theory came from". It is very understandable that he turned to Gauguin (without, however, altogether giving up what he had learnt from Divisionism), for Gauguin's work confirmed the Fauve painter in his quest for an art of imagination rather than representation, in his attempt to achieve greater power of expression by juxtaposing patches of colour or emphasizing outlines, and in his desire for a new kind of colour relationship based not so much on the systematic opposition of complementary tones as on accords between kindred tones. With their calculated spontaneity and direct lyricism, the first canvases painted at Collioure are rather sketchy and lack artistic impact. The same cannot be said of those that followed, for, thanks to Gauguin, Matisse was learning to organize colour. "An avalanche of colours has no real power", he remarked. "Colour is fully expressive only when it is organized, when it corresponds to the intensity of the artist's emotion." This development is illustrated by four important canvases: *La Fenêtre ouverte* (The Open Window), *La Femme au chapeau* (Woman with a Hat), *La Sieste* (The Siesta; Pl. 31) (Private Collection, Switzerland) and *La Femme à la raie verte* (Woman with the Green Stripe) (Statens Museum for Kunst, Copenhagen). Whatever the subject, there is no trace of naturalism; the artist desired only to express the feeling inspired in him by contemplation of the object. Thus light ceases to exist as a realistic element modelling the object. In *La Sieste*, for example, it introduces no variations in colour to indicate distance from the spectator; the same red verging on orange is used in the foreground as in the background, but it nevertheless appears to vary in intensity through the interplay of colour relationships alone. Thus, space is no longer based on light but on colour expressive of the artist's feelings. This handling of space may be termed "lyrical" since it is so dependent on the artist's innermost self. In the same fashion as *La Sieste*, *La Fenêtre ouverte* shows Matisse resolutely interpreting space in terms of his own sensations. Each of these pictures contains a window which could well serve as a pretext for setting inner and external space in a harmonious or conflicting relationship (one need only mention Manet's *Balcony*). In fact, Matisse unites both kinds of space in his emotional reaction, which makes no distinction between the atmosphere of the landscape and that of the room. He is striving to avoid the naturalistic rendering of space on segregated planes, preferring a poetic concept of space that can be expressed only through a combination of coloured surfaces. A definition given by Matisse in 1935 had already been valid thirty years earlier: "The picture consists of a combination of differently coloured surfaces, a combination that results in an act of expression."

As well as exhibiting some works (now impossible to identify) at Berthe Weill's, Matisse took part in the Salon d'Automne, of which he was not only a member but assistant secretary, showing only recent works painted at Collioure. Two can be identified with certainty, since they were reproduced in *L'Illustration* of 4 November 1905: *Fenêtre ouverte* and *Femme au chapeau*.

At that time critical opinion was sharply divided on the subject of Matisse. Camille Mauclair waxed sarcastic about how little time Matisse must have spent on his pictures. G. Jean Aubry even thought that the painter was playing a practical joke on the public: "I have heard", he said, "young artists repeating 'He is the most gifted of us all!' I admit that his painting is quite often pleasing to the eye, but why didn't he simply exhibit his palette instead of this Chinese puzzle called, contrary to appearances, *Young*

Woman in Japanese Costume or that *Open Window* which remains shut to me? As for his *Woman with a Hat*, I cannot agree with those who defend it; it strikes me as ugly in drawing, colour and expression." Denis, for his part, understood Matisse's experiments, but found fault with them as the product of "a systematizing spirit". "You are never satisfied", he said to Matisse, "until every feature of your work is intelligible. Nothing must remain conditioned or accidental in your universe." He sees another danger in Matisse's painting, that of "engaging in dialectic" and thus arriving "at ideas, at noumena of pictures". Denis's theme was taken up by Gide, to whom Matisse's works seemed to present "the aspect of demonstrations of theorems... [His art] is the product of theories. Everything in it can be deduced, explained; intuition has no place in it... Yes, this sort of painting is certainly rational, but, more than that, it is disputatious. How far we are from van Gogh's lyrical excess!"[37] Matisse always protested against this interpretation of his painting, since he felt that there is no art without passion. It is, in fact, a misrepresentation to treat Matisse's painting, even in 1905, as essentially systematic and dialectical, for it is quite the contrary. This does not mean that it is the product of brute instinct or chance; Matisse had a very lofty idea of the creative act in which both the intelligence and the will played a part. In his view a picture was the product of an integral poetic process in which inspiration and technique were combined in such a way that the first could not be betrayed nor the second deprived of sense. On this point the painter was explicit: "Thus, for me, Fauvism was a testing-ground for media: placing a blue, a red, a green side by side, assembling them in an expressive and constructive way. It was the result of a need I felt in myself and not a voluntary attitude, not a deduction or a rationalization, for these have no part in painting." It cannot be denied, however, that there is a tendency towards distortion, or even abstraction, in this kind of art. This is a logical consequence of the search for equivalencies which characterized Matisse's efforts at Collioure; the descriptive rendering of forms is replaced by what Denis termed "noumena of pictures", a kind of sign language.

Matisse established a completely new figurative system resulting in the total destruction of the traditional concept of space. This system was the product of a highly logical train of thought, a series of precise conclusions immediately acted upon. He recognized that it was essential for him "to learn passionately and regularly, to further each study in a definite direction". This logical turn of mind fascinated Derain, who also pondered a great deal on his art. "As regards logic and psychological speculation," he wrote to Vlaminck from Collioure, "he is a much more extraordinary person than I should ever have believed."

Marquet

We have seen that the enthusiasm that drove Marquet towards Fauvism in the years 1899-1901 soon changed to a more reserved attitude; this produced a very personal manner of painting which did not, however, exclude Fauvist features. He continued to work in this manner until the beginning of 1905.

Matisse dans l'atelier de Manguin (Matisse in Manguin's Studio) (Musée National d'Art Moderne, Paris), painted incontestably in the winter of 1904-5, shows the extent to which Marquet rejected the relinquishment of the traditional treatment of space; his planes are arranged with a rational strictness and the Pointillist technique is restrained so as to avoid any confusion of the pictorial space. Similarly, Marquet drew the nude with clear contour lines that helped place it in the foreground. The fact that the tones are considerably heightened does not in itself give the picture a particularly Fauve character. A comparison with the "companion piece" painted by Matisse at the same time and in the same place, *Marquet peignant un nu* (Marquet Painting a Nude) (Musée National d'Art Moderne, Paris), is revealing. The colours are applied with divided brush-strokes and their degree of saturation is the same all over the canvas so that the foreground is distanced and the background brought forward, with the result that all planes meet, as it were, on the picture surface. Matisse preferred the plastic potential of the surface to a logical treatment of space. Marquet rarely went so far.

At the Salon des Indépendants of 1905 Marquet showed eight canvases, only one of which is known now because it was purchased by the state—*Notre-Dame, soleil* (Notre Dame, Sunshine; Pl. 24) (Musée des Beaux-Arts, Pau). It had already been exhibited at the Indépendants in 1903.

In the summer, when Matisse and Derain were in Collioure, Marquet and Camoin were painting at Cassis, Agay, Menton and St. Tropez. Camoin had developed a great admiration for Manet after seeing forty of his works at Durand-Ruel's in May 1899. He must have tried to convert Marquet to his views, which no doubt explains the echoes of Manet we can trace in the latter's painting. At St. Tropez Marquet and Camoin were still so full of Manet that they gave the nickname "Le Bon Bock" to the Bar des Roses where rather coy models posed for them; and Marquet intended to name a canvas showing one of these women *Nouvelle Olympia* (in imitation of Cézanne).

Marquet's Mediterranean output is well known thanks to several pictures that have been preserved. Two of them, identified beyond dispute, which were among those sent to the Salon d'Automne, might be taken as points of reference: *Le Port de Menton* (Menton Harbour; Pl. 71) (Hermitage, Leningrad) and *Vue d'Agay* (View of Agay) (Musée National d'Art Moderne, Paris). These two works can be considered Fauve since Marquet—without going so far as schematization—used a decidedly synthesizing idiom, and also because colour is used as an essential means of expression. However, there are some other noteworthy points to consider. Although Marquet expressed the overall impact the southern landscape made on him, there was nothing abrupt or instinctive about it. It was not set down as it was; it was the outcome of careful refining which shows in

the revised drawing and the carefully thought-out harmonies. Marquet in no way aimed at communicating a particular feeling experienced at a given moment: he wanted his picture to be the sum total, the synthesis of the feelings experienced over a period of time, so that we might speak of composite sensations—what Matisse in 1907 called "the condensation of sensations". Marquet certainly was one of the less intuitive Fauves; we must not be taken in by the apparent simplicity of his style. His chromatic system, above all, made him an especially lucid and sophisticated painter. *Le Port de Menton* (Pl. 71) has a very sober, delicate harmony in which complementary tones practically never lie adjacent to each other, and if they happen to be close together, they are not of equal colour intensity: pale pinks are matched with saturated greens; like Manet, Marquet chose the rarest harmonies—blue-greens, green-yellows, blue-mauves. And in both *Le Port de Menton* and *Vue d'Agay* the brush-stroke has none of the unruliness generally found in the other Fauves. Here, by contrast, the paint was applied thoughtfully because it was the instrument of a fully controlled emotion. Although Marquet used the contrast of coloured planes in his treatment of space, he also resorted to a complex play of lines and a succession of segregating planes. In *Le Port de Menton* (Pl. 71), for example, the curve of the quay, the obliqueness of the yacht, and the horizontal line of the boat compel attention. We can also see that Marquet varied the consistency of his paint, applying it fairly thickly in the foreground and very thinly in the background features, thus creating an effect of depth. The *Vue d'Agay* uses a different system: the foreground and the background converge beyond the stretch of sea, whose blue creates a pictorial link; line plays a lesser part here than the contrast between cold and warm shades.

Marquet shows us two views of southern reality: one in which pale forms are drained of colour by warm light reflected in the harbour, the other in which luxuriant, vividly coloured nature is intensified by burning light. We must stress the fact that these are accurate images, for although Marquet, like all Fauve

39. Derain *La Seine au Pecq*, late 1904.

40. Derain *Le Vieil Arbre*, late 1904.

painters, gave greater weight to the picture-image at the expense of the reality-image, the equivalents and the signs nevertheless remain true to the object. In fact, Marquet had not entirely shaken off his naturalist approach. When he painted the water in the port at Menton, he saw it not solely as an artistic feature but in its reality, a liquid and reflecting element. Note, too, the accuracy of the forms, rendered by faithful, though simplified, drawing, the exact treatment of light, the precision of the tones, heightened but not transposed, and true to reality.

Fauvism is more in evidence in the *Port d'Agay* (Private Collection, France). Here Marquet does not confine himself to heightening the tones; they are equally saturated over the whole surface so that the suggestion of space comes from the contrast between the tones and not from their shading.

Marquet did not show any of the pictures painted at St. Tropez at the Salon d'Automne. These were precisely the ones—executed after his stay at Menton and Agay—that show a much more definite and complete orientation towards Fauvism. Carried away by a lyrical feeling that opened his eyes to the essence of Mediterranean nature, he simplified, abbreviated, eliminated, accentuated, recomposed, transposed and, above all, used colour as the equivalent of light and space. In other words he expressed himself as a true Fauve, but that does not mean as a Fauve who has lost his head; we can see this in *Le Port de Saint-Tropez* (Pl. 32), in the geometrical rhythm of the composition, the measured play of sustained lines, and the rejection of violent tones in the chromatic system.

This wholly Fauve idiom seems to have come as the end result of an evolution which Marquet's art underwent in 1905 and not just as a transitory manner of painting inspired by the Mediterranean environment. Admittedly, some geographical features of the Mediterranean region might have played a part in the heightening of colour and the treatment of space; this is true of Marquet as much as of the other Fauves. But we must not exaggerate the importance of this aspect, for we must remember, first of all, that a great deal

may be due to the influence exerted by a fellow painter (Camoin's on Marquet at St. Tropez, Matisse's on Derain at Collioure) and, secondly, that the decision to work in the South was surely taken with at least some awareness of the consequences it might have. We must also bear in mind the example of Vlaminck, who never went to the South during his Fauve period. While we do not entirely discount the influence of the natural setting in which the artist is working, we think that it is reasonable to suppose that the motivation of a Fauve painter was aesthetic rather than geographical. In Marquet's case, too, the Fauve manner persisted in the works executed in the course of the autumn and winter after his return from the South. Thus *Le Soleil à travers les arbres* (Sunshine through Trees) (Pushkin Museum of Fine Arts, Moscow) and its two variants, *Le Quai de la Mégisserie*, which actually represents the two works *Le Quai du Louvre* (Anonymous Collections) as well as *Le Quai des Grands-Augustins* (Musée National d'Art Moderne, Paris) belong to the same family as the intensely Fauve works of St. Tropez, although they had a more subdued palette simply because Marquet was conveying a reality other than that of the Mediterranean; it goes without saying that the Paris quays are not the same as the port of St. Tropez—this is a matter of light. Marquet's interest in light alone would give him a place apart among the Fauves. He was undoubtedly the only Fauve whose picture-image remained more or less an image of reality.

His interpretation of art has often been misunderstood. As early as 1905 his painting seemed difficult to understand, yet it was not really fundamentally different from Matisse's or Derain's; but it was less immediately shocking because the drawing had no distortion and the colour no violence. The critics of the time generally regarded Marquet as a new Impressionist. And this is not altogether wrong when considering his exhibits at the Salon des Indépendants, but glaringly wrong when it comes to the Mediterranean pictures shown at the Salon d'Automne. The critics of the time simply decided whether a work was Fauve or not according to the intensity of its colours.

41. Derain *Paysage de l'Ile-de-France*, 1904.

42. Signac *Au Temps d'harmonie. L'Age d'or n'est pas dans le passé, il est dans l'avenir*, 1894.

43. Ingres *L'Age d'or*, 1862.

It is true that Marquet's painting is exceptionally difficult to analyse because it is full of subtleties. Although there was an element of realism in his approach, he did not aim at the exact reproduction of the physical world. His spirit was no less lyrical than that of Matisse and Derain; his lyricism is different, made up of a subtle, even pensive poetical feeling for the appearance of things. The painter's emotions are always superimposed on reality. He is a colourist, and the fact that he is a subtle colourist does not make him any less of a Fauve. Is it really necessary to roar like Vlaminck to be considered a Fauve? Some critics seem to think so, and perhaps Marquet himself shared their view to some extent. He did not always apply colours of equal saturation because he wanted to retain a suggestion of aerial perspective by means of shading and the modulation of coloured planes. It is unlikely that he really wanted to discard the traditional treatment of space altogether; the fact is that he neither wholly accepted nor wholly rejected it, but compromised with it. He rarely adopted the Fauve manner of creating pictorial space by means of vivid colours; he never used the contrast of discordant colours; he preferred the alternation of emphatic and light planes. To say that Marquet was an independent Fauve is meaningless. On the whole, Marquet's position was that of a Fauve painter. As we have said, a work is not Fauve simply because it contains the sum total of elements defining Fauvism. The Fauve character of a work stems from the relationship it creates between the various elements: in Marquet's case, that relationship distinguished his art fundamentally from that of the Impressionists, Manet or Corot, with whom it has often been compared; it shows that he truly belonged to the Fauve family, which must not be considered a homogeneous *bloc*.

Derain

The Fauve tendencies we have analysed in some of Derain's work at the end of 1904 developed strikingly during 1905.

At the Salon des Indépendants Derain exhibited eight canvases. Two of these we can identify with certainty—*Le Vieil Arbre* (The Old Tree; Pl. 40) (Musée National d'Art Moderne, Paris) and *Bougival* (Pl. 21) (Private Collection, France), for we have reconstructed the circumstances in which they were bought from Derain at the time of the Salon by Ernest Siegfried (uncle of André Siegfried) for his son-in-law Olivier Senn, on whom he wanted to play a practical joke.[38] Thus we have two sure points of reference. We have discussed the importance of *Le Vieil Arbre* with regard to the new idiom Derain was attempting to formulate; in this connection *Bougival* is an even more important work, for it clearly shows his determination to transpose reality, to substitute a lyrical interpretation for the naturalist approach to the physical world, even if there is still some illusionist treatment of space. These two works go back to, and confirm, the experiments already contained in *Le Pont du Pecq* (Bridge at Pecq), which doubtless was simultaneously exhibited at the same Salon.

A canvas bearing the date 1905, *L'Arbre, paysage au bord d'une rivière* (Tree, River Landscape) must be dated from before his summer stay at Collioure. We suggest that it was the last, the most Fauve, interpretation of the subject of the "old tree" which absorbed Derain at the end of 1904. It is equally possible that a canvas called *Banlieue* (Suburb), which shows a landscape that seems similar to that of *Bougival*, may date from the beginning of 1905.

In the summer Derain was working at Collioure together with Matisse, who had urged him to join him. From the point of view of Fauve experimentation, Derain was no less go-ahead than his friend, although he was eleven years younger. At the Indépendants that year Matisse was able to show *Luxe, calme et volupté* and a *Vue de Saint-Tropez* which heralded a new era in painting, but Derain was able to show *Bougival* and *Le Pont du Pecq*, which were no less promising. Moreover, the two painters had the greatest esteem for each other and knew that they stood to gain a great deal from working together. They had known each other since 1899 and were very close. Gertrude Stein

44. Van Dongen *Manège de cochons*, 1904.

tells us that "at that time Derain was always with Matisse and of all Matisse's friends he was Madame Matisse's favourite." Matisse must have felt a high regard for his friend's painting since he helped him obtain a contract from Vollard in February and urged him to exhibit at the Indépendants. He made the trip to Chatou with his wife to persuade Derain's parents to let their son go to Collioure. We might be tempted to add that Matisse encouraged him to come to Collioure because he fully realized that his experiments and Derain's had a great deal in common. Speaking of that particular period, he said later to Francis Carco that Derain "knew more about it than anyone".

Derain's output during the months of July and August which he spent at Collioure was prolific. Before returning to Paris he told Vlaminck that he would have "thirty canvases completed, twenty drawings and some fifty sketches".

Of the thirty Collioure canvases he himself mentioned we now know only about twenty, which perhaps constitute the most important collection in the whole of Fauve painting. It is not easy to establish their chronology, but we do not think it impossible. Four letters from Derain to Vlaminck give us some idea of the direction in which the artist was evolving.[39]

In his first letter (which, in our opinion, should be dated to the beginning of July) Derain said that he was working a lot, that he found it difficult to convey his emotion fully and that he had come to convince himself that "it is silly to use a street corner to express the whole synthesis of feelings a landscape arouses in you." Above all, he told his friend of his great revelation: the light of the country, "a fair golden light that does away with shadows"; then he added: "This is a maddening job. Everything I have done so far seems stupid to me."

The second letter (written no doubt during July) confirmed his enthusiasm for working with Matisse, whom he surprised, he said, with his "science of colour". There is an enigmatic comment: "My cure dates only from today." What had been the matter with him? Not simply the vague anxiety of wondering whether he was on the right road; we feel there must be a more definite answer, and we shall attempt to give it. A little later Derain admitted that he was not altogether cured, which is not surprising when we remember his anxious character, constantly doubting his painting. But it would be wrong to exaggerate Derain's anxiety for, in the same letter, he told his friend: "I shall have thirty studies finished by the time I get back. I have never before done work as complex and as different, quite disconcerting for the critics."

In his letter of 28 July he again mentioned his "difficulties in synthesizing", for which he blamed the "radiant sun" which compelled him to do "acrobatics with light". He then told Vlaminck of his discoveries: having defined "a new conception of light that consists of this: the negation of shadow", and having been able to "stamp out any kind of division of tone", he said that Matisse continued to use the Divisionist method but that he himself "hardly used it any more". "It's logical", he said, "in a luminous and harmonious picture. But it is detrimental to anything that takes its expression from deliberate disharmonies." In the same letter he complained of his own excessive lyricism, his strained transpositions: "My nerves are getting me down. I am getting more and more besotted with this kind of painting into which I put everything that one can't see anywhere... I even want to put too much of myself into it. I'm overloading it, I'm stifling it." Thus we can see that Derain is still beset by doubts: he had gone so far so fast that by July he was in a state of crisis.

Given these circumstances it is not surprising that he told Vlaminck, on 5 August, that he was not cured; at the same time he explained why he had thought earlier that he was: "I told you I was cured so that, with your usual need to be the first, you might feel more cured than I was. In reality, it's not true. I strain my brain and have poorer results than before."

Taking the letters as a starting-point we can reconstruct the evolution of Derain's art at Collioure. We believe there were three phases.

We are tempted to regard *Le Séchage des voiles* (Sails Drying) (Hermitage, Leningrad) as one of the

45. Van Dongen *Le Moulin de la Galette*, 1904.

first works he painted at Collioure, one of those in which he attempted, in a relatively limited view, to synthesize all the new emotions he was experiencing. In some ways this canvas is not very different from the *Pont du Pecq*, painted a few months earlier; it suggests the same restraint in the use of transposition; we would even say it is less arbitrary, both in drawing and colour; the picture also reverts to an earlier manner in which coloured areas are associated with broken surfaces. But there are some entirely new features—on the one hand, the treatment of light through a total elimination of shadow, and, on the other, the use of the white of the canvas to convey the glare of noon.

During a second phase Derain continued to experiment with Divisionist methods; we can see this in the landscape called simply *Collioure* (formerly Daelemans Collection, Brussels). The variety of serried brush-strokes creates an impression of density, of fullness of form, which is absent from the earlier phase. The dazzling, wholly arbitrary colour constructs space through equal saturation of tones; but, more than anything else, it interprets the artist's inner vision which puts into the painting, as he himself said, "everything that one can't see anywhere".

This second phase was traumatic for Derain, who became aware of the difficulty of following his inner vision without damaging the picture and the difficulty of balancing subjective and objective distortion, of reconciling lyricism and style. This, we feel, lies at the heart of the sickness which, he told Vlaminck, could not be cured. Thus we can distinguish two types of works during this second phase, that is, when he was exploring methods for dividing tones. The first group comprises canvases in which the calculated organization of the painted surface shows that the lyrical spirit is perfectly under control; this is the case in *Collioure, le village et la mer* (Collioure, Village and Sea) (Folkwang Museum, Essen). The second category includes canvases in which Derain, to cite his own words, "lets himself go with colour for colour", "strains his brain" and wants to put too much of himself into the picture, so that his transpositions lead to virtual distortions, to abstraction—a typical

46. Matisse *La liseuse*, 1906.

47. Marquet *Fête foraine au Havre*, 1906.

48.   Derain *Pont sur la Tamise*, 1906.

49.   Vlaminck *Voilier sur la Seine*, 1906.

50.   Van Dongen *La belle Fernande*, 1906.

51. Dufy *Le bal champêtre*, 1906.

52. Friesz *Le port d'Anvers*, 1906.

53. Braque *L'Estaque*, 1906.

example can be seen in *Barques amarrées* (Boats at Mooring).

Derain very soon realized the pitfalls of Divisionist excess; hence the third phase, which comprised notably three versions of the suburb at Collioure, the last of which was doubtless the one in the Musée National d'Art Moderne in Paris (Pl. 72). Here Derain chose to create a "deliberate disharmony", that is, a chromatic construction based on less attractive, less stimulating relationships of colour than before—for instance, blue and green, ochre and orange, violet and blue. He no longer used complementary but kindred groups of shades and at the same time substituted the technique of flat areas for the breaking-up of colour. This was probably due to the revelation of Gauguin's paintings which he saw at Daniel de Monfreid's at Corneilla-de-Conflent. Thus Derain, like Matisse, was helped by Gauguin to free himself from Divisionism.

In September Derain returned unwillingly to Paris to prepare his submission to the Salon d'Automne which, we know, included *Le Séchage des voiles*, reproduced in *L'Illustration* of 4 November 1905. He also exhibited works we cannot identify at Berthe Weill's and at Prath and Magnier's.

Derain always asserted that he stayed in London on two occasions, once at the end of 1905 and then again during the following year. We can assume that his first visit must have been in the autumn or winter of 1905 and that it did not last more than two weeks; he must have concentrated on reconnoitring subjects and painted only studies. The second stay would probably have been in the winter and spring of 1906; he stayed for three months, leaving in April at the earliest.

It is impossible, from the twenty or so surviving canvases, to establish any chronology or even to distinguish those of 1905 from those of 1906. There is not sufficient evidence on the subject. Two letters sent to Vlaminck from London are unfortunately not dated. A single canvas bears the date 1906—*Le Parlement et le pont de Westminster* (Houses of Parliament and Westminster Bridge; Pl. 62) (Private Collection, New York).[40] We know from Derain himself that he painted another in April 1906, the *Bassin de Londres* (Pool of London) (Tate Gallery, London). Critics usually date the canvases in the Divisionist manner, like *Big Ben* (Pl. 63) (Pierre Lévy Collection, Troyes), from the first stay, and the canvases with flat areas of colour and linear composition like *Hyde Park* from the second. This methodology seems highly questionable and makes unwarranted assumptions. Why should we proceed from the premise that Derain followed the same course in London as at Collioure? We think that it would be more sensible to assume that when he arrived in London in 1905, soon after his stay at Collioure, he was determined at first not to use a Divisionist method, but that he came to use it subsequently because he found it better suited for conveying the effect of the fluid subject he was treating; note that the divided brush-stroke appears each time there is a sky-water relationship. We must be careful to remember that in Derain's case everything is much more complex than might at first appear. We think his problem did not consist in choosing between divided tones and flat tones. At the outset he probably did not care which of the two techniques he used: upon counting we find that there are about as many canvases in the one manner as there are in the other. The main problem for the artist was how to convey his vision artistically—with all that this implied as regards technique—a non-realist vision, admittedly, but one linked nevertheless to a specific geographical environment more changeable than Collioure. This explains why the hesitations and relapses were more frequent in London than at Collioure. In these circumstances it seems more sensible to analyse the London pictures as a whole, without trying systematically to establish their chronology; since the stay ended in the spring of 1906 we shall postpone this analysis until the next chapter.

The year 1905 ended with an event of great importance for Derain: his discovery of African art. He bought a Congolese mask from Vlaminck, which the latter had acquired in an Argenteuil café during the summer. Of course it would be absurd to say that this purchase produced an immediate upheaval in Derain's art—there would hardly be any evidence of that. All we can say for the moment is that Derain saw something in that African mask that brought back Cézanne's teaching, which had been forgotten during the period of intensive Fauve experiments but was now revived. Derain did not yet feel any need to break with Fauvism. Indeed, for the time being African art and Fauvism were not incompatible—far from it.

Vlaminck

Vlaminck first exhibited at the Salon des Indépendants of 1905. The circumstances that led him to take part in that Salon are obscure. While there is no doubt that Matisse, who was the chairman of the hanging committee of the Indépendants, encouraged Derain to exhibit, it is difficult to imagine him doing the same for Vlaminck, whose work, at the end of 1904, was so insignificant compared with Derain's; and the canvases he painted at the beginning of 1905 do not seem to have been any better. It is hard to believe that Matisse, on seeing *Le Quai Sganzin* (Pl. 7), which dated from the end of 1904, could have advised Vlaminck to exhibit at the Indépendants. We think it more likely that it was Derain who, out of friendship, recommended him to Matisse so that he would also be in the exhibition. After all, the Salon des Indépendants was completely open to anyone, as there was no jury. It was quite like Vlaminck to decide to exhibit without asking anyone for anything.

Of the eight canvases he exhibited, three have been identified. At an anonymous collector's we have found one entitled *Les Bords de la Seine à Nanterre* (Banks of the Seine at Nanterre; Pl. 22) (Private Collection, France) which had been believed lost. It was one of a lot, which also included three canvases by Derain, bought by Ernest Siegfried for his son-in-law Olivier Senn.[41] This provides us with an absolutely certain chronological reference. The work has a totally naturalist approach: no trace of lyricism modifies the reality of the subject-matter; there is no distortion in the drawing and the colour is true to the local colour. There is nothing revolutionary in it, no attempt at transposition, no novel treatment of space. At the beginning of 1905 Vlaminck was by no means so far advanced on the road to Fauvism as he has claimed. We cannot even say that the painting he exhibited was a much earlier work, for the signature "M. de Vlaminck" was in the manner that came between his "M. de V." at the end of 1904 and "de Vlaminck", which first appeared in the summer of 1905 when the initial of the Christian name was omitted altogether.

Vlaminck also showed *Les Bords de la Seine à Bougival* (Banks of the Seine at Bougival; Pl. 7), now more commonly known as *Le Quai Sganzin* (Private Collection, Geneva). We have seen that this canvas, which bears the signature "M. Vlaminck" (just prior to "M. de V.") must date from the summer or autumn of 1904 and that in its quest for a new form of representation it was no more promising than its predecessor.

La Fille de ma voisine or *La Fille à la poupée* (My Neighbour's Daughter or Girl with Doll) is the third of the canvases we know; the date "1902" inscribed on the picture by the artist is not trustworthy—it is inconsistent with the type of signature it bears. Vlaminck had never signed in this manner, in joined lower-case letters with no underlining, before 1905; he used this form of signature for a very short time since he took to underlining his name at the beginning of 1906 and continued to do so until 1908. There is every reason to believe that Vlaminck added his signature and the date 1902 in about 1905-6, perhaps in April 1906 when he sold the picture with his entire output to Vollard. We think it would be more accurate to date the picture from the end of 1904 or the beginning of 1905. In the first place, the spirit and execution of the work are far better than anything Vlaminck painted between 1900 and 1904. It is, in fact, a work of major interest. Vlaminck described the circumstances in which the portrait was painted: "On the same floor lived a coal merchant with his wife and daughter. As the child often called in to see us, I

54. Matisse *Le Port d'Avall, Collioure*, 1905.

55. Matisse *Vue de Collioure*, 1905.

suddenly thought I would do her portrait." What is even more important, the artist described what was in his mind at the time: "I wanted to do portraits, a series of portraits of the people, character portraits, real ones, like living landscapes, human landscapes, sad or beautiful, with all their flaws, in all their poverty and dirt." There really is a great deal of feeling in this rough portrait of a working-class child in drab clothes solemnly clutching a pathetic doll, against a background of faded wallpaper, a little girl who seems to be overcome by the responsibilities of her make-believe motherhood, with a joyless face, though her eyes are brimming over with the blue of the sky. We cannot say that this work is in any way Fauve; it belongs to the Intimist and Expressionist tendency of the Nabi painters, such as we find in Vallotton, for instance, although we must remember that Vlaminck's Expressionism took a very special form: it had nothing of the unexpected charming humour of the Nabis or of Vallotton's caustic irony, but was infinitely more pessimistic, rather in the spirit of van Gogh.

During the summer Vlaminck took the plunge: his naturalist approach became a poetic one and he brought imagination into his art. This is borne out by the works he exhibited at the Salon d'Automne. *L'Etang de Saint-Cucufa* (The Pond of St. Cucufa) could not possibly date from 1903, as has generally been claimed. First of all, the signature, "de Vlaminck", is the way he signed in the summer of 1905, and there seems to be no reason why Vlaminck should have waited so long to exhibit it when he had every reason to do so sooner. Moreover, it is a work in which the painter is not describing, but is trying to transpose; his colour (even if muted) has a spatial function (admittedly a relative one); he creates an artistic reality other than the physical reality. Here Vlaminck achieved a Fauve work.

The pictures shown at the Salon d'Automne probably included *La Vallée de Port-Marly* (The Valley at Port-Marly) and *La Maison de mon père* (My Father's House) (sold at Sotheby's, London, in December 1971), two canvases signed "de Vlaminck", which had all the qualities that partake of the fundamental definition of Fauvism. A rather rudimentary Fauvism, admittedly, both as regards the organization of the painted surface and the colours, which are limited to a few vivid tones: chrome yellow, cobalt blue, Veronese green, vermilion red. But it seethes, it blazes, it is alive.

We know of three other paintings signed "de Vlaminck" that might legitimately be dated from the summer of 1905: *Les Régates à Bougival* (Regatta at Bougival; Pl. 38) (Private Collection, New York), *Les Coteaux de Bougival* (Hills of Bougival) (Staatsgalerie, Stuttgart) and *Voilier sur la Seine* (Sailboat on the Seine; Pl. 49) (Private Collection, New York). These show Vlaminck's difficulty in mastering the rendering of space and the relationships between coloured areas, whether the tones are divided or not. But the variety and frenzy of the brush-strokes convey the artist's dynamic participation in the scene. What chiefly mattered to Vlaminck was that the picture should be the fervent equivalent of the emotion he experienced. "By instinct," he said, "unmethodically, I expressed a human, not an artistic, truth."

It is impossible to identify the works Vlaminck exhibited together with his fellow Fauves at the end of the year at Berthe Weill's and at Prath and Magnier's.

In the list of works painted in 1905 we would include canvases such as *Châtaigniers à Chatou* (Chestnut Trees at Chatou), on which the signature "Vlaminck", not underlined, is relatively horizontal and painted in rather fine separate letters. Their style is different from that of works of 1906, the composition more deliberate, the treatment more elaborate and the spirit more lyrical.

In 1905 Vlaminck's Fauvism assumed a highly individual manner which did not change very much until 1907-8. It was a very instinctive kind of Fauvism with little subtlety in the treatment; it was not yet very aggressive, but even so its eloquence was uncluttered by fine details. There was little attempt at careful composition (the most powerful lines were often submerged in the colour) and there were only six or

56. Marquet *Le Soleil à travers les arbres*, 1905.

57. Derain *Port de Collioure, le cheval blanc*, 1905.

130

58. Derain *Le Phare de Collioure*, 1905.

seven colours (primary colours systematically set off by their complements). Until the end of 1905 the tones are generally heightened rather than transposed. Some cold shades show that Vlaminck was not yet bold enough to use a screeching palette, but we can sense that the time was not far off when he would do so. In formulating his idiom the painter rejected all preconceived notions and did not prefer one kind of brush-stroke to another. He had not yet decided whether form was to be broken up or not; it was usually both flat and divided at one and the same time; he regarded this as a relative problem depending on the kind of feeling to be expressed, and trusted his intuition. Generally the brush-strokes were separate, even very separate, and extremely varied: commas or rods, squares or wiggly lines—his repertoire was inexhaustible. On the other hand, for Vlaminck the flat area did not necessarily demand a contour line any more than separate brush-strokes excluded one. In other words Vlaminck chose, without constraint, the form of expression best suited to his temperament. We might even say that he chose the most direct, the most spontaneous, form that allowed him to express his feelings; we could call it automatic writing in the service of his lyricism, which is poured out almost without restraint. "I try to paint with my heart and my guts," he said, "without worrying about style." No other Fauve rejected all tradition, all teaching, all influence as completely as he did. Van Gogh helped him to see his inner self, Derain gave him a vocabulary, and Vlaminck himself did the rest.

Van Dongen

At the end of 1904 several features in Van Dongen's painting heralded Fauvism but did not yet show a decidedly Fauve attitude. Nor were the first months of 1905 very different from the preceding period.

At the Salon des Indépendants he exhibited paintings of the Moulin de la Galette and the Carrousel. These cannot be precisely identified but must have been in the same vein as the versions we know from the end of 1904 (if indeed they were not the same).

Of the submissions to the Indépendants we can identify with certainty *Le Boniment* (Hanky-panky). Van Dongen's treatment consisted of demolishing illusionist modelling and space by means of a Tachist technique which carries a very distant echo of Impressionism and Divisionism. The extreme breaking-up of tones created a kind of distortion, while the use of a range of closely related hues made the figure on the right, for instance, fade into its surrounding colour and created the confusion of horizontal and vertical planes. Here Van Dongen reached the same point Matisse and Derain had—the idioms differed a little, admittedly, but the conclusion was the same: substituting a lyrical for a naturalist approach to the world.

After the Salon des Indépendants Van Dongen went more deeply into Neo-Impressionist painting. At the Salon he had seen the example of Seurat, of van Gogh (several of whose works used Divisionist techniques) and of Matisse's *Luxe, calme et volupté*. Thus in the summer of 1905 Van Dongen's Fauvism went through its Divisionist phase. It doubtless began with a new and final version of the *Moulin de la Galette* and another picture closely connected in its subject-matter, *Le Violoncelliste* (The Violoncellist; Pl. 59) (Private Collection, Switzerland). These were the only occasions when Van Dongen followed Seurat closely as regards the layout, the (relative) accuracy of the composition and the systematic breaking-up of tones. On the other hand, the disequilibrium of the complementary colours and the presence of continuous lines in the composition show that he did not intend to conform rigidly to Seurat's doctrine. Van Dongen's main concern was to find new ways of heightening the tones.

The works he painted during the summer months he spent (with his wife and new-born daughter) at Fleury, on the plain of the Pays de Bière, were freer and more personal. Nineteen of them were exhibited at Druet's from 23 October to 11 November 1905. The—unfortunately—few we know show an amazing audacity. Composed in a very special manner—

59. Van Dongen *Le Violoncelliste du Moulin de la Galette*, 1905.

which must have affected the whole series he exhibited, if we are to believe a remark made at the time—in which the sky occupied almost the whole of the canvas (Pl. 73), must at first sight have given the impression of studies in atmosphere. They were not: the Fleury-en-Bière series was no more Impressionist than Derain's 1905-6 series of London townscapes or Dufy's 1906 series of the Fourteenth of July. Van Dongen did not reproduce a momentary view of nature; far from it, he let his imagination transform the somewhat ordinary, monotonous scene of the Bière plain. "A fine picture", Van Dongen said, "is not a photograph of life, but something artificial, like something out of a dream; and art in a picture begins where nature and reason leave off." The technique he adopted was a very individual Tachist system which has only a vague kinship with Seurat's manner of fragmentation. He confided to L. Chaumeil: "I did that warm series with generous brush-strokes to show that I was able to go back to Seurat, pick up his manner, and add something to it." In fact, it is that "something" he added that is important: an ecstatic lyricism that created the most fantastic forms imaginable. There was also something allusive in his treatment of the subject; his tendency toward abstraction is clearly visible in these views of Fleury-en-Bière. The landmarks by which we can identify the scene or views are reduced to a minimum because the figurative organization of the picture surface takes precedence over representational reality.

We must compare this series with the canvas called *Nuages ou Guus et Dolly portées aux nues* (Clouds or Guus and Dolly Praised to the Skies) (Private Collection), painted at Fleury and composed in the same manner as the landscapes: the plain of Bière, where we can distinguish two haystacks, occupies a narrow strip at the bottom of the canvas, while all the rest is taken up by clouds, in the midst of which are Guus and Dolly. This is a kind of Fauve version of a subject akin to the Assumption.

The summer of 1905 marked Van Dongen's complete adherence to Fauvism. Like the other Fauves he came to Fauvism by way of Neo-Impressionism in which he hoped to find the components for his new idiom: a very free Tachism from the start—more immediately free than even Matisse's or Derain's. But Van Dongen could not, any more than the other Fauves, remain satisfied with this position. A new manner appeared in his works at the Salon d'Automne, where he exhibited *La Chemise* (The Shirt) and *Torse* (Torso), which marked the starting-point of this new style, a complete elimination of broken-up tones to which, in fact, Van Dongen never reverted. The artist preferred to use flat areas of vivid and contrasted colours organized by thick contour lines that facilitated the differentiation of planes. While *La Chemise* is a harmoniously measured organization of the painted surface in which the planes are suggested mentally by the opposition of tones of equal saturation, the *Torse* by contrast initiates a new type of nude for Van Dongen, which was also Fauve in concept. The feminine body is subject to the same phenomenon of transposition as an image of nature. Van Dongen did not intend to give a faithful likeness of the woman or to endow her with conventional beauty: the drawing is sketchy, the modelling inaccurate, the fiery colours (set off by the cold blue background) unreal. The *Torse* is a lyrical interpretation of the female body, the transposed image of sensuality, an animal image that conveys the artist's keen sexuality.

Thus the course Van Dongen followed in 1905 was very much like that followed by Matisse and Derain. At the same time and with the same deliberateness he rejected the naturalist approach of Impressionism, investigated the colour potential of Tachism in the Divisionist framework, and then became aware that the breaking up of tones was detrimental to expressiveness and that line, as much as colour, had to play its part. We have proof that Van Dongen realized before August 1905 that art was taking a new direction and that Impressionism was finished. This is the reply he gave to Charles Morice's opinion poll, which appeared on 1 August in *Le Mercure de France*. Another important fact to emerge from that reply was his interest in Gauguin and then in Cézanne. "Gauguin has left us a fine body of work," Van Dongen stated, "and I consider him the precursor of a new religion of art." In other words, Van Dongen was studying Gauguin's art in the summer of 1905 (at exactly the same time as Matisse and Derain were doing so at Collioure) and this explains the works he sent to the Salon d'Automne.

Dufy

We have to wait until the Salon des Indépendants of 1905 to see a profound change in the art of Dufy. At that Salon the painter first saw Matisse's *Luxe, calme et volupté*. "At the sight of that picture", he was to say later, "I understood the new *raison d'être* of painting, and Impressionist realism lost all its charm for me as I looked at this miracle of creative imagination at work in colour and line. I immediately grasped the mechanics of art."

Until the Salon des Indépendants Dufy had remained faithful to Impressionism. To Ch. Morice's opinion poll he replied that "Impressionism is not finished", that "the influence of Manet, Monet, Sisley, Renoir, Degas, Seurat and Pissarro weighs too heavily on today's art for any signs of a truly new direction to be discernible". Questioned on Gauguin and Cézanne, he thought that he did not know enough about Gauguin's work to talk about it and that "Cézanne was determined to assert his exclusive concern with technique". Thus we can see how much credit must go to Matisse for inspiring such a complete conversion in Dufy.

It did not take Dufy long to change from an objective approach to reality to lyrical transposition. He undoubtedly did so most spectacularly in 1906 when the works exhibited by some of his friends at the Salon d'Automne of 1905 (in which he himself did not participate) confirmed his new course. However, the revelation of seeing Matisse's picture in the spring of that year had a strong enough impact to produce fundamentally Fauve works. This is obvious if we compare two canvases on the same subject: *Le Yacht*

pavoisé (The Dressed Yacht; Pl. 37) (Musée des Beaux-Arts, Le Havre) and *Bateau pavoisé* (The Dressed Boat; Pl. 36) (Musée des Beaux-Arts, Lyons), which must have been painted some time in the summer of 1905. "Impressionist realism", to quote Dufy's own words, is obvious in the first picture, in the suggestion of air as a surrounding element modifying both line and colour, in the way the paint itself tells us that the water is liquid and even choppy, that the flags are pieces of cloth waving in the wind. In the second picture, by contrast, reality has been revised and corrected by the artist, who has superimposed his inner vision. For real light and space he has substituted an artistic rendering: the water loses its liquid property to become a pretext for the repetition of pictorial forms; similarly, the flags cease to be cloth and become blotches of colour linked to one another. The drawing, too, has changed, and we can sense the concern for simplifying line as much as colour. It would be an exaggeration to say that until the spring of 1905 Dufy worked with a thoroughly detailed drawing, but his respect for form resulted in a fairly accurate drawing. But from then on this was finished. Imagination was introduced into drawing as well as into colour; the painter's main concern was to express himself in a quick drawing that did not check his lyricism, whether he was dealing with vigorously outlined flat forms or forms that blazed out in stenographic brush-strokes.

During the summer of 1905, Dufy used his new manner on his usual subject, the breakwater, and on a new theme, regattas, of which we know three versions, including the *Fête nautique* (Boat Party) (Galerie Beyeler, Basle). He applied his colours unmixed on to the canvas as if in a feverish hurry, striving to convey his emotions as simply and directly as possible. The blots of primary colours run over the picture surface like the scrawl of an agitated handwriting or the notes of a passionate symphony. The artist abandoned his customary concern with composition and the density of form; the careful use of white lightened his canvas. These elliptical forms and this system of equivalents create a sense of life that is much more real than anything in, for instance, the earlier pictures of the beach at Ste. Adresse.

Of course the impact Matisse's picture made on Dufy was essentially aesthetic. In other words, Dufy did not see in it only a special technique—an almost Pointillist technique, as he fully realized. He did, however, linger for a time on the lyrical potential that a Neo-Impressionist technique might offer so long as one steered clear, as Matisse had done, of orthodox rules. As a result Dufy's output during the rest of 1905 was marked by a very free Neo-Impressionism. He fastened on a certain manner that is rather well illustrated by *Les Gymnastes* (The Athletes) (Musée du Havre) in which the breaking up of the painted surface rendered the effect not of the natural light but of a fictitious light that fashioned the picture. But, to tell the truth, this was not yet Dufy's definitive Fauvism, but only an aspect that had recurrent revivals until the end of 1907.

Friesz

The year 1905 brought no profound changes in the painting of Friesz, who continued to work in the Impressionist manner begun in 1900.

At the Salon des Indépendants, besides the *Foire aux chevaux à Guibray* (Horsefair at Guibray), of 1903, he exhibited canvases whose titles suggest that they conveyed effects of atmosphere. These works, together with those shown at Berthe Weill's on two occasions and those sent to the Salon d'Automne, have disappeared. Nothing has survived from the year 1905. It seems likely that Friesz destroyed his work of that period. Did he want to wipe out the traces of paintings that were too Impressionist for 1905? Here we come to a curious problem that concerns others besides Friesz. In 1906-7 it was rather important to be regarded as an avant-garde artist, even if success was due only to notoriety; indeed, notoriety, or shocking the public, was becoming profitable and useful for attracting the attention of new art dealers, like Druet and Kahnweiler, who at last were willing to remunerate audacity.

Friesz's attachment to Impressionism was such that he did not hesitate to join the First Exhibition of Impressionist Artists held in July at Prath and Magnier's bookshop; his works hung beside those of such artists as M. Luce, R. Florès, and E. Diriks. It is difficult to regard this exhibition as anything but a first gesture by a group of artists who deliberately intended to maintain the fundamentals of Impressionism. It seems logical to assume that this was Friesz's intention, too, for it is borne out by his artistic output. It was also confirmed later, in November, by his participation in the Third Exhibition of the Société des Peintres du Paris Moderne at Chaine and Simonnson's. This society, presided over by Léonce Bénédite, and which included Raffaëlli among its honorary members, welcomed some young painters who were interested in a certain form of Impressionism (not that of Monet)—R. Florès, Boutet de Monvel, F. Jourdain and J. Villon. The last-named felt ashamed at having been taken in by this genre; "an unavowable period", he said;[41] Friesz contented himself with drawing a veil over his output of that time.

Friesz's biographers have dated to the end of 1905 or thereabouts a visit which the artist made to Antwerp and assumed that he stayed there long enough for several pictures to be dated to this period. It is possible that Friesz made a quick trip there, but it is difficult to see how he could have stayed there for any length of time at the end of 1905 when his presence would be required in Paris at a number of exhibitions he was taking part in and which occupied him fully. What is even more significant is the fact that during the months that followed he did not exhibit a single landscape of Antwerp; at the Salon des Indépendants of 1906 he showed only landscapes of Normandy. Views of Antwerp first appeared at the Salon d'Automne, and these were canvases painted during the time Friesz and Braque stayed on the banks of the Scheldt in the summer of 1906. All the views of Antwerp we know either bear the date 1906 or are undated; not a single one bears the date 1905.

Even more hypothetical is a stay Friesz is supposed to have made in the South of France in 1905; we shall

60. Dufy *Marché à Marseille*, 1905.

come back later to this problem which concerns far more than a mere biographical episode.

Braque

At the end of 1904 Braque rented a studio in Montmartre. During the summer of 1905 he stayed at Honfleur and Le Havre and, back in Paris, got in touch again with his friend Friesz.

We know that the painter destroyed nearly his entire artistic output prior to 1906. However, we know that the landscape *La Côte de Grâce à Honfleur* or *Vue du parc à Honfleur* (View of the Park at Honfleur) (Musée des Beaux-Arts, Le Havre), date from before 1906, i.e. before the opening of the Salon des Indépendants at which it was probably shown; it must have been painted during the summer of 1905, and was a strictly naturalist work. We think that the *Bateau dans le port du Havre* (Boat in the Port of Le Havre) was executed several months later, for it has the signs of approaching change—a determination to transpose reality which is chiefly evident in the chromatic expression.

In 1905 Fauvism was still at an experimental stage which drew generously upon the example of Divisionist painting. Matisse and Derain, at Collioure, took all that could be gleaned from it until the need arose for an antidote. A closer acquaintance with Gauguin led them to abandon Divisionism and to use new means of pictorial expression. The Fauve picture increased in spontaneity, in lyricism, in expressiveness, while affirming its specific quality: to convey through colour the essence of each object, the intensity of the emotional impact and the equivalent of space. Van Dongen, after a rather slower start, followed the same evolution as his friends and finally overcame the same ambiguities. While Marquet restrained his lyrical flow, Vlaminck, by contrast, gave it free rein in a riotous lyricism, although he did not reach that stage until the summer. At the end of the year Dufy had broken with Impressionist naturalism, but Friesz, and no doubt Braque too, were still faithful to it. Collioure must undeniably be a shrine in the history of Fauvism, and so van Gogh's prediction of 1888 was realized, when he prophesied that a "colourist school" would take root in the South; Matisse and Derain must also incontestably be regarded as the pioneers of the new manner of painting. It is impossible to say which of the two was the first; we might perhaps say, in comparison with the school of Pont-Aven, that Derain was the Emile Bernard of Fauvism and Matisse its Gauguin, for Matisse seems to have found in Derain's company and youthful audacity the psychological stimulus which he could hardly have found in Marquet's composure.

Chapter IV   1906—Imagination and lyricism

By the beginning of 1906 the Fauve system was almost completely perfected: all that it needed now was to gain confidence, to dominate, as it were, its technique so that the artist's imagination and innermost feelings could be expressed with ease. Fauvism was gaining recognition and we might even say, in view of the originality and quality of Fauve works, that 1906 was one of the finest years in the history of painting.

Matisse

In the spring of 1906, from 19 March to 7 April, Matisse had a one-man show at Druet's comprising fifty-five canvases as well as sculptures, drawings, watercolours, lithographs and wood engravings. The majority were works painted at Collioure, including *L'Idole* (The Idol) (Jacques Koerfer Collection, Berne) and *La Gitane* (The Gipsy) (Musée de l'Annonciade, St. Tropez). The generally unfavourable reaction of the critics, who regretted that the artist had abandoned his earlier manner, shows how difficult it was for Matisse to change his image and break with his past as an Intimist painter. This exhibition included a *Study* for the picture of *Le Bonheur de vivre* (The Joy of Living; Pl. 69) (The Barnes Foundation, Merion, Pennsylvania), the only work Matisse showed at the Salon des Indépendants and one in which both subject and style marked a turning-point in the painter's evolution.

It seems to have been at Collioure, in 1905, that Matisse first thought of integrating nude figures into a landscape, not so much to create a composition on the subject of women bathing, as he had done earlier, but in order to attempt a special type of pastoral. The first picture of this genre was probably the one in the Musée du Petit-Palais in Paris. In fact, pastoral subjects in painting were not new in 1905, as we have seen, and should no doubt be seen in the context of a kind of Humanist quest for a new ideal of happiness. Several artists attempted them—Bonnard, Cross, Denis, Maillol and, in his own way, Signac in *Au Temps d'harmonie* (In the Age of Harmony; Pl. 42) (Town Hall, Montreuil-sous-Bois). The iconography of *Le Bonheur de vivre* was actually better suited to the theme of the golden age, in which allusions to leisure, love, games and dancing were traditional components. That is why we think that Matisse first had the idea for such a composition not at Collioure but in Paris, at the time of the Salon d'Automne of 1905, when he saw Ingres's works exhibited there, notably a drawing of *L'Age d'or*. Thus he went back to a landscape painted at Collioure (Statens Museum for Kunst, Copenhagen) and introduced the figures in an overall arrangement reminiscent of Ingres. Several of the figures clearly have a kinship with Ingres's composition: the entwined couple standing and the woman picking flowers, who is based on the man kissing Astraea's dress. The young woman standing and raising her arms to adorn herself with leaves was taken from the *Le Bain turc* (Turkish Bath) which was shown at the Salon d'Automne; this, too, was the source of the recumbent woman who is being embraced by a man.

The influence of Ingres lay not only in the iconography, but also affected the artistic expression. Matisse was rediscovering Ingres's art and he saw it with fresh eyes. Ingres struck him as a draughtsman full of imagination who certainly did not render form objectively and whose contour lines suggested the underlying structure; Ingres also struck him as a painter who could use bright colours with restraint but without adulterating them. This new approach to Ingres, however, would not have been possible without Gauguin, whom Matisse had been studying since his stay at Collioure in 1905 and whom he regarded as "coming from Ingres". In other words, Ingres's teaching strengthened Gauguin's; it came at the very moment when Matisse felt he had not paid as much attention to the transposing potential of drawing as he had to that of colour. At that stage in the evolution of Matisse's painting we must also take into account the influence of Oriental art. The painter later said that he had been interested in the linear experiments of Muslim art; he certainly visited the exhibition of Islamic arts in 1903 at the Pavillon de Marsan. "Through its accessories", he said, "this art creates an impression of greater space, of three-dimensional space." Unfortunately we have no contemporary writings by Matisse, but Derain, who followed a parallel evolution, clearly explained the same problems in 1906. Matisse, like Derain, was absorbed by the problem of linear expression, the integration of drawing into the new figurative system; in other words, the relationship between form and colour. When speaking of a piece of Persian pottery, Matisse said that "here the relationship of colour and form achieves a kind of perfection". Of course the painter already knew that Oriental artists used colour as a means of expression whereas, since the Renaissance, colour had been regarded in the West as a complement of drawing. But this was not enough: in Oriental art Matisse rediscovered the lessons of purity, harmony and expression. It was in this light that he reconsidered Japanese prints.

Thanks to Ingres, Matisse found a way of bringing imagination to drawing and thus of strengthening the

61. Matisse *Jeune marin II*, 1906.

62.   Derain *Le Parlement de Londres*, 1906.

63. Derain *Big Ben, Londres*, 1906.

64. Vlaminck *Bords de Seine à Carrières-sur-Seine*, 1906.

65. Van Dongen *Le clown*, 1906.

66.   Dufy *Les ombrelles*, 1906.

67.   Dufy *Les affiches à Trouville*, 1906.

68.   Braque *Le port de L'Estaque*, 1906.

expressive power and lyrical content of the painting. The new method, which enriched the plasticity, was applied not only to the human figures of *Le Bonheur de vivre* but to the natural setting whose supple and sensitive lines harmonize with the general feeling of the composition. Matisse strove to give proportion to all the terms of his idiom, not really with some vague notion of a formal equilibrium (though this idea would not in itself necessarily be detrimental) but in order to increase the expressiveness of his picture. In this way he avoided a conflict between colour and line; he chose, on the contrary, an active combination of colour and form—that is, he did not hesitate to modify his drawing to obtain a better expression of colour.

With *Le Bonheur de vivre* Matisse abandoned the technique of broken-up colour which he had used to some extent until then; he now regarded flat colour areas as a technique that was better suited to his new needs; the harmony of flat colours is obviously more expressive than the Pointillist *vibrato*. This picture marks a complete and definitive break with all dividing of colour, of form, of the contour line, and with the entire purely physical communication of the perceptible world. We can well understand why Signac was extremely annoyed by that canvas.

Shortly after the opening of the Salon des Indépendants and the exhibition at Druet's, Matisse left for Algeria, at a time when his friend Derain chose to go to London. There, on the banks of the Thames, Derain probably was in terrible danger of being infected by the ghosts of Impressionism; Matisse, on the brink of the desert, would run no such risks. Although he went as far as Biskra, his stay in Algeria was short, probably two weeks; he brought back fabrics and ceramics which he posed in his next still lifes. We do not know what prompted Matisse to make this visit, but it may have been partly that he wanted to see the living Islam.

Upon his return from Algeria, Matisse stayed at Collioure, where he seems to have painted fewer pictures than in the previous year; some of them, which he showed at the Salon d'Automne, can be identified: *La Liseuse* (Woman Reading; Pl. 46) (Musée de Peinture et de Sculpture, Grenoble), *Nature morte, tapis rouge* (Still Life with Red Carpet) (Hermitage, Leningrad) and *Nature morte à la statuette* (Still Life with a Plaster Figure) (Yale University Art Gallery, New Haven). In each of these the artist has inserted felicitous chromatic inventions: here, a kind of tenderness in the tones which creates an atmosphere of quiet reading; there, black combined with vibrant reds and calming greens in the manner of Algerian weavers. His main purpose was to create harmonies of great expressive power.

We can understand Matisse's creativity when we compare two figures also painted at Collioure—*Jeune Marin I* (Young Sailor I) and *Jeune Marin II* (Young Sailor II; Pl. 61) (Private Collection, Mexico City). The expressiveness of the latter is achieved through the simplicity of the form; that is, through a work of paring, of eliminating accessory features and all explanatory detail; through the integration of the line into a generous living synthesis of rhythm and colour; through a precise relationship of the coloured areas. In 1908 Matisse explained this method of working very clearly: "There is a necessary proportion of tones that might make me change the shape of a figure or transform a composition. Until I have achieved it in every part, I go on looking for it and go on working. Then comes a moment when all the parts have acquired their definitive relationship, and from that point on I couldn't possibly change anything in my picture without redoing it completely."

We can see how decisive the year 1906 was for Matisse, who began to make use of line in his pictorial idiom and to determine its correct relationship to colour in order to achieve expressiveness. As for colour, after striving, in 1905, to use non-imitative tones, he now began to experiment with the relationship of the tones to each other. From now on the painter's ultimate aim was to strive for expressiveness—that is, to find the most adequate manner in which the artist could convey his feelings, which were the basis of the work of art. In fact by 1908 Matisse himself actually had used the word "expression"

69. Matisse *Le Bonheur de vivre*, early 1906.

150

70. Matisse *Nature morte au tapis rouge*, 1906.

when asked to define his doctrine, and it remained the key to his whole art.

Marquet

Although the examination of Marquet's art in 1906 raises no major difficulties, thanks to the reliable dating of a number of pictures, we know little of the artist's output at the beginning of the year; we can get no help from the list of works exhibited at the Salon des Indépendants where Marquet had eight canvases, all of them titled *Paysage* (Landscape). At the beginning of 1906 Marquet's manner of painting does not seem to have been any different from that of the previous year. We believe that several paintings executed at that time must have slipped into the catalogue of works for 1905, so that there is an apparent gap until the summer of 1906.

We are much more fortunate with Marquet's output during that summer. Several works bear the date 1906; the works exhibited at the Salon d'Automne, painted between July and September, have sufficiently distinctive titles for almost all of them to be identified; one of them is even known with complete certainty because it was purchased by the state.

Marquet's submission to the Salon d'Automne comprised eight landscapes, three of Paris and five of Normandy. We know that he stayed in Normandy in the summer of 1906, together with Dufy, notably at Le Havre, Trouville and Ste. Adresse; sometimes both of them treated the same subject. The celebration of the Fourteenth of July provided the inspiration for about a dozen of Dufy's canvases, each constituting a different artistic variation, executed not on the spot but in the studio because the artist's imagination was such that he did not need to go out into the street. For Marquet there was no pictorial problem absolutely independent of reality; he always needed the prompting of nature, he never ceased his dialogue with it. He painted only two or three versions of the Fourteenth of July in Le Havre because the subject itself is not inherently susceptible to many changes in the course of a day.

Le 14 Juillet au Havre (Fourteenth of July at Le Havre; Pl. 101) (Musée de Bagnols-sur-Cèze) seems to have been the version exhibited at the Salon d'Automne of 1906. In it Marquet's palette takes on decisively Fauve accents; it is particularly interesting to see the generous use of vermilion, which is otherwise extremely rare for him. He even chose or invented a Union Jack simply so that he could add its especially brilliant red to his picture. But in spite of this strong emphasis on colour, Marquet's work was still muted compared with Dufy's *La Rue pavoisée* (Street with Flags and Bunting) (Musée National d'Art Moderne, Paris), painted from exactly the same viewpoint. Dufy needed no Union Jack to sustain the brilliance of his composition. Indeed, the basic difference lies in the fact that Marquet had difficulty in admitting that pure colour could in itself be the equivalent of light; that is why he applied touches of white and cold blue here and there to introduce light and shadow into the picture. Thus light-space was still much more familiar to Marquet than colour-space. In two other versions of *Le 14 Juillet* (Fourteenth of July; Pl. 102) (Musée des Beaux-Arts, Bordeaux and Private Collection, Switzerland), Marquet could not bring himself to build up space by means of planes in pure discordant colours; he employed the method he had used in the previous year, alternating lightly coloured (white or ochre) and deeply coloured planes. As he disliked dissonances, and even somewhat violent harmonies, he had to use the contour line (which he did abundantly in the Swiss picture) to avoid confusion between the planes and to make his composition as clear as possible. Marquet never ceased to aim at being clear, at being obvious, as we have already said in connection with his works of 1905.

Why is the painting listed as *Quai du Louvre et Pont-Neuf, soleil* (Quai du Louvre and Pont Neuf, Sunshine) (The Hermitage, Leningrad) in the catalogue of the Salon d'Automne so commonly identified with *Le Pont-Neuf au soleil* (Pont-Neuf in Sunlight) (Boymans-van Beuningen Museum, Rotterdam), when the latter in no way corresponds to the former title? The latter showed the Pont-Neuf in the fore-

71. Marquet *Le Port de Menton*, 1905.

ground with the statue of Henri IV on horseback and, on the left, Quai Conti and the Institute; the Quai du Louvre, on the right, is not shown at all. We think the picture hung at the Salon was, in fact, the one now in the Hermitage.

We do not know which picture was shown under the title *Notre-Dame*. By contrast, the one named

Trouville can be identified with certainty as the picture in a private collection, New York.[42] Here Marquet shows himself a true Fauve, without reservation or reticence. Exceptionally, he has no oblique line in his composition: the planes succeed one another horizontally, from the foreground to the back, and the colour of the background (the sky) is more

153

saturated than that of the foreground, which brings it closer to the viewer; space is organized on the surface according to very brightly coloured areas in vigorous contrast to each other. However, we cannot really speak of a totally arbitrary transposition of colours because Marquet contented himself with heightening the tones of a subject that was inherently colourful.

It is absolutely certain that *Le Port de Fécamp* (The Port of Fécamp) (Musée des Beaux-Arts, Quimper) was shown at the Salon d'Automne, for we know that the picture was bought by the state at the Salon and placed in the Museum of Le Havre on 29 December 1906 (it was taken to the Quimper Museum in 1913). This was one of Marquet's most Fauve pictures; long strokes of colour indicate abbreviated forms, and arbitrary, very intense tones create—almost by themselves—the equivalent of space. The same stark treatment, the same elliptical style and the same fantastic colour are found in *La Plage de Fécamp* (The Beach at Fécamp) (Musée National d'Art Moderne, Paris), which was shown at that Salon.

The works we have identified constitute a perfectly coherent group in which the Fauve tendency predominated, expressing itself in abbreviated forms, emphatic brush-strokes facilitating the movement from one plane to the next, and in bright contrasted tones which can be unhesitatingly arbitrary. We also find some special features characteristic of Marquet's style during the summer in Normandy. The paint is thin, fluid, as if coloured in, and does not cover the canvas completely; this technique, commonly used by the Fauves, made the picture resemble a sketch and gave it an appearance of spontaneity enhanced by perfunctory drawing. Moreover, in almost each of these pictures there was a cold zone, varying in size, composed of blue and of red ochre which acted as a counterbalance to the warmly coloured forms. Marquet never lost this need to establish a contrast, however limited, between light and shadow; works with no cold tones are exceptional.

Of the other canvases Marquet painted in Normandy during the summer, *La Passerelle de Sainte-Adresse* (The Jetty at Ste. Adresse; Pl. 84) (Private Collection, Paris) deserves special mention. The subject of the picture, the jetty so dear to Dufy, is pared down to produce a simple, powerful effect: a few figures, some cold patches of blue and red standing out against the light of a sky with green blots illuminated by a white, yellow and blue sun. Never before had Marquet achieved such paring down of the subject nor such spareness of means, reducing them to a few essential signs. He hid the reality, so to speak, in order to convey nothing but the raw sensation. This was undoubtedly the one and only occasion on which Marquet allowed himself to be swept away by such a keen impulse, by such a spontaneous spirit of lyricism. This work has a more general importance, too, because it shows that Fauve lyricism at its climax could lead to a sort of abstraction, a distortion, as a result of the abbreviation and arbitrariness in the treatment. Dufy went very far in this vein, without, however, crossing the frontier of true abstract art, at least until 1907. But what for Dufy was a deliberate consistent quest remained no more than a passing curiosity, in the experimental stage, for Marquet because his character was fundamentally unsuited to this kind of experiment.

When we examine the works executed after his return to Paris, we can see that some of them continued in the manner in which he had painted during the summer; *Le Pont-Neuf* (Pl. 76) (The National Gallery of Art, Washington) and *Le Pont-Neuf au soleil* (Boymans-van Beuningen Museum, Rotterdam), for example, have many features in common with *La Plage de Fécamp* (Musée National d'Art Moderne, Paris) and even with the daring *La Passerelle de Sainte-Adresse*. But there are others in which Marquet retreats: the composition becomes more structured; lines again combine to express space; and fine chromatic harmonies are chosen in preference to brilliant colours. The most typical example of this is found in *Les Toits de Paris* (Rooftops of Paris) in which the structure of the composition shows clearly through the play of crossing contour lines, and the colour harmony is confined to shaded greys with a light patch of white and green in the centre. We can see that Marquet has gone back to drawing and shading, even adding a new note of austerity which he undoubtedly felt was called for after his colour excesses of the summer.

At the end of 1906 Marquet broke with the lyrical outbursts to which he had probably been pushed by his friend Dufy. He reverted to a more restrained and subtler feeling for nature which was more in keeping with his personality. But the adventure of the summer had not been useless. It confirmed him in his predilection for seascapes and ports—for places where the elements of nature exhibit their most changeable features, where they are composed of light; that is, water and sky. Marquet seems to have felt a greater need than in the previous year to convey differences in atmosphere, which obviously put him at a remove from typically Fauve concerns, even if a "composite feeling" was substituted for the immediate sensation. His experience that summer enabled him to make his art more expressive, with simple means, whether in the use of colour or drawing. In this sense he achieved the same results as Matisse and Derain. But whereas they remained fundamentally Fauve, Marquet evolved a wholly idiosyncratic idiom which cannot be analysed in terms or Fauve or non-Fauve; in any case, pure colour became an integral part of his system of painting and he continued to lean towards lyricism, but one that owed more to Apollo than to Dionysus.

Derain

As we have seen above, it is impossible—except in the case of two canvases—to decide which of Derain's pictures of his visits to London dated from the first stay (autumn–winter 1905) and which from the second (winter–spring 1906); however, we can assume that the majority must have been painted during his visit of 1906, when he seems to have stayed at least three months, whereas previously he had stayed only two weeks.

Critics have wondered why Derain chose to work in London. It has often been said that Matisse had advised him to look at the Turners he himself had seen in 1898. In fact, the foremost reason (which does not exclude others) lay in the suggestion made by Ambroise Vollard (Derain's dealer since the beginning of 1905) who hoped that his gallery would achieve a success similar to Durand-Ruel's with Claude Monet's views of the Thames in 1904. This is proved by a letter Derain wrote in 1953[43] in which he stated that he had been "sent" to London by Vollard; the latter, filled with enthusiasm by a visit he had made to England, wanted "paintings inspired by the atmosphere of London" and hoped that Derain would do in a completely new way what Monet had done before. Derain confirmed to Pierre Lévy, the collector, that it was really a matter of being "one up" on Monet.[44] And, in fact, he was a complete contrast to Monet. In the twenty or so canvases of his London collection there is no trace of anything Impressionist whatsoever. He did not set out to convey objectively the fleeting changes in the townscape according to the quality of light; his arbitrary palette alone suffices to show that he had wholly rejected the naturalist approach. If Derain painted the glints of the setting sun on the Thames, this was not because he wanted to cling to the momentary phenomenon of light but because it takes on a special character in London which easily excites the imagination: thus the picture stems from the artist's inner vision and not from his reference to reality. He was trying to create an autonomous picture in which forms did not depend on the dissipating action of light but owed their existence to a deliberate chromatic order bound up with an act of poetic creation; when Derain painted the Thames it was not a mirror of the sky but its artistic counterpart. Writing to his friend Vlaminck, he said he considered Turner superior to Monet because he saw in him something additional that he called "humanism", the artist's inner dream that is superimposed on—or even substituted for—the raw perception of reality. "Painting", he wrote, "is too beautiful to be reduced to a vision like that a dog or a horse has. We have to get out of the rut in which realism has trapped us."

We may wonder why, in about half his canvases, Derain used the division of tones which in the previous year, at the end of his stay at Collioure, he had decided to use less and less. To this we must reply that Derain had not decided to abandon it completely, but to reserve it for "luminous and harmonious pictures" in which, he felt, it had a logical purpose; and when he was creating "deliberate disharmonies" he preferred the technique of flat areas. His technique, in fact, was determined by the subject, or rather by his reaction to the subject; his method would vary in every case. Whichever technique Derain used (sometimes one, sometimes the other), he always showed tremendous imagination in drawing and colour; this was undoubtedly the most noteworthy feature of his London series, for in this realm he surpassed anything he had painted at Collioure. As for the drawing, we have the vertiginous bend of Westminster Bridge, St. Paul's leaning like the Tower of Pisa, one bank of the Thames higher than the other, vehicles about to overturn, barges larger than cargo boats, human figures exempt from the laws of gravity. As for the colour, it is more fantastic than anything Derain had ever produced: here a boat is coughing up red smoke, there the Thames has been cut into two slices, a green one and a yellow one; elsewhere the sun (blue, surrounded by a green circle and another red one) casts multi-coloured match-stick rays that ignite a fantasy fire. Derain had never gone so far in lyrical expression; here it is like a frenzied intoxication, whose effect is a true distortion of the work of art. This irrealist, we might almost say phantasmagorical, quality is somewhat reminiscent of Turner's fairyland of colour. It is quite possible that Matisse, surprised by his friend's paintings done at Collioure, had had the perception to realize that Turner might help Derain's poetic genius to unfold.

Thus, in the series of London paintings, we can see an accentuation of Derain's Fauvism towards non-realism and abstraction. For instance, in the *Effet de soleil sur la Tamise* (Sunlight on the Thames; Pl. 80) (Musée de l'Annonciade, St. Tropez) it is striking to see Derain's abstract treatment of a landscape that had

been the subject of an earlier version, *Le Pont de Charing Cross* (Charing Cross Bridge; Pl. 79) (Private Collection, New York); the canvas in the Annonciade clearly is an abstract replica of the earlier one. Derain ignores the bridge and the view of London to show simply a chromatic composition with practically no reference to reality. In our opinion, it is on the basis of this observation that there would be some chance of identifying the last canvases painted in London. We should also add that *Le Bassin de Londres* (The Pool of London) (Tate Gallery), which Derain said he had painted in April 1906, is one of the most poetic works in the series.

At the Salon des Indépendants Derain exhibited three works, which have not been identified; two of them were probably compositions and not landscapes. During his Fauve period he seems to have painted several compositions which have nearly all disappeared. Fortunately, *La Danse* (The Dance; Pl. 113) (Private Collection, Switzerland)[45] has survived; it is undoubtedly contemporaneous with the London works in view of the special colour range, notably the violent reds. It is extremely difficult to decipher the subject of the picture, for Derain clearly did more than describe a dance: he told a story.

At first we are struck by the Oriental appearance of the scene, although it is impossible to determine if it is Hindu, Cambodian or what. Is the painter alluding to some adventure of the god Krishna in which the snake Kaliya is involved? Is it an allegorical battle, such as we find in Javanese Wayang religious drama, between Good and Evil, the good spirit and the evil spirit, in a setting of symbols? The general composition of Derain's picture bears a strange resemblance to a Khmer sculpture in the Musée Guimet; the pediment from a temple of Shiva at Banteay Srei (Pl. 114) shows two brothers fighting over an *apsara* (one of them is seizing its forearm). Derain could not have seen this work, which has been in the Musée Guimet only since 1937, but may have seen other Khmer pediments at the Indochina Museum in the Trocadéro, where there were reconstructions of major sections of buildings from Angkor Vat, Ta Prohm and the temple of Bayon.

72. Derain *Le Faubourg à Collioure*, 1905.

No doubt Derain interpreted and condensed several works so that the scene of *La Danse*, which is both precise and vague, does not refer to one particular myth. On the other hand, we know that, on his way to L'Estaque in the summer of 1906, the painter went through Marseilles at the time of the colonial exhibition, which he certainly would not have missed. There he could have seen all kind of works, some original ones, some reconstructed, like the bas-reliefs of Angkor Vat. Above all, he may have gone to see the ballets

157

performed at the Indochina Theatre by the troupe of Cambodian dancers in the retinue of King Sisowath (those dancers whom Rodin joined in Marseilles); the idea for his picture may have come to him through mimed scenes and dances evoking the myths of *Ramayana*. In the wood panels (Pl. 116) sculpted at the time he was painting the picture, Derain took up in a more explicit manner the subject of the dance, giving his figures characteristic attitudes derived from both Cambodian sacred dances and figurative works such as representations of Shiva (Pl. 115), of which there are many in the Musée Guimet.

We are also struck by the medieval character of *La Danse*, which appears not only in the figures but in the subject itself. During the Middle Ages the West was familiar with such representations, in which the idea of Good and Evil had some kinship with Far Eastern thought—for example, on the pier of the former portal of the abbey of Ste. Marie at Souillac, the figures gripping each other are supposed to be vices exercising their hold over man; a bas-relief in the abbey also shows a demon clutching a soul by the wrist. Derain could have seen these works—without going to Souillac—at the Musée des Monuments Français.[46]

The major interest in Derain's composition definitely lies in this fundamental association of Romanesque and Cambodian art (which approaches Rodin, who saw in the *Ange* of Chartres the attitude of a Cambodian dancer). The study of both medieval and Far Eastern art[47] was undertaken by Derain, as by Matisse, to increase the expressive power of the painting with the help of the rhythmic potential of line. In the case of Matisse, this study referred back to Gauguin, who wrote to D. de Monfreid: "Always keep the Persians, the Cambodians and a little of the Egyptians in mind."

At the Salon d'Automne Derain showed eight landscapes, mostly of l'Estaque, where he must certainly have been in the summer of 1906. This enables us to date a letter written during that stay to Vlaminck, who filed it—wrongly we think—among the correspondence of 1905.[48] Given its importance, it is surprising that this letter has not attracted more attention. In it Derain sets out very clearly the contradictions in his art, which are basically the contradictions contained in Fauvism. He was fully aware of what was illogical in his manner of creating a picture: he wanted to go beyond the physical facts, yet it was from these facts that the picture took its origins and it is to these facts that the finished picture will refer. Derain thought that the "composition" might resolve this dilemma—that is, a picture that grew not out of a view of nature but was imagined; not the "visible composition" in the manner of Denis which creates "the things we see", but a composition in which "forms are grouped in the light and at the same time harmonized with the material at one's disposal". Derain thus gives a good definition of the total or ideal Fauve picture, in which subject, line and colour would be purely arbitrary creations; this is also a definition of abstract painting reminiscent of Gauguin: "A word of advice: don't paint too much after nature. Art is an abstraction, wrest it away from nature by dreaming over it, and give more thought to the created work that will come of it." Unfortunately, Derain never painted that kind of composition.

We can thus get an insight into Derain's state of mind when he was painting at L'Estaque. It certainly explains why he did only a very few pictures, which are, incidentally, little known. The canvas called *Pont sur le Riou* (Bridge over the Riou) at the Salon d'Automne was probably the picture now in the William S. Paley Collection in New York. We suggest that another one, called *Vers la fontaine* (To the Fountain) can be identified as *L'Estaque, route tournante* (L'Estaque, Winding Road; Pl. 86), now in the Museum of Fine Arts, Houston. If we link these two pictures with *Les Trois Arbres* (The Three Trees) (Art Gallery of Ontario, Toronto), we have a series of three pictures on the same subject and undoubtedly contemporaneous which closely reflect the anxieties Derain mentioned in his letter to Vlaminck. His poetic art concerned drawing, purified by synthesis and set off by contour lines as much as colour; this created a truly artistic arrangement not dependent on

73. Van Dongen *Nuages*, 1905.

the object, to which was added the chromatic treatment, fundamentally unrealistic, at the absolute limit of saturation. The painted landscape thus had a non-objective character deliberately created by the artist: these might almost be the "compositions" of which Derain dreamed in which everything, except the subject, is imagined—line, form, colour, light and space.

At the end of the summer Derain's Fauvism suddenly took an individual turn. Under the pretext of purging his transpositions of reality the painter in fact achieved rigorously disciplined constructions; his quest for ever greater simplification finally made him express himself through a geometrical form, as in the *Paysage à Cassis* (Cassis Landscape), dated 1906 by the artist. Here we have to acknowledge a basically different kind of lyricism: this is no longer the impassioned lyricism of most of the earlier works; it is, by contrast, a measured lyricism that owed more to Apollo than Dionysus. Weary of forcing his emotions, Derain allowed reflection to take its rightful place again. This evolution may owe something to the influence of African art. The letter Derain sent to Vlaminck from London on 7 March 1906 mentioned his lively interest in the works he had seen in the African section of the British Museum. However, he did not really confront the implications of African art for his own painting until the end of the year. He posed the problem of light in fresh terms: he thought of expressing it no longer as colour but in close relation to form and volume. But Derain was only hypothesizing—the actual experiment was not attempted until the beginning of 1907. For the time being, all he seemed to retain from African art was a vague geometrical stylization.

Vlaminck

The year 1906 did not mark any profound change in Vlaminck's art compared with 1905. The painter was spared the anxieties and perpetual doubts that assailed his friend Derain. He made no attempt to change the manner in which he expressed himself. Convinced that he was on the right course, he tried only to perfect his idiom, to gain perfect control over it so that it would better express his inner being. Unlike the other Fauves, he felt no call for new horizons. The banks of the Seine were more than enough for him; at Chatou, at Bougival, at Argenteuil, at Le Pecq, he painted barges, tug-boats, bridges, towpaths. Sometimes he left the Seine to paint gardens, cornfields and woods.

Attempts to establish a catalogue of his œuvre comes up against insoluble difficulties when identifying exhibited works. The titles were too vague and have often been changed in the course of time, for how can anyone assert that this or that view of the banks of the Seine was at Bougival, Chatou or Le Pecq? The difficulties are further compounded by the fact that we are dealing with a large number of canvases; in fact, commencing in April 1906, Vollard purchased Vlaminck's entire output, which enabled the artist to devote himself entirely to painting. Moreover, during 1906 and at the beginning of 1907 he signed his paintings in more or less the same way: the signature is painted in fine letters, separate or joined, mostly horizontal, and always underlined with a long or short line, usually straight, rarely slanted.

Of the eight canvases hung at the Salon des Indépendants we know for certain only *La Cuisine (intérieur)* (In the Kitchen–Interior) (Musée National d'Art Moderne, Paris), which has been persistently dated 1904, or even 1903; no one seems to have wondered why its author should have waited until the spring of 1906 to exhibit it. We are convinced that this mistake is due to a misreading, for we are not dealing with a pre-Fauve attempt on the level of *Le Quai Sganzin*, painted at the end of 1904. Just as the latter reveals a complete lack of understanding of Fauvism, *La Cuisine*, by contrast, shows that the author has gained a great deal of experience in handling pure colours. It would have been unthinkable for the Vlaminck of 1903-4 to produce a work like this. We think that the error is commonly made because Vlaminck was treating an Intimist subject, which was exceptional for

160

74. Friesz *L'Entrée d'une corvette dans le port d'Anvers*, 1906.

Fauve painters, who were above all landscapists, and because he used some cold colours. As for the subject, we must remember that before April 1906 Vlaminck was unable to devote all of his time to painting; he was only able to paint during rare moments of leisure, which he also had to share with his family. This would explain why he found it easier, especially in winter, to paint interiors and still lifes, as he seems to have done.

The fact that he used cold tones should not be regarded as a lack of boldness, a reluctance to use vivid colours. We know that he rejected any form of *a priori* ruling, any systematic acceptance of things: he felt completely free to use only such Fauve idiom as suited his purpose. And, in *La Cuisine* especially, he showed an amazing mastery of himself and his medium. He knew precisely how to adapt his pictorial vocabulary to his inner vision, to convey the emotion he felt, an emotion that sprang from a certain sensation of colour and light. Vlaminck was at home in his own kitchen, with his wife, who was busy with the housework: a bright light falls into the room, the play of colours expresses both a sense of peace and vitality. This is not the kind of anecdotal Intimism, rendered in half-tones, that we find in Vuillard; this is a more sensual Intimism expressed in a more direct manner. Vlaminck relied solely on colour, a totally imagined colour, clear and warm, in which a few cold shades suggest the intimate darkness of the room, creating a highly poetic chiaroscuro effect.

The Salon des Indépendants had not yet closed its doors when, during April, Vollard decided to buy all of Vlaminck's existing stock and future output. This was an event of the utmost importance. On the one hand, Vlaminck no longer had any material worries. The relief was such that he was able to paint more light-heartedly, more joyfully; his lyricism soon took on an exuberant, riotous character. On the other hand, when Vlaminck realized that his painting, like that of other Fauves, could at least interest a dealer like Vollard, he was convinced that he must on no account deviate from his course.

It is difficult to identify with any accuracy Vlaminck's artistic output after the Salon des Indépendants and especially during the summer of 1906. It is very easy to confuse these works with those of 1907. Examining the artist's signature is of little help since it did not vary much until the end of 1907; during that year, however, Vlaminck tended to sign rather more elliptically.

Not a single one of the seven works exhibited at the Salon des Indépendants can be identified with certitude. But a number of well-known canvases painted during 1906 enables us to understand the main lines along which Vlaminck's art was evolving. There were two phases separated by the vital psychological moment of the contract with Vollard in April. The happy effects of Vlaminck's new financial security must have made themselves felt from May onward. Before that date his manner of painting was to some extent a continuation of that of 1905; despite a growing boldness, he still reveals a certain stiffness in composition and form; we have the feeling that here is a painter setting out to paint a picture who applies himself to the task in an almost naïve way. This creates a somewhat heavy overall impression. The first phase of 1906 also coincided with Vlaminck's rather Pointillist manner. And whereas the broken brush-strokes should result in bright and vivid harmonies, Vlaminck's often come out very differently: the painter overworked his colours with an excessive jostling of minute strokes (when there is no added impasto) which ultimately destroy the chromatic harmony. Often, too, the accumulation of tiny strokes of all shapes, going in all directions, creates an incoherent riot of colour that totally demolishes the painted surface and makes the rendering of space illegible. An example of this is the *Berge de la Seine à Chatou* (Bank of the Seine at Chatou; Pl. 87) (Musée d'Art Moderne de la Ville de Paris). It took Vlaminck some time to get the better of his technical inexperience, which vitiated his inspiration. A typical example of the period before May is *Les Pêcheurs à Nanterre* (Anglers at Nanterre). On the canvases belonging to this first group we can see that the signature consists of fine, separate letters, well aligned (even if the signature itself slants); thus it is like his signature at the end of 1905, but differs from it by always being underlined. The second phase, which began in May and continued into 1907, was Vlaminck's finest Fauve period. It may have started with such canvases as the *Bateaux-lavoirs* (Musée de l'Annonciade, St. Tropez) in which we can still sense a meticulous striving to organize and balance the surface but which succeeds, nevertheless, in giving the colour its full effusiveness, or with *La Partie de campagne* (The Picnic) (Marcelle Bourdon Collection, Paris), the Fauve version of the theme of the *Déjeuner sur l'herbe*, which shows great progress in the (now coherent) distribution of small patches of colour. From that moment on Vlaminck's Fauvism was expressed with total freedom and ease, and there was no conflict between his inspiration and his skill;

75. Braque *Le Port d'Anvers, le mât*, 1906.

the idiom remained very simple, flexibly adapted to the artist's lyricism. The composition lost its somewhat contrived character, the drawing yielded to the subjective distortions, the vision released its full power of synthesis and the force of its transposition, the colour became daringly arbitrary and, above all, predominant, that is to say, it was the soul of the picture, it was light and space; the paint itself, finally, was applied more lightly, in supple, clear, dynamic brush-strokes of tremendous variety. At the same time, the signature had undergone a parallel transformation; it also came to life, it slanted, it curved, it writhed; the component letters remained separate and the underlining had not yet disappeared, but the letters became thicker and the line was rarely straight. It was in this second group of works, which included many masterpieces, that we find the most exuberant lyricism, in such works as *Bords de Seine à Carrières-sur-Seine* (Banks of the Seine at Carrières-sur-Seine; Pl. 64) (Private Collection, Paris) and the *Jardinier* (Gardener). In the drawing and especially in the colour, Vlaminck let himself be carried away by the liveliest flights of imagination and reached the peak of Fauvism, if Fauvism is the art of being as arbitrary and Dionysian as possible.

Vlaminck was one of the Fauve painters who were most attracted by the human face, which he did not treat simply as an artistic subject-matter. For Vlaminck a face, a portrait, was always charged with all sorts of psychological connotations. To explain his art, especially his tendency toward a kind of Expressionism, he often referred to his Nordic origins. To this we might also ascribe his interest in human beings and his manner of treating them. Here we clearly have a parallel with van Gogh, who remained his exemplar and teacher much more than Gauguin or Cézanne; and through van Gogh he made a connection with his friend Van Dongen, another Northerner.

Vlaminck does not seem to have painted any figures during that first period of 1906 we have discussed; by contrast, there are many from the second period. We think that there is a simple reason for this: Vlaminck had no studio, and as he painted mainly nudes he

76.   Marquet *Le Pont-Neuf*, 1906.

77. Derain *La Tamise*, 1906.

78. Derain *Les deux péniches, Londres*, 1906.

79. Derain *Le Pont de Charing Cross, Londres*, 1906.

80.   Derain *Effet de soleil sur la Tamise*, 1906.

81. Vlaminck *La danseuse du Rat Mort*, 1906.

82.   Van Dongen *La ballerine borgne saluant*, 1906.

83.   Dufy *Vieilles maisons sur le bassin à Honfleur*, 1906.

could only do them in Derain's studio in Paris, but he was not able to go to Paris until Vollard's contract enabled him to devote himself entirely to painting—that is, from April to May on. In fact Vlaminck went to stay with Derain, who rented a studio in Montmartre, rue Tourlaque, on several occasions during 1906. The two friends also met sometimes at the Azon restaurant, place du Tertre, where they had interminable discussions on art with Apollinaire, Max Jacob, Van Dongen and others. But Vlaminck said that this "intellectual bohemian" atmosphere was not at all to his liking and that he preferred the banks of the Seine. One of the dancers from the neighbouring cabaret, Le Rat Mort, came to pose at the studio in rue Tourlaque. Around April or May, Derain and Vlaminck painted the same model, with Vlaminck on her right and Derain on her left. Derain's picture, *La Femme en chemise* (Woman in a Slip) (Statens Museum for Kunst, Copenhagen), confirmed its author's break with Divisionism, while, by contrast, Vlaminck's *La Danseuse du Rat Mort* (The Dancer from the "Rat Mort"; Pl. 81) (Private Collection, Paris) showed a persistent interest in the breaking-up of form. We know that Derain had come to prefer flat coloured areas with contour lines to give greater expressiveness to form and more density to space. To Derain Vlaminck's picture was an example of what one should no longer do; it is true that Vlaminck's exaggerated use of Divisionist methods (especially as he did not apply them with any great discipline) caused a splintering of the painted surface that detracted from the expressive power of the image.

Van Dongen, whom Vlaminck met often, was faced with the same problem, which he solved in the same way as Derain had done. Thus Vlaminck had two examples close to him, and decided to follow them; we can see a swift evolution in the course of 1906. At the starting-point, around May, we may put *La Danseuse du Rat Mort* and *La Femme au chapeau de paille* (Woman in Straw Hat) and, shortly afterwards, works like *Portrait de femme au chien* (Portrait of a Woman with Dog) and *La Fille* (The Girl), in which the painter has fully succeeded in letting the figures stand out from their Pointillist setting and giving them greater density.

Although Vlaminck's Fauvism continued to evolve until the end of 1906, it remained basically the same as in 1905. Subjectivity predominated: the expression of feeling always prevailed over artistic problems, in which the artist still showed little imagination and taste. He saw Fauvism chiefly as a means of expressing his own vital impulses. "Painting", he said, "should be as lively, emotive, tender, fierce and natural as life."[49] He was one of those who went furthest in their quest for a new relationship between the artist and nature: "I felt no jealousy, no hatred," he wrote, "but a consuming passion to create a new world, the world as I saw it with my own eyes, a world of my very own. I was poor, but I knew life was good. And I wanted nothing more than to find new ways of uncovering the deep ties that bound me to the soil. I heightened all the tones, I transposed all the feelings I was conscious of in an orchestration of pure colours. I was a barbarian—tender and full of violence."[50] That was why Vlaminck's Fauvism at that point was so direct and spontaneous, but also so limited, for sensations cannot be revived at will, however great the artist's vitality, and the saturation of reds, blues and yellows is subject to chemical limitations.

Van Dongen

Thanks to Picasso, who told him of a vacant studio, Van Dongen was able to move with his wife Guus and his daughter Dolly to the Bateau-Lavoir in December 1905, where he stayed until February 1907. These chronological facts enable us to attribute a number of works to the year 1906, although not with complete certitude for none of them is accurately documented. There is another odd discrepancy, which applies only to Van Dongen in any significant degree: the catalogues of the time are more or less useless because, in the first place, the titles of the works exhibited in no way correspond to any work now known and, in the second place, because many surviving works, often the most characteristic ones, are not found in the catalogues of the time and do not seem to have been exhibited, which makes them difficult to date. In fact, between 1906 and 1908, Van Dongen generally showed few of his recent works either in collective or one-man shows, although his output was prolific during these years; exhibitions of his work were often retrospective.

His submissions to the Salon des Indépendants, with one exception, comprise works on the circus, dance and music-hall. All the sources tell us that Van Dongen, together with Picasso, went to the Médrano circus several times a week. Therefore it seems reasonable to date from 1906 a number of canvases showing clowns, acrobats and circus riders. We also know that Van Dongen, who adored dancing, went regularly to balls, notably those at the Moulin de la Galette where the *maxixe* was popular. After moving to the Bateau-Lavoir, he seems to have been more interested in café and music-hall floorshows. We do not know if Picasso's influence had anything to do with this. As for the Folies Bergères, it was certainly through Nini, a prostitute he met towards the end of 1905, that he got to know the back-stage world; she was a *Petite Marcheuse sur le plateau* (A Bit-player on the Stage).[51] She sat for him on several occasions. It is logical to date from 1906 the canvases based on Nini, especially as two drawings called *Nini* and *Nini sur la chaise-longue* (Nini on the Chaise-longue), were shown at an exhibition in Amsterdam in July and August 1907; as the painter stayed in Holland from February to August 1907, it follows that February 1907 was the latest possible date for works showing Nini, who was replaced by other models in 1907.

At the Bateau-Lavoir, Picasso's companion, Fernande Olivier, would also occasionally pose for Van Dongen. We think that the picture shown at the Indépendants under the title *Une Femme en gris* (Woman in Grey) can be identified with the portrait of *Fernande Olivier*. The greyish-mauve dress of the model stands out against a light grey background; contrasting with these subtle, rather cold tones, the face is coloured bright yellow, green and red. There is

a deliberate accent on the outline of the figure created by a wide contour line leading from the plane of the figure to the surrounding plane; the contour line itself is duplicated by a coloured band of varying width, modulated and discontinued—an intermediate plane which helps the figure blend less abruptly into its surrounding space and raises the dynamic intensity of the tones. This was a method frequently used by Van Dongen, which suggests that, for a time at least, he was indifferent to the planes farthest from the figure he was painting. This method generally emphasized the figure itself and made the most of the line and pose. We shall see that his treatment of pictorial space was extended to include the whole surface when he wanted to make the picture more expressive.

From 24 May to 17 June Van Dongen exhibited sixty-two paintings and eleven drawings at the Cercle d'Art in Rotterdam. Almost all the works were earlier than 1906 (one of them dated even from 1894); only two were followed by the mention "1906": *Portrait d'enfant* (Portrait of a Child) and *A la Galette*. Thus the catalogue of this exhibition is not much help to us. Nor can we hope for more from the list of works hung at the Salon d'Automne (*Montmartre, Mademoiselle Leda, Parisienne*), which cannot be identified, at least not without venturing into hazardous assumptions. A document of the time may help us reconsider the date of one picture. This was the list of works bought from Van Dongen by Felix Fénéon, the art director of the Bernheim-Jeune Gallery, on 23 December 1906.[52] It mentions a canvas called *Jarretière* (The Garter) which, we suggest, can be identified with *La Jarretière violette* (The Violet Garter), a picture often dated—wrongly, we think—to 1910. The treatment of the nude seems to correspond exactly with the style used for the nudes of 1906.

As we can now see, the list of works painted by Van Dongen in 1906 falls into three groups: the first dealt with the circus and music-hall (the nude can be associated with this group), the second with Nini, and the third with Fernande Olivier. Clearly, we cannot ascribe each of these groups to a particular period in 1906; Van Dongen was not in the habit of devoting

174

84. Marquet *La Passerelle de Sainte-Adresse*, 1906.

himself to one subject for a certain time to the exclusion of all others; he liked to vary his work, going from one subject to another as the spirit moved him or as circumstances prompted. As we have no absolutely certain chronological reference within the year 1906, it is difficult to follow Van Dongen's creative course during that period with any accuracy. However, we can see that he evolved towards a complete mastery of the Fauve means of expression adapted to representation of the human figure. Thus *La Ballerine borgne et son enfant* (The One-Eyed Ballet Dancer and her Child), which we think should be considered as the first work of the period beginning with Van Dongen's move to the Bateau-Lavoir, is derived not so much from Fauve art as from that of Degas, Toulouse-Lautrec and Manet, with its simplified style, its drawing discreetly set off by contour lines, its modulated areas of colour, its subtle chromatism and intangible space. This work was undoubtedly also influenced by Picasso's contemporaneous experiments with a manner that was astonishingly spare and yet at the same time rich in artistic expression, illustrated, for example by the series on circus people. Subsequently, Van Dongen's figures took on more body and vividness, while space became animated and denser. The artist showed his preference for curved lines and rounded rhythms, as we can see in *La Femme au collier* (Woman with a Necklace). The play of arabesques gives a measure of elegance to the rather coarse figures of the dancers and circus riders who have not yet acquired the slimness of the women painted after 1908. The outline of the figure becomes dynamic thanks to a method peculiar to Van Dongen—the superimposition of a broken line on to the continuous line defining the form; but this was probably motivated by a concern with space, since the broken line is often replaced by thick perpendicular hatching on the contour line. The broken line or the hatched area create an immediate plane surrounding the figure and make it stand out from the picture surface by virtue of its tones and colours, which are identical with the tones of the background planes. We can see the same kind of concern in the drawing; even

when Van Dongen was expressing himself in black and white, he used the same methods as in painting to achieve similar ends. He seems to have attempted to combine the concepts of outline and volume so dear to him with the Fauve concept of space; the portrait of *La Belle Fernande* (Beautiful Fernande; Pl. 50) (Private Collection, Paris) confirms our interpretation of the artist's aims at the beginning of 1906.

In the treatment of figures the flesh is rendered with no concern for anatomical accuracy; yellow is mixed with pink in wide modulated flat areas with green shadows; faces are strongly coloured: vermilion lips, black eyes lined with mauve. At first the figure stood out light against a dark—sometimes even black—background; then the background took on vivid colouring and became a cold blue that grew progressively warmer until it finally changed to yellow. But black was not discarded entirely; it was reserved for certain details of clothing—a vest or stockings, for instance. The setting of a light figure against a dark space, an unusual procedure contrary to the traditional rule that dark planes push back light planes, should be interpreted as more of a Fauve feature than would appear. Van Dongen rejected all illusionist space in favour of a purely plastic treatment of space constructed through contrasts of pure colours of equal saturation. At first the artist moved from one plane to the next through a wide coloured band that duplicated the contour line and seemed to put a halo round the figure. Then he abandoned that method and instead used the juxtaposition of brightly coloured areas without any—or with only very few—contour lines. This resulted in a more expressive organization of the painted surface. Van Dongen was moving towards a progressive assimilation of the Fauve treatment of space but without the use of abrupt contrasts; he always showed a concern for chromatic subtlety that was alien to the Fauves. At first, space was a sort of void, undifferentiated or treated with simple decorative motifs; the artist then introduced definite motifs connected with the subject (for instance, in the pictures of clowns) which were obviously meant to enrich the painted surface and thereby increase its

85. Derain *Le Pont de Waterloo*, 1906.

86. Derain *L'Estaque, route tournante* ou *Vers la Fontaine*, 1906.

expressiveness. Basically, Van Dongen's approach at the beginning of 1906 was more that of a draughtsman anxious to accentuate certain attitudes, certain movements, than that of a colourist. During the year he progressively came to follow a more strictly pictorial course: he rejected anything descriptive, anything anecdotal in even the poetic rendering of an action or gesture; he stripped away, as it were, the memory of Degas and Toulouse-Lautrec and came to express himself essentially through colour, which he used

with marvellous imagination and the utmost arbitrariness. From around the end of 1906 we would date *Le Clown* (The Clown), with strongly contrasted tones, and *Le Clown* (Pl. 65) (Private Collection, Paris), with kindred tones in the manner of Gauguin. Both these pictures show not only Van Dongen's perfect mastery of the Fauve means of expression but his gift for well-matched powerful resonances and rare harmonies in which—as in Gauguin—red plays a predominant role.

178

87. Vlaminck *Berge de la Seine à Chatou*, early 1906.

Dufy

The tendency toward Fauvism that Dufy had shown since the summer of 1905, after the impact made on him by Matisse's picture *Luxe, calme et volupté*, became more marked, but this did not happen very quickly. A childhood friend of Friesz and Braque, Dufy nevertheless drifted away from them and grew closer to Marquet, with whom he felt a greater affinity. This affinity was not confined to personal feelings: Dufy liked working with Marquet because he felt he could gain much more from him, in painting, than from his Le Havre friends. The Salon d'Automne of 1905 confirmed Dufy in the course he had been shown by Matisse, but that Salon also had a retrospective of Manet, whose art did not seem at all anachronistic to Dufy and Marquet. Their intellectual closeness increased their friendship for each other and their eagerness to paint together, and it is not surprising that in 1906 their output shows a great similarity in subjects and style.

We cannot judge Dufy's art at the beginning of the year because not a single one of the eight pictures he exhibited at the Salon des Indépendants has been identified. But such titles as *Neige* (Snow) (three works by that name) and *L'Hiver* (Winter) rather suggest that the painter still retained an Impressionist approach. These must have been older works, since Dufy had not yet had time to produce pictures in the new style to which Matisse had opened his eyes.

His output in the summer of 1906, by contrast, is well known. Some of the works executed during that period were shown in October, either at Berthe Weill's (who organized the painter's first one-man show) or at the Salon d'Automne (in which Dufy took part for the first time). We know nothing of the exhibition at Berthe Weill's, but can identify four of the seven canvases the artist showed at the Salon d'Automne. These show two styles adopted by Dufy that are neither contradictory nor mutually exclusive but coexistent. The first was compact, dense, deliberate; the coloured areas were in direct apposition, the tones lively. This is illustrated by *Les Ombrelles* (The Umbrellas; Pl. 66) (Private Collection, Houston) with its intense and refined harmonies. Here the handling of the concordances of the flat areas varying in size required great assurance. Dufy did not attempt any systematic, banal, even automatic, opposition of complementary tones. Without discarding them altogether, he replaced them with a more subtle play of very close, almost identical shades: blue-violet and even blue-blue, pink-red and, most unusual for a Fauve painter, he did not leave out black. There is no doubt that this subtle colouring and the use of greenish whites carried echoes of Manet. The second style, by contrast, was fresh and spontaneous-looking. Intermediate areas, whether black contour lines or white zones, link the colours to each other. This was a kind of very free Tachism which had absolutely no connection with Divisionism, in which Dufy, who did not like any form of systematic theory, was not at all interested. We can see this style in *Les Affiches à Trouville* (Posters at Trouville; Pl. 67), of which two versions are known, one of which is now in the Musée National d'Art Moderne in Paris, although it is impossible to tell which of them was shown at the Salon d'Automne. Here Dufy was very close to the art of his friend Marquet.

The two canvases at the Salon d'Automne called *Rue pavoisée (Le Havre)* (Street with Flags and Bunting) correspond to a series on bedecked streets on the Fourteenth of July of which eleven versions have been counted. It is generally believed that of the versions Dufy showed at the Salon d'Automne, one is now in the Musée National d'Art Moderne in Paris and the other in the Alphonse Bellier Collection, Paris. Dufy's mastery was such, and his artistic imagination so rich, that he was capable of infinite variations on a chosen theme, of giving a multitude of interpretations, each of them a poetic creation in which the subject was merely the peg on which to hang an inexhaustible lyricism. The painter's methods are reminiscent of those of musical variations: like a musician, Dufy executed several compositions on a given theme. This, as we can see, has nothing in common with the series by Monet who, in

88. Dufy *La Balançoire*, 1906.

each version of the same subject, relied on the exceptional keenness and skill of his eye to render faithfully the fleeting changes in nature. Dufy listened far more intently to himself than to the outer world so that each artistic variation is the product of an inner vision, constantly renewed, which leaves its mark on the physical reality. Thus no comparison is possible between Dufy's interpretations of the Fourteenth of July and Monet's; nor are they anything like van Gogh's, who treated the same subject, for his were fundamentally no less Impressionist than Monet's. On the other hand, there are certain similarities between some of Dufy's variations (for instance, *Le 14 Juillet* in the A. Bellier Collection, Paris) and some versions of *La Rue Mosnier pavoisée* (Rue Mosnier with Flags and Bunting) by Manet (for example, the one in the Bührle Collection, Zurich), in the artistic autonomy through which the work transcends reality, in the concern for composition and layout and even in the simple technique.

We must mention a characteristic detail of the *Rue pavoisée* in the Musée National d'Art Moderne: the transparency of the flag that lets us see two passers-by behind it. This was the kind of representation we find in Dufy's later work, but it is significant that it appeared as early as 1906 (and, as far as we know, in Dufy alone); proof of his originality and the outstanding mastery of his vision. To Dufy the picture was an artistic summary, a general impression of a series of views; the transparent feature conveyed two impressions superimposed in time: one refers to the moment when the two passers-by were visible, the other to the moment when the flag hid them. Nothing could be more anti-Impressionist than this manner of interpreting a scene, for it presupposes a concept of continuous observation whereas the Impressionist painter treated only the immediate moment.

Dufy's output, which was very prolific at the end of the year, showed that the artist had not yet solved all his problems, especially that of deciding whether to contain his lyricism or, on the contrary, be swept away by it. On the whole the lyricism seems rather measured, held in check, in the views of Ste. Adresse

and of Honfleur, as in *Vieilles Maisons sur le bassin à Honfleur* (Old Houses at Honfleur Harbour; Pl. 83) (Private Collection) and much more spontaneous and fiery in the views painted at Le Havre, which can be reliably dated to 1906 as is noted on most of the canvases. We think that these were the last to be finished by Dufy, after the Salon d'Automne of that year, where two artists seem to have interested him in particular—Gauguin and Derain. Dufy's *Nature morte en plein air* (Still Life Outdoors) (Private Collection),[53] dense, luxuriant, arbitrary in its colouring, was a real homage to Gauguin. And his *Port du Havre* (Private Collection, Paris)[54] was very close to Derain's views of London which had been shown at the Salon; never before had Dufy been so completely detached from "objective things", in Derain's words, nor had he ever achieved such a degree of expressiveness, imagination and lyricism, or come so close to abstraction. The examples of Marquet and Monet had been replaced by those of Gauguin and Derain, who now were more apt to encourage the flowering of Dufy's art.

Friesz

We must not be deceived by the fact that in December 1905 Friesz exhibited at Prath and Magnier's beside Matisse, Marquet, Derain, Vlaminck and Van Dongen. Friesz had not yet reached the stage of reappraising his painting; he continued along Impressionist lines. This is confirmed by his submission to the Salon des Indépendants. Although the eight canvases he exhibited have disappeared, the titles, or rather subtitles, like "sun", "dull weather", suggest that the painter's approach remained fundamentally focused on objective physical reality. Oddly enough, Friesz even did some history paintings: he showed a picture called *La Mort d'Auguste* (Death of Augustus). How can we explain this except by assuming that he wanted to show the critics who were hostile to the Fauves that he himself had not turned his back on tradition?

In the summer of 1906 Friesz and Braque stayed in Antwerp. From that moment onward Friesz's art becomes more comprehensible. The pictures of the Antwerp series (some twenty) have been preserved and have been shown frequently. In September of that year some works (oils? watercolours?) were shown at Le Havre under the general title *Vues d'Anvers* (Views of Antwerp). In the following months, at the Salon d'Automne, Friesz hung four canvases, three of which are known: *Le Croiseur pavoisé* (Dressed Cruiser),[55] *Les Péniches* (The Barges) and *L'Entrée d'une corvette dans le port* (The Arrival of a Corvette in the Port of Antwerp; Pl. 74) (Musée du Petit Palais, Geneva). He exhibited only four, whereas he had a right to eight items. Why? It must have been that he had no more canvases completely finished in October. But there may have been another reason: Friesz knew what the Fauves were doing; he knew, for example, what his friend Dufy was engaged on; he realized that he could not show canvases still imbued with Impressionism beside those of his friends—he thought four would be enough. Precisely the three views we know that were hung at the Salon d'Automne show a strong Impressionist spirit. The Antwerp series contains a few more in the same manner which may have been finished before the opening of the Salon d'Automne but which Friesz did not want to add to his exhibits. On the other hand, if we examine the views of Antwerp as a whole we find that they consisted basically of three subjects—that is, each subject gave rise to several versions, some derived from Impressionism (painted at Antwerp), some with a Fauve look (certainly done in the studio in Paris).

We think that it was at the time of the opening of the Salon d'Automne that Friesz decided to change his manner of pictorial expression under the impact made on him by the works his friends were going to exhibit at the Salon, which he saw in their studios. From that time we might date the *Port d'Anvers* (The Port of Antwerp; Pl. 89) (Cabinet des Estampes, Liège) and the *Fête foraine à Rouen* (Fair at Rouen) (Musée Fabre, Montpellier). But Friesz gave his work only a Fauve appearance by heightening the colour. This was surface Fauvism, for the act of painting did not come from an inner dynamism, from the artist's own passion, from an intoxication that played havoc with reality. Friesz thought he was becoming Fauve by changing from the local tone to an arbitrary one; he forgot that his approach remained fundamentally naturalist, that his concept of space remained subject to light. His mistake lay in thinking that he was executing Fauvist works while using essentially Impressionist means. It is significant, incidentally, that he did not appreciate either van Gogh or Gauguin, accusing the first of "sensual turmoil" and the second of "exoticism"; Cézanne, by contrast, retained his approval, for he regarded him as an Impressionist who tried "to give solidity to things".[56]

Braque

We must admit that Braque's approach at the beginning of the year was as naturalist as Friesz's, if we are to judge by *La Côte de Grâce à Honfleur* (Côte de Grâce at Honfleur) (Musée des Beaux-Arts, Le Havre), the only surviving picture of the seven exhibited at the Salon des Indépendants. Although this approach did not change radically, there are nevertheless signs of a change in *Bateau dans le Port du Havre* (Boat in the Port of Le Havre), which, we believe, must have been painted shortly after the preceding work; here we can see attempts at chromatic transposition which suggest that Braque had looked at his friends' exhibits at the Indépendants with great interest.

Braque was with Friesz in Antwerp during the summer. The works he painted, which do not seem to have been very numerous, show as little will as those of Friesz to renew the pictorial idiom radically. Even when Braque used a very vivid palette in order to transpose physical reality (and in this field he probably went further than Friesz), he retained the illusionist treatment of space whose links with Impressionist naturalism are obvious.

But Braque did not share Friesz's past as an Impressionist painter; this explains why he detached himself from Impressionism more easily than his

89. Friesz *Le Port d'Anvers*, 1906.

friend. Friesz rightly said that Braque did not have "to clear the ground like his elders". Braque was more determined than Friesz: the latter exhibited little at the Salon d'Automne, Braque did not exhibit at all.

Unlike Friesz, Braque appreciated Gauguin. He decided to break with naturalism and settled at L'Estaque, which was a revelation to him. "It was in the South", he said, "that I felt all my passion wake in me." Braque's output during the winter of 1906 (more than twenty canvases, often dated) shows the painter's total adherence to Fauvism. A Fauvism, moreover, with a fine poetic quality: imagination and control, lyricism and lucidity went hand in hand, as in the dynamically structured view of *L'Estaque*, or the

90. Braque *Port de l'Estaque*, 1906.

Paysage à L'Estaque (Landscape at L'Estaque) whose arbitrariness both in colour and drawing borders on abstraction.

The essential feature in the development of Fauve art in 1906 was the new role of drawing, which now participated much more actively than in 1905 in the expression of the Fauve picture; it now assumed the capacity for transposition which had previously been confined to colour. Line thus became a main part of the Fauve vocabulary and posed the problem of the relationship between form and colour in new terms. Here, too, Matisse and Derain were the first in the field and took their place as leaders of Fauvism. It is also important to realize that they advanced by way of an appraisal of Islamic and Far Eastern art, for this introduced a cultural pluralism in the painters' sources of inspiration: the tired art of the West could regenerate itself through non-Western sources.

Like Matisse and Derain, Van Dongen became aware of the need to reject drawing that depended more or less on the object and resolutely to adopt a more or less arbitrary line with greater lyrical power. The Fauves' lyrical impulse took on such a frenzied character that we can almost speak of Dionysiac lyricism. Even Vlaminck, who did not bother much with such questions, let himself go into an equally frenetic Fauvism, but came up against the difficulty of reviving his flagging sensations. Marquet's lyricism was less elated, and to him drawing was above all the art of structuring a picture; Dufy's was more muted, although he had great imagination. Friesz's hesitation was countered by Braque's swift enthusiasm.

The lyrical impulses of many of the Fauves were such that they blurred reality to the point of creating almost abstract works. Derain alone was fully aware of the ambiguity of painting the object and the artist's subjectivity at one and the same time and he alone envisaged a solution by imagining pictures that would be "compositions" not based on nature. After arbitrariness in colour, after arbitrariness in line, came arbitrary treatment of the subject.

Chapter V 1907—New lyricism, meditation, abstraction

The year 1907 was of the utmost importance to Fauvism since it marked its end. But until the year was over the Fauve picture continued to grow increasingly expressive, first because Fauvism simplified its idiom even further, to the point of starkness, and second because the arbitrary treatment of the drawing multiplied the lyrical power of the image. The consequences, which had been apparent to a lesser degree in 1906, became increasingly accentuated in the case of many Fauves who pushed back the boundaries of representation until their work approached abstract art.

Matisse

The art of Matisse did not undergo any fundamental change during 1907; the painter only clarified, filled in some gaps, and refined his artistic system. His contribution to the Salon des Indépendants consisted of two drawings, three wood engravings which cannot be identified, and a *Tableau No III*, which has been identified, though not with absolute certainty, as the *Nu bleu, souvenir de Biskra* (Blue Nude, Memento of Biskra; Pl. 117) (Baltimore Museum of Art). Actually, there is no room for doubt if we look at L. Vauxcelles's comments in his review of the Salon. He wrote: "A naked woman, ugly, lying in the opaque blue grass, under the palm-trees... The drawing here strikes me as rudimentary, the colour cruel; the right arm of the mannish nymph is flat and heavy; the line of the hips of the deformed body defines an arabesque of leaves, unless it is really the curve of the foliage that determines the curve of the woman."[57]

Contrary to what has frequently been asserted, the *Nu bleu* could not have been painted at Collioure in 1907 since Matisse stayed there after the Salon des Indépendants. The picture must have been executed during the winter of 1906-7. The subject of the nude is derived from the *Bonheur de vivre*, which in turn was no doubt based on *Le Bain turc* by Ingres. The drawing of this *Nu bleu*, transposed into an African setting, is less supple than the figure of the *Bonheur de vivre*; the lines often converge in sharp angles, creating a rather harsh rhythm—somewhat unexpected in an exotic figure that suggests the comforts of life. Matisse no doubt refused to give his figure any form of superficial pleasantness, any sentimental or picturesque connotations, to avoid any resemblance to an odalisque by Ingres; plasticity replaced the anecdote. Whereas the *Bonheur de vivre* had human figures that were flat or whose mass was roughly suggested by an arabesque, the *Nu bleu*, by contrast, has exact indications of the form which depend not only on the suggestive power of the contour lines but on contrasting colour values. Of course, Matisse would never introduce an objective light to give the form an illusion of volume; the lighting remains arbitrary, rendered by colour playing the role of a figurative equivalent, here the blue Matisse called "structural".[58] The urge to give the nude a certain plastic solidity and at the same time a strong structure reveal Matisse's personal preoccupations, which reflect the fact that he was working on sculptured figures at the same time. The *Nu bleu* has its companion-piece in sculpture, the *Nu couché I* (Recumbent Nude I) (bronze, Museum of Modern Art, New York; Museum of Art, Baltimore; Musée d'Art Moderne de la Ville de Paris). It would be futile to speculate whether this statuette was made before or after the *Nu bleu*. Whether the picture was modelled on a living person or on the statuette itself is of no importance. Matisse has said himself that he often worked on a painting and sculpture simultaneously. "Thus, to express form, I sometimes indulge in sculpture, which enables me to walk round the subject and get to know it better instead of being confronted with a flat surface." "Now, convey the curves of this body as in a sculpture", he advised his pupils in 1908. "Find out their mass and their fullness. Their outlines must be enough for that... A drawing is a sculpture."

What is striking about Matisse is the sureness of his art, the coherence of his ideas, which he would soon be able to define in writing, to publish and to teach. In this he differed from the other Fauves, notably the anxious Derain, whom Matisse, incidentally, visited twice during the summer, at Cassis. The first visit, which must have been in or around June, lasted about a week; Derain wrote to Vlaminck that Matisse "is rejuvenated", that he was "happy as a lark and doesn't seem to worry about anything".[59] Matisse saw his friend again at the beginning of July, when he was going to Italy with his wife. In another letter to Vlaminck, Derain wrote: "He has shown me photos of his canvases; they are absolutely amazing. I think he is going through the gate of the seventh heaven, that of happiness."[60] At a time when Derain was going through a dramatic reappraisal of his painting and even questioning all the premises of painting itself, Matisse evinced the quiet assurance of the artist who had found his way, who had constructed a sound form of expression. From his stay in Italy, which was fertile in ideas, he did not bring back questions but affirmations. He probably started off on his trip at the beginning of July; the date of his return is more certain—around 15 August.[61] We know that Matisse went to Venice, Padua, Florence, Fiesole and Siena,

91.   Matisse *Les voiliers*, 1906.

92. Vlaminck *Nu couché*, 1906.

93. Van Dongen *Anita, nu couché*, 1906.

94.   Dufy *La plage de Sainte-Adresse*, 1906.

95.   Braque *Le port de La Ciotat*, 1907.

96.   Friesz *Arbres à Honfleur*, 1906-1907.

97.   Friesz *Paysage à La Ciotat (Le Bec-de-l'Aigle)*, 1907.

98. Braque *La Ciotat*, 1907.

and that he was particularly taken with the works of Duccio, Piera della Francesca, and above all Giotto, who always remained an examplar for him: "Giotto is my ultimate wish." Matisse could not help but see similarities to his own painting in the art of the Italian fresco painter. The expressiveness of Giotto's art, achieved through simple painterly means, would naturally attract the author of the *Bonheur de vivre*. "When I look at Giotto's frescoes in Padua," Matisse wrote in 1908, "I don't care which scene in the life of Christ I am looking at, but I immediately understand the feeling it exudes, for it is in the line, in the composition, in the colour, and the title only confirms my impression." Perhaps it was the example of Giotto's supple manner that helped divert Matisse completely from the rather stiff manner of the *Nu bleu*. After Islamic art, it was probably the example of Giotto that helped Matisse to achieve, before the end of 1907, an extremely sparse form of art.

Of the seven items by Matisse hung at the Salon d'Automne, two have been identified: *La Musique* (Music) and *Luxe I* (Luxury I; Pl. 99) (Musée National d'Art Moderne, Paris). The first work has a great soberness of line and colour; Matisse had cut away a great deal to let the harmonious synthesis of the outline and of the simple contrast of two tones predominate. In the second picture, *Trois Baigneuses* (Three Women Bathing), which we think was based on a composition painted at Collioure in the summer, Matisse adopted a triple composition with a hieratic standing figure, a second one crouching, and a third moving in the background; an arrangement that is very similar to that of *La Musique. Luxe I* was a sketch, and no doubt Matisse was planning to make the necessary changes to achieve another picture in which the expressiveness would be enhanced. If we refer to earlier works, like *Jeune Marin I* and *Jeune Marin II* (Young Sailor I and Young Sailor II), we can see that in the first conception Matisse imagined a composition based to some extent on the observation of reality, in which colour and drawing were not yet purified, just as the form-colour synthesis was not yet stabilized. The artist had not yet decided on the most

essential lines in his drawing, on the extent of the flat areas, or on the equilibrium of his tonal harmony. That is why, logically, *Luxe I* is a less harmonious, a less expressive composition than *Luxe II* (Pl. 100) (Statens Museum for Kunst, Copenhagen), executed a little later, undoubtedly at the beginning of 1908. This seems to have been something entirely peculiar to Matisse, who tried to combine both the feeling aroused by nature or any other emotion and the artistic demands of the work of art, the first penetrating the second, and the second correcting the first; Matisse's attitude toward the relationship between the artist and nature and the artist and the work of art was very special.

L'Enfant au filet à papillons (Child with Butterfly Net) (Institute of Art, Minneapolis), definitely painted in 1907, reflects the same concerns as *Luxe I*, but here Matisse achieved a sufficient overall expressiveness so that he did not think it necessary to do a second version. We cannot avoid comparing Matisse's *L'Enfant au filet à papillons* with Picasso's *L'Enfant au pigeon* (Child with Pigeon), painted in 1901, which reveals a similarity in the experiments of the two artists. Was this fortuitous? Or had Matisse seen the picture in Picasso's studio in 1906? Conversely, in some of Picasso's canvases painted in 1906 at Gosol, like *La Toilette* (Dressing) (Albright-Knox Art Gallery, Buffalo) and *Le Harem* (The Cleveland Museum of Art), we find an orientation towards an expressive style through the use of simple means such as had been initiated by Matisse in *Le Bonheur de vivre*. The two works by Picasso cited also contain figures that have too much in common with Matisse's for the similarities to be entirely fortuitous.

Matisse's artistic output in 1907 included very few landscapes or still lifes. His lack of interest in landscape manifested itself at that time and soon became total, whereas still life shortly regained its special place. Matisse favoured the human figure. "What interests me most," he wrote in 1908, "is neither landscape nor still life but the figure. It best enables me to express the almost religious feeling I have for life." In this field Matisse created a special kind of composition in which one, two or at most three monumental figures are shown in a landscape which the painter suggests with only a few lines. We could not call them figures integrated into a landscape because it is not a natural setting but an artistic decor or accompaniment. This does not mean that there is no harmony between the setting and the figure—far from it. The degree of simplification, we might almost say abstraction, affects all the artistic components of the picture: the very imprecise nudes of *Luxe I* are matched by a setting, a background in which the allusions to reality are slight, whereas the less approximated nude of *Nu bleu* has a background in which the references to reality are obvious, although schematic. It is a curious fact that Matisse's figures are never shown in a studio setting although the pictures were actually executed indoors. The idea of the open air was probably still firmly rooted in Matisse's mind, although the lighting on the forms is wholly arbitrary and invented. Perhaps the outdoor setting was used by Matisse as a banal excuse for vivid tones, or perhaps he simply had not yet shaken off that habit of the eye which had so long been trained in the open air.

Far more marked experiments in the way of structure and volume than those we have seen in the *Nu bleu* (Blue Nude; Pl. 117) (Baltimore Museum of Art) are found in the *Nu debout* (Nude Standing) whose date, 1907, is certain. The *Nu bleu*, with its volume conveyed as much by the contour line as by the relationship of tones (although their range was limited), belonged logically to the experiments Matisse had been undertaking since the *Bonheur de vivre*; it belonged entirely to the Fauve system that had not yet drawn on African art although Matisse had been familiar with it since 1906. This is certainly not true of the *Nu debout* which must be the outcome of a simultaneous appraisal of Cézanne's painting and African sculpture. It was not a composition aiming at the same kind of expression as the *Nu bleu*; from the chromatic style Matisse moved on to the volumetric one so that he created an anti-Fauve work. However, we must not attach too much importance to this in an assessment of Matisse himself since he soon moved on

from this theory. By contrast, it directly heralded the *Nu debout* by Braque finished in 1908.[62] Matisse does not seem to have taken as much interest in African art as some of his fellow painters. But it is undoubtedly true that African art encouraged him in his quest for the autonomy of the plastic object; in other words, it confirmed the course on which he had already been launched by the Japanese print, Gauguin's painting and Islamic art.

It is not difficult to define Matisse's art in 1907, especially when we consider that the ideas he expressed with great precision in the following year actually applied from the time of the *Bonheur de vivre*.

First of all, Matisse rejected all immediate grasp of reality which could only be superficial, ephemeral and deceptive; his break with naturalist Impressionism was unambiguous. He sought to express the permanent, true essential character of beings and objects, at the expense of charm—what he called, "to condense". "I'll condense the meaning of this body", he wrote, "in seeking the essential lines. At first sight its charm will be less obvious, but it must eventually emanate from the new image I have obtained, which will have a wider, more fully human meaning." He also said: "I want to reach that stage of condensation of sensations that makes up the picture." The important thing for him was to express not the object itself but the emotion the object aroused, so that the feeling and the means for conveying it were closely linked. "I can't distinguish", he wrote, "between the feeling I have for life and the way I convey it." This shows the importance of expressiveness: "What I seek above all is expression"—a word that cannot be misunderstood if we remember the definition Matisse gave it: "Expression for me does not lie in the passion that lights up a face or bursts out in a violent gesture. It lies in the whole arrangement of my picture: the place occupied by the bodies, the empty spaces around them, the proportions, all play their part." It is clear that expressiveness is linked with composition, which Matisse defined as "the art of arranging in a decorative manner the various elements

99. Matisse *Luxe I*, 1907.

100. Matisse *Luxe II*, 1907-8.

the painter has at his disposal for expressing his feelings." This "decorative manner" has often been misinterpreted. There is a derogatory meaning to "decorative" which has nothing to do with Matisse's art. Magnelli said that when the artist "stayed on the surface of things his work will be nothing more than decorative"; this could not be said of Matisse. Matisse's manner of painting, too, was fundamentally different from decorative technique for his forms are always defined in relationship to the setting and the surface to be covered. "The composition, which must aim at expression", he wrote, "is modified according to the surface to be covered. If I take a piece of paper of a given dimension, I shall sketch a drawing on it that must have an inevitable relationship with its format. I would not repeat the same drawing on another sheet

199

of different proportions, for instance a rectangular one instead of a square one. And I would not just enlarge it if I had to transfer it to a similarly shaped sheet ten times larger. The drawing must have a power of expansion that enlivens the things that surround it. If an artist wants to transpose a composition from one canvas to another larger one, he must modify its features, not simply square it up." To Matisse, then, the "decorative manner" was a way of establishing harmonious and expressive relationships between the various figurative components of the picture which are not based on the physical reality of the object.

We can never exaggerate the importance Matisse attached to the study of ratios, of the relationships of forms to one another; the specific character of a form is modified by its relationship with other forms; the whole is entwined "like a rope or a snake", Matisse said. In his system, drawing and colour were subject to the same rule of "anything that is not essential to the picture is actually detrimental". Thus line and colour combine to create the same effect of expressiveness. Matisse wrote that "the predominant function of colour is to be of the greatest possible service to expression". He implied that the same was true of line. It would be wrong to regard this as a simplistic method. Our examination of the evolution of Matisse's art has shown that the painter succeeded in defining and mastering his idiom perfectly after diverse and profound experimentation. The simplicity of Matisse's art is all that is apparent. As early as 1907 Apollinaire realized this fully and was able to discern all the novelty of this art. "You have often been blamed", he wrote "for this summary way of expressing things, my dear Matisse, but no one has acknowledged that you have thus accomplished one of the most difficult things: you have given plastic life to your pictures without the aid of an object, except to arouse feeling."[63] This opinion must, of course, not be taken to suggest that Matisse was deliberately trying to be abstract. This would have been very unlike Matisse, who may give us a figurative equivalent of nature, admittedly, but one that was meant to be a truer image because it was more concentrated.

At the end of 1907 Matisse's authority was greater than ever; he was still the leader of the new way of painting. All the Fauves respected him, followed his work with interest, and often drew inspiration from it; many counted on him to show them the way out of the crisis they were going through. Some of his friends, especially Hans Purrmann and Sarah Stein, urged him to open a school. The critics were becoming less reserved about him; admittedly, they often dissociated him from the other Fauves and thought he had sobered down; Apollinaire interviewed him; he took part in numerous exhibitions in Paris and abroad, where his influence was growing.

Marquet

For Marquet the year 1907 began with a one-man show at the Galerie Druet, quite an important one, too, since there were thirty-nine items, the earliest of which did not go back further than the summer of 1905, while the most recent dated from the autumn of 1906. This exhibition left the critics cold, except for P. Jamot, who saw in Marquet's art a variety of Impressionism.[64]

There is some difficulty in gaining any deeper insight into his artistic output in 1907 since very few of his works of that year have survived. Thus the year 1907 was not at all represented at the Bordeaux–Paris retrospective of 1975. He may have been so upset by his mother's death in May that he did not produce very much. We must reject any hypothesis of an artistic crisis, for that would have been out of character; he did not tend toward anguished self-questioning. At the time when most of the Fauves were trying to break the deadlock of colour orchestration and to check some of their excesses, Marquet had no cause to be troubled in the least by such considerations. He had not previously indulged in the kind of colour hysterics that would now make him want to exclude all vivid colours; he had not given way to the kind of Dionysiac frenzy that would at this point make him want to reject all lyricism; his painting

101. Marquet *Le 14 Juillet au Havre*, 1906.

never had the kind of systematic character of which even Vlaminck grew tired; and there was no need for him to seek a structured idiom since his pictures had always had a solid framework. It is reasonable to suppose that Marquet's art did not undergo any profound change of direction in 1907.

In the spring he exhibited three canvases at the Salon des Indépendants, each of which bore the vague title *Paysage* (Landscape), so that no identification is possible. In March and April he exhibited some drawings at B. Weill's; in May he was showing another drawing at the Nemzeti Szalon in Budapest. In autumn, he exhibited in three different places: first in Prague, at Manes's, beside Bonnard, Monet, Signac, etc., then, at the same time, in Paris, at the Galerie Eugène Blot, where he showed ten canvases (all old ones) which were criticized as showing hasty synthesizing and a lack of nuances,[65] and also at Berthe Weill's. Finally, his submission to the Salon d'Automne consisted of only two items. The first, which has disappeared, showed a London bridge; it was painted during Marquet's visit to London, with Camoin and Friesz, in May 1907, a visit that was interrupted when he had to hurry back suddenly to his dying mother. Marquet, incidentally, was the only one who brought back a picture from London; no known canvas by Camoin or Friesz is based on their London stay, which must have been very short. The second picture shown at the Salon d'Automne was a view of the *Quai des Grands-Augustins*, which may be the one painted in 1906, one of the many works dating from that year in which Marquet's synthetic language took on a remarkable expressive power.

Whereas in 1906 Marquet's disturbing contrasts of light and colour had brought a passionate lyricism to some landscapes, we find nothing of the kind in 1907. That year, by contrast, was characterized—as far as we can judge from the few surviving works—by a perfectly serene lyrical spirit. We can see this in the very fine picture of the *Place Dauphine*[66] which can be dated with certainty from 1907 and in which the transition from light to dark layers has great smoothness. It is amazing to find an idiom that is both so pared down and so complete, an idiom that says so much in so few words.

In summer Marquet stayed at Saint-Jean-de-Luz, a rather longer stay than his London visit since he painted at least four pictures there.

The picture of *Saint-Jean-de-Luz* in the Hermitage, although concise in style, has rather limited expressiveness because Marquet did not follow his usual custom of applying colour in large, spread-out areas: here, we do not know why (perhaps it was only a study in which the harmonies had not yet been worked out), the artist broke up the surfaces. The composition, on the other hand, reverted to the plan he had adopted long ago and from which he rarely deviated except when painting a river bank or a quay: a curving line giving depth and another, horizontal one, for width. This is actually a method of composing, of dividing the surface, we also find in Seurat and which was taken up by almost all the Fauves; it suited Marquet particularly well because he always wanted to back up, as it were, colour-space with linear perspective.

There was more expressiveness in the other views of Saint-Jean-de-Luz, which were very similar versions of the same subject. The one now in a Geneva collection went furthest in this direction; it was certainly chronologically the last, if we assume that the artist was evolving towards increasing spareness. This view of Saint-Jean-de-Luz is pared down as much as possible; Marquet extracted the essence of reality, which is conveyed in the picture by the most evocative lines and colours; this is what gave Marquet's œuvre its expressive force. First came appraisal, meditation on the subject—not in order to let the artist's ego penetrate reality, not in order to exalt that ego through the picture, but to grasp the essentials, eliminate accessories, to achieve what we have called the composite sensation, the perfect summary, we might almost say the objective summary, which proves deep and total involvement with the subject. This approach was obviously not Impressionist; moreover, it was not really fundamentally naturalist, since it aimed at going beyond the appearance of the

102. Marquet *Le 14 Juillet au Havre* ou *Fête foraine au Havre*, 1906.

103. Van Dongen *Le Vieux Clown*, 1906.

quet's eye was practised in constructing and abbreviating. If we examine a few of his drawings, we can see that he can say everything with a few strokes of a brush dipped in ink. Marquet transposed on two levels—that of drawing and colour. But in his case all transposition in drawing is contained within limits that definitely retain the legibility of the form. The transposition of colour is subject to a double limitation. The first limit is set by the demands of harmony, which Marquet wanted to be subtle and expressive, not violent or dissonant; only Matisse had an equally highly developed skill in the use of colour, in producing a daring play of dynamic surfaces that relate to each other. The second limit Marquet felt he had to respect was the clear definition of the subject, that is, the need to make the chromatic treatment faithful to the subject's intrinsic, not apparent, character. Thus arbitrary treatment is exceptional and transfers excluded: the colouring of *Saint-Jean-de-Luz* is not interchangeable with that of the *Quai des Grands-Augustins*. This need to retain a sort of reference to reality kept Marquet from the trend to abstraction towards which some of the Fauves were sliding.

Derain

For Derain the year 1907 was truly dramatic, a year in which he totally reappraised the art of painting and which ended with the destruction of part of his artistic output. During the summer of 1906 at L'Estaque he had already clearly realized that there was something illogical and inconsistent in seeking to go beyond physical reality while continuing to work from nature. At the same time, Derain—with remarkable lucidity—began to see that the solution lay in painting abstract compositions; but he never did any. He also wanted strictly to eliminate any picturesque feature from his painting and to purify the transposition of nature both in line and colour. 1907 marked an accentuation of this new trend.

It is not surprising that this state of mind might appreciably diminish the artist's output, which had

physical world; it was Fauve. It was Fauve even though nature was not treated as a pretext for exalting the ego, although the painter did not choose to express it according to his own imagination, for Marquet was more concerned with nature than with himself. Thus the synthesis was achieved in the artist's mind, inside him, before being expressed on canvas. Marquet was not only a marvellous technician; he was, above all, a poet who knew nature and was capable of inventing the syntheses it evokes, syntheses that were faithful in their essence. These were generated swiftly, for Mar-

104. Dufy *Les Bains de Marie-Christine à Sainte-Adresse*, 1906.

already begun to fall off, as we have seen, at the end of 1906. Derain would never regain that creative impulse, the happy fertile inspiration which had given birth to the marvellous landscapes of Collioure and London. This does not mean that his output in 1907 was insignificant—far from it. Derain, who was one of the first creators of the Fauve idiom, was also one of the first to transform it. This transformation seems to have owed less to the influence of the art of Cézanne (which critics tend to exaggerate) than to that of African art.

Of the four works Derain exhibited at the Salon des Indépendants, two can be identified with certainty thanks to the indications given by L. Vauxcelles in his review.[67] He mentions, on the one hand, *La Femme en chemise* (Woman in Slip) (Statens Museum for Kunst, Copenhagen), painted, as we have seen, in 1906, and, on the other, *Baigneuses* (Women Bathing),[68] a little-known work which, we think, must be considered contemporaneous with Matisse's *Nu bleu* with which it has some points of resemblance, but these are really only superficial—the presence of blue, the emphatic line, and the strict rhythm. We must not lose sight of the essentials: unlike Matisse, Derain did not use the Fauve system. In Derain's canvas, volume, light and space do not arise from the relationship of colours. The figures sketched in ochre stand out solidly against the blue background; green in the shade, a very light ochre for the light; the painter avoided the usual intense light of Fauvism and chose instead a very dim undergrowth lighting. What remained unchanged compared with his work of 1906 was the use of the contour line. In *Baigneuses* Derain launched on a new form of pictorial expression which, quite frankly, had nothing to do with Cézanne, however much this may annoy those critics for whom there can be no women bathing outside the domain of Cézanne. Derain's picture sprang from a determination to integrate ideas inspired by African sculpture. We have seen that, in 1906, the visit to the collection of African art in the British Museum raised a number of questions for Derain to which he had not chosen to formulate a reply until now. We know that he

thought it possible to express light and its effect on form through the relationships of volumes (these were his own words); this is precisely what he was attempting to do here. We can clearly see features borrowed from African sculpture: the geometric synthesizing of form, the adaptation of a mask for the face of the woman in the foreground, the cylindrical treatment of her fingers. We may also wonder, along with E.C. Oppler, if Picasso's *Les Demoiselles d'Avignon* did not play a part at that juncture in the evolution of Derain art,[69] but it is difficult to reply to that question because, to begin with, we do not know precisely when Derain finished *Les Baigneuses*, and then we also know very little about the chronology of the *Demoiselles d'Avignon*. During the winter of 1906-7, Derain may have seen preparatory studies for the *Demoiselles d'Avignon* in Picasso's studio, at a time when Picasso was interested in Iberian art which might, to some extent, raise some of the same questions as were posed by African art.

During the summer Derain worked at Cassis. We can be certain of the dates of two letters sent at that time to Vlaminck, who inverted them and filed them incorrectly—a mistake he often made—with the series of letters dated 1905.[70] Both of them mention a stay by Braque and Friesz near Cassis, and we know for a fact that they were staying at La Ciotat and then at L'Estaque during the summer of 1907. In the first letter Derain said that Matisse had come to visit him for about a week; we do not know whether this visit took place at the time when Matisse was on his way from Paris to Collioure or whether he left Collioure specially to go and see Derain, so that the date of this visit cannot be ascertained with accuracy. In the second letter, however, Derain wrote that he had seen Matisse "a second time", when Matisse was going to Italy with his wife, a detail that enables us to be fairly accurate in dating this visit to early July.

The content of the letter deserves notice. Derain said that he was going through a crisis: "Impossible to do anything decent", he wrote. "Physically and mentally very tired... I have no mental energy at the moment... I am very lonely." And he added that his

105. Friesz *Automne à Honfleur*, 1907.

friends had more confidence than he had. Speaking of Matisse, he wrote in the first letter: "He is rejuvenated. He is happy as a lark and doesn't worry about anything." In the second: "He has shown me photos of his canvases; they are absolutely amazing. I think he has gone through the gate of the seventh heaven, that of happiness." About Friesz and Braque he wrote to Vlaminck that they "are very happy". "Their idea", he added, "is youthful and seems new to them. They will change their mind; there are other things to do." Derain's problem was to decide to treat drawing the way he had treated colour. "There is a lot to do," he wrote, "in painting we must do for drawing what we have so far done for colour." We do not think this should be interpreted as a decision to treat line in exactly the same way as colour; Derain certainly would have envisaged changing the drawing at the expense of the colour. This was undoubtedly what he tried to say in this rather obscure phrase: "Until now the colour has served only to demonstrate the formula of deliberate pureness; but I don't think this is the right way." The *Baigneuses* was already a work giving drawing precedence over colour.

Derain did few pictures during the summer at Cassis. "I am doing nothing or almost nothing," he wrote to Vlaminck, "only sketches. And I have several big pictures in my head. But it's nothing... I try to store up as many sensations as possible. I shall try to get things in order this winter." There were perhaps only some ten pictures, two of which are known: *Paysage à Cassis* (Landscape at Cassis; Pl. 112) (P. Lévy Collection, Troyes) and *Cyprès à Cassis* (Cypresses at Cassis) (Musée de Peinture et de Sculpture, Grenoble). Both clearly illustrate the worries the artist discussed in his letters. Derain had never been so detached from reality, which he interpreted very arbitrarily. There was transposition of both line and colour, but more of the first than of the second. For Derain transposition was chiefly a means of simplification. At first, a simplification of forms, seen as absolutely flat areas and outlined with extremely thick lines that had nothing more in common with the contour line he had used previously, for instance, in

106.   Vlaminck *Paysage aux arbres rouges*, 1906-1907.

107. Dufy *Les pêcheurs à la ligne*, 1907.

108.   Friesz *Le Bec-de-l'Aigle, La Ciotat*, 1907.

109. Braque *Petite baie à La Ciotat*, 1907.

110.   Braque *Maison derrière les arbres, La Ciotat*, 1907.

111.   Braque *Paysage à L'Estaque*, 1907.

112.   Derain *Paysage à Cassis*, 1907.

113.   Derain *La danse*, 1906.

his landscapes of L'Estaque. It is wrong to draw a comparison with Gauguin here, as has sometimes been done. Gauguin had never used such contour lines; to him, the contour line played a strictly intermediary role, a scanning role. For Derain, the contour line had become a necessary means of interpreting physical reality, of expressing the image transposed by his inner vision. Next Derain went on to simplify colour; his palette was restricted: dark blue for cypresses, a green or two for other trees, ochre for the soil, an attenuated blue for the sky and a few light patches to set off the general harmony. Very little colour, in fact, and above all mostly colours with no warmth, without saturation, applied strictly within the areas previously defined by a contour line. Thus there was a retreat from pure colour, but this does not mean that Derain was totally indifferent to it. When discussing with G. Duthuit the period of his detachment from Fauvism, he told him: "The most inert, the most monotonous colour can have an insurpassable potency." Nor does this mean that Derain had abandoned the Fauve principle of rendering space by means of colour signs. We can get a better insight into the new creative line the artist was taking when we compare three works (less well known than the preceding ones), three versions of the same subject (a road in a Cassis landscape) which we shall list as, first, that of the Hermitage, then that in the Rupf Collection in Berne, and finally the one in the Museum of Modern Art in New York. In these we can see Derain progressively abbreviating and pruning back: he began with an already relatively economical canvas, richly coloured, and finished with an austerely coloured work of geometrical schematization.

These Cassis landscapes show a deep evolution in Derain's Fauvism. An austerity produced by an extreme spareness of language, monumentality of stylized forms, a tendency toward abstraction resulting from abbreviated symbols, controlled emotion and a studied carefulness in the expression which attenuate the lyricism—all these were new characteristics which foreshadowed an even more radical transformation in the near future.

At the Salon d'Automne Derain certainly exhibited three landscapes of Cassis that cannot be identified. It is worth mentioning that he also exhibited two wood engravings. The style of painting he had developed by the end of the summer, with thick lines and wide flat areas, was perfectly suited to the technique of wood engraving, and it is not surprising that Derain found it a means of expression well adapted to his experiments.

There is some mystery about Derain's artistic output after the Salon d'Automne, especially as it was around that time that the painter destroyed many of his works. The subject of women bathing seems to have preoccupied him more from the end of 1907 on. Should a canvas of *Nus* (Nudes),[71] with its schematic form, flat tones and, especially, thick contour lines typical of the Cassis landscape period be dated from 1907, as is usually thought? A picture entitled *Toilette* (Dressing) (Unknown Collection)[72] was probably executed during the winter of 1907-8; this was undoubtedly the one exhibited at the Salon des Indépendants of 1908 which attracted Gertrude Stein's attention.[73] It belongs logically to Derain's experiments of that time. But the style of the figures attending to their appearance is confined to strokes that are more abstract than real and went further than any of the previous works. The colossal and hieratic treatment of these figures, rigid as if they were made of wood, and the severity of the drawing that consists of a series of straight lines arranged in an angular fashion show the accentuation, even the systematization, of the characteristics we have noticed in the earlier works. Derain clearly was not following Cézanne any more than he had done before: here, rather, we should see the influence of Gauguin combined with that of African sculpture.

Through constant reappraisal and a whole range of experiments that were never divorced from logic, Derain finally may have achieved his aim of getting away from "objective things" by means of the extreme simplification of the transposed image and the distortion of line. He found out that increasingly spare transposition demolishes objectivity and distorts more effectively than the simple transposition of colour alone; a tree, for instance, did not entirely cease to be a physical reality when fantastic colour was applied to it, but it did cease to be real when it was given an arbitrary outline. We can see how dangerous this discovery would be for Fauvism, since it put colour, its life blood, in second place. But we can also see its importance as it opened up a new range of artistic possibilities for painting.

Vlaminck

Vlaminck, in whom man and artist were perfectly combined, was not troubled by the anxieties that tormented most of the Fauve painters in 1907; for him, that year as a whole was very much the continuation of 1906. However, the frenetic inspiration which had given rise to the most exuberant works of Fauvism became attenuated, not because Vlaminck deliberately wanted to change his idiom but because any feverish state finally subsides and because nothing can go beyond paroxysm.

Vlaminck was unable to avoid inaccuracies both in his account of the moment when he abandoned Fauvism and of the motives that inspired him. Just as he claimed to have been, chronologically, the first Fauve, so he also claimed to have been the first to abandon Fauvism; he must have thought that this, too, was somehow to his credit.

None of the six canvases he showed at the Salon des Indépendants can be identified with certainty. His submission must have consisted, as was generally the case, of works finished in the previous year to which he might have added some finishing touches just before the opening of the Salon. It is mainly from the works exhibited at the Salon d'Automne, at least as far as we know them, that we can get an idea of the way the Fauve painters were evolving; this does not apply to Vlaminck whose contribution to the Salon remains a mystery. Thus we must look for the works painted in 1907, whether shown at the Salon d'Automne or not, and examine them.

During 1907 Vlaminck adopted a new type of signature. At the beginning of the year he continued to sign in the same way as in 1906, and then, at a moment we cannot precisely determine, he began to use a form composed of rather thick, less well-formed, connected letters; it is also very drawn out, almost illegible, and the underlining, used consistently until then, rarely appeared in 1907 and disappeared completely in 1908, when his signature had almost taken its definitive form (except for growing rather more elliptic).

We shall divide Vlaminck's 1907 output into two groups. The first group of works, painted before the summer, hardly differed in style and signature from those of the second period of 1906, so that some of them could have been executed in 1906; by the same token, some canvases we have dated from the end of 1906 could very well have dated from the beginning of 1907; the list we have drawn up for 1906 is very copious compared with that for 1907. Two works in the first group are particularly significant: *Paysage à Chatou* (Landscape at Chatou) (Private Collection, Paris), and *Paysage aux arbres rouges* (Landscape with Red Trees; Pl. 106) (Musée National d'Art Moderne, Paris). Whereas the first is simply a continuation of the landscape series of 1906 (although the lyrical spirit is more subdued and the colour more restrained), the second one strikes a new note: on the one hand, the obvious concern with structure and rhythm gives emphasis to the drawing and, on the other, the colour is not based on a violent contrast between complementary tones but on the meeting of kindred tones applied thinly on flat areas. This method was derived from Derain, who exhibited his landscapes of L'Estaque at the Salon d'Automne of 1906; these, as we have shown, were certainly influenced by a study of Gauguin's art. Thus, not long after Derain, Vlaminck also became aware of the need to discipline his inspiration and to give structure to his canvas by concentrating more on line and abandoning broken brush-strokes.

The second group of works owes nothing to Gauguin but much to Cézanne. *La Seine à Chatou* (The

Seine at Chatou) in the Grenoble Museum shows that concern with structure now predominated. The palette, although retaining some warm tones, is no longer brilliant. The transposition in line and colour has lost the poetic strength of the earlier lyrical works and is introduced through the intermediary of a synthesizing approach that seeks what is essential and permanent. The colour, applied as in Cézanne's work in slanting and parallel strokes, suggests planes not through the effect of contrasts but through that of modulation. Vlaminck now approached the work of art in a spirit of discipline and austerity that went very far since it accentuated the schematic treatment, thereby giving form a geometrical appearance. The transition from one phase to the other is clearly discernible if we compare two pictures entitled *Le Pont de Chatou* (The Bridge of Chatou),[74] one of which is in a private collection in Paris.[75] Although the tendency toward geometrical treatment was still rather inconspicuous in 1907, it became accentuated during 1908 together with the elimination of the basic feature of Fauvism—colour-space. Vlaminck was probably not particularly enthusiastic about abandoning Fauvism. At the end of 1907 he was still trying to make his mark as a Fauve painter and not as anything else; at the Berthe Weill exhibition his painting was described as "wild colouring", whereas Matisse's was judged "sober".[76] And when Derain was writing to his friend, he tried to overcome the latter's obstinacy in retaining pure colour. As the pressure of events brought Cézanne to the foreground, the influence of this artist, whom Vlaminck called "the sad friend", was certainly more decisive than the latter's personal convictions. But it would be unfair to say that Vlaminck was any less aware than his friends of the dead end to which Fauve painting had come; he simply refused for a time to admit it objectively. Unlike the other Fauves, he was not keen to overthrow what he had so recently worshipped.

On various occasions, if not always coherently, Vlaminck has explained the reasons for which he rejected Fauvism: we can distinguish four. The first was the mechanical, automatic character which trans-position ultimately assumed, owing more to an acquired style and great skilfulness than to a poetic vision. "To work by pressing a tube directly on to a canvas," Vlaminck said, "soon leads to excessive cleverness; in the end you transpose mathematically... Emerald green becomes black, pink a flamboyant red, etc. Suddenly numbers stand out and success is deadened." On several occasions he compared himself with an orchestra conductor who can easily raise his score by several tones. But it was precisely in this field that the Fauve painter had to recognize limits. This was the second reason, which we might call the impossibility of going beyond the potential of pure colour. "The play of pure colours", Vlaminck wrote, "the extreme orchestration into which I threw myself unrestrainedly, no longer satisfied me. I could not stand not being able to hit harder, to have reached the maximum intensity, to be limited by the blue or red of the paint-dealer." And he added: "Could I have gone on blowing into the trombone, letting myself be winded playing the saxophone till I spat blood? I discovered sadly that my compositions boiled down to coloured rhythms—harmonious, discordant, monotonous—and that, from simplification to simplification, I made shift with the play of pure colour. By arbitrarily doing without tones and the whole gamut of possibilities they offer, I lapsed into mere decoration." This danger of doing no more than decorating was Vlaminck's third reason for reacting against Fauvism; this was undoubtedly the most important one and it did not affect only Vlaminck but all the others. All the Fauve painters except Matisse, who saw it in a different light, were frightened of falling into the trap of decorative art, that is, of ending up with a kind of gratuitous art whose final result would have been the harmonious distribution of forms on the surface of the canvas into which emotion did not enter at all. "I wasn't going into things any more," Vlaminck said, "I didn't touch them in depth. The decorative spirit was going to make me forget painting." Vlaminck also had a romantic view of the picture as a state of mind; for him, it could never come down to simple figurative statements. There was a

114. Khmer Art *Fronton du temple de Çiva à Banteay Srei*, A.D. 967

220

115. Hindu Art *Çiva, roi de la danse*, Chola period, 11th century.

116. Derain *Trois Danseuses*, 1906.

fourth reason why Vlaminck turned against Fauvism: colour had been taken over by fashion. "This childish riot of colours", the painter wrote, "was becoming unbearable. Pure colour played the starring role everywhere. It was vulgarized and demeaned for commercial purposes. I came to loathe it and decided never to use anything but browns and ochres." And, indeed, a number of painters far less gifted than the Fauves were trying to imitate them and colour in all its excesses was becoming commonplace.

When discussing his reasons for turning against Fauvism, Vlaminck did not at any point suggest that a fresh look at Cézanne's art had played a part. This is somewhat surprising for, after 1907, Vlaminck himself did not hesitate to borrow some methods from the Aix master; these, however, were only matters of technique. In fact, Vlaminck's chief concern was with pure colour, whereas Cézanne's art was obviously not dominated by a concern with pure colour but by the determination to establish a new relationship between

117. Matisse *Nu bleu, souvenir de Biskra*, 1907.

the painter and nature in the treatment of space and of light. These were questions to which Vlaminck gave only summary answers.

Vlaminck seems not to have drawn on African art either, although he was probably the first to notice African statuettes. Between 1905 and 1907 there is no trace of any direct influence of black art in his work; he took some superficial ideas from African culture, but these only reinforced his earlier views. Coloured African sculpture, for instance, would serve only to confirm Vlaminck's use of subjective, not imitative or broken colours, applied in flat areas. And he would naturally be sympathetic to an art that was, like his own, opposed to academism because it was a primitive art, that is, an art without tradition.

At the end of 1907 African art did not play an important role in Vlaminck's painting; only superficial comparisons can be made between, for instance, the *Baigneuses* (Women Bathing; Pl. 120) (Galerie Schmit, Paris)[77] and the famous Congolese mask

Vlaminck sold to Derain (Alice Derain Collection). The schematized face of the two women seen from the front might be an adaptation of that mask. Without actually realizing volume, Vlaminck suggested it by means of a modulated brush-stroke which resembled the light relief given by the African artist to his mask. From him, too, the painter may have borrowed the simplification of form which he applied to the whole of his composition. As for the drawing, all curves and arabesques, it may have been derived from the Congolese mask. But we may wonder whether on these points Vlaminck, who was not very inventive, who hated studying sources in depth, and who preferred to use his friends' acquired conclusions as his starting-point, did not simply content himself with drawing on the works of Derain and Matisse. Although African art did not determine the direction taken by Vlaminck's painting, it nevertheless confirmed his choice of a subjective, spontaneous, and synthesized art in which the heightening of expression always played a major role.

At the end of 1907 Vlaminck must have gone through a period of upheaval: on the one hand, he had to admit that it was impossible to continue to paint with pure colours; on the other, he witnessed the advent of a speculative form of art for which he felt no vocation. Yet it was the second course he would follow for a while before retreating progressively into a romantic naturalism.

Van Dongen

In January 1907 Van Dongen was still at the Bateau-Lavoir; he left in February for Holland. His wife had fallen ill and he wanted to take her to his family to be looked after. He also seems to have been commissioned by F. Fénéon to get van Gogh's paintings together for an exhibition the Galerie Bernheim-Jeune was planning to organize in January 1908. Van Dongen stayed in Rotterdam until August, which explains why he did not take part in the Salon des Indépendants. In July and August he exhibited drawings and pastels—all of them apparently early ones—in Amsterdam. He returned to Paris alone. After staying for a time with Picasso, in September he rented an apartment in rue Lamarck, where his family joined him. Van Dongen did not make a journey to Uruguay in 1907; it was after 1911, when he was beginning to become famous and liked mystifying the critics, that he first claimed to have done so. Although he was in Paris, he did not exhibit at the Salon d'Automne. We know the reason for this omission thanks to a letter he wrote to his wife, who had stayed in Rotterdam: he wanted to devote himself entirely to a one-man show promised him by Fénéon at the Galerie Bernheim-Jeune;[78] this show did not actually take place until November and December 1908. Towards the autumn of 1907 Van Dongen committed himself by a verbal contract to Kahnweiler, who had just opened a gallery in rue Vignon.

Numerous models came to his studio in rue Lamarck, including Anita la Bohémienne, who was a dancer at a dive in Pigalle. Not all the canvases based on Anita necessarily date from 1907—some may have been painted in 1908. Actually, there is no major difference in style between them, although they differ from the works of 1906. First of all, we are struck by the extraordinary chromatic subtlety which goes far beyond Van Dongen's earlier accomplishments. He now played most skilfully on the reds and blues, which he endowed with a variety of dull rather than clear shades; the reds usually turn into orange and the blues into violet; sometimes the reds predominate and colour the background, sometimes the blues. We find the same careful shading in the rendering of flesh tones; the ground of yellow and green is reminiscent of 1906, but the brush-strokes, more modulated and better blended, hug the relief of the body with real concern for anatomical accuracy. The determination to emphasize the plastic values of the modelling is the second characteristic of these works which extol Anita's sensual beauty. In the earlier works transposition, with its implications for distortion of colour and line, played a greater part. Although transposition or, if we prefer to call it lyrical interpretation, was still

118. Van Dongen *Nu allongé*, 1907.

present, it was subject to the accurate indication of volume. We must interpret this as Van Dongen's own way of dealing with the concern for plasticity which worried the Fauve painters in 1907; Van Dongen, incidentally, like Matisse and Derain, was also trying his hand at sculpture at the time. The treatment of space, too, differed radically from that of 1906. Van Dongen no longer surrounded his figures with a band as an intermediary to the adjoining plane; he practically abandoned the use of contour lines altogether and instead used the juxtaposition of areas in contrasting colours to create planes at varying distances from the viewer. The human figure stands out firmly against the background; the abruptness of the transition is barely softened by small blobs of the background colour applied to the figure, but this was a chromatic necessity for the equilibrium of the painted surface rather than a solution to the problem of space. Van Dongen no longer bothered to give equal colour saturation to all the planes, which would give the same density to all parts of the picture; there is little saturation of the flesh tones, as if it now went against the painter's grain to present a many-coloured image of Woman. To tell the truth, the expressiveness is no less intense than in the earlier works where colour saturation came into full play, but now it had a different content; it arose from the feeling of uneasy sensuality with which the painter endowed his images. We think that Van Dongen's new way of painting the female body conveyed a new kind of relationship between the artist and his model. His nudes of dancers and circus performers at the Folies-Bergères were chaste nudes, in which the painter's eye transposed without *arrière-pensée*, in cheerful colours. This is no longer true of the nudes of Anita, notably *Nu couché à la jarretière* (Recumbent Nude with Garter), for they are transposed into a cheerless space, whose carnal seductiveness is sustained and betrays sexual overtones. We believe that this is the source of the Expressionist character Van Dongen's art assumed at times in 1907, which attracted a painter like Pechstein, who visited Van Dongen that year and invited him to exhibit among the *Brücke*. Unlike the other Fauves, who were more concerned with the problem of the artist's relationship with nature, Van Dongen expressed himself through Woman. His fellow painters felt that art was basically a means of taking possession of the cosmos, of recreating the world; Van Dongen saw it as a means of possessing Woman. His voluptuous and lewd nudes are hymns to eroticism. "I exteriorize my desires", he said, "by expressing them in pictures. I love anything that glitters, precious stones that sparkle, fabrics that shimmer, beautiful women who arouse carnal desire... painting lets me possess all this most fully."

Some of the works exhibited at Bernheim-Jeune's in 1908 were listed in the group dated "1905-7": these include two well-known canvases which can legitimately be dated from 1907: *Liverpool Lighthouse* (Rotterdam) and *Le Chanteur Modjesko* (The Singer Modjesko). These are two Fauve masterpieces testifying to their author's rich artistic inventiveness. *Liverpool Lighthouse* returned to a theme he had previously treated in a watercolour and a painting; the changes in the subject are insignificant, but, by contrast, the boldly simplified drawing and daringly transposed colour in the last version show all the skill Van Dongen had acquired. There is great freedom in the treatment of space which is rendered through strong contrasts of tones (not complementary) generously applied, most of which—notably the blues and reds—are taken to the utmost intensity and brought into direct apposition without any intervening contour lines. In *Le Chanteur* (The Museum of Modern Art, New York) the palette is completely different from that of the preceding picture: it is based on the harmony of light colours, less restricted and perhaps more arbitrary, and uses the play of complementary contrasts (red-green, blue-orange) around a bright yellow. Van Dongen also uses contour lines and even a band of perpendicular hatchings on the outline, all of which is close to his manner of 1906. The comparison of these two works is interesting for it shows that the greatest expressiveness accompanies the greatest simplification. This dual orientation seems to have characterized Van Dongen's art in 1907. The *Portrait* de Kahnweiler (Portrait of Kahnweiler), for example, shows how Van Dongen sought to achieve the greatest degree of expressiveness by using a sober palette of rather dull tones; the change from one tone to another is very direct, giving the forms an exceptional density which contributes to the power of the plastic expression. We must add that here Van Dongen introduced a procedure that was soon to become a habit: the use of red as the background in his portraits, a practice he did not actually invent since Degas, Gauguin and Picasso had used it before him, but he systematized a method that had until very recently been regarded as heretical since it was agreed that red came in front and could therefore not be used for the background.

As for simplification, Van Dongen went very far at that time if we are right in accepting 1907 as the date of the *Nu allongé* (Recumbent Nude; Pl. 118) (Private Collection, France). It has never been pointed out that this picture reverts, with extreme simplification, to *Nu couché à la jarretière* and that it must therefore logically be a later work. In our opinion it must have been painted not long after the *Nu couché* for it has the dull, strong chromatism of the nudes of Anita and of the *Portrait de Kahnweiler*. On the other hand, it seems difficult to ascribe such experiments to 1905, although Van Dongen, as we have seen, started very early to express himself in an abbreviated style. Nowhere outside the *Nu allongé* (Recumbent Nude) had the painter achieved such an elliptical, we might even say abstract, manner. We can cite no similar examples from 1907 because Van Dongen certainly would not regard such an extreme formula as definitive. His position amounted to a rejection of abstract art, a rejection of any tendency toward illegibility, and in this he was not unique. Even Derain, who went much further towards abstract painting, did not cross the boundary of total omission of any reference to nature, although he clearly expressed, as we have seen, the logical need for such an approach. Van Dongen probably took a passing interest in an almost abstract manner of painting at the time Derain was consciously experimenting with it, that is, in 1907.

Van Dongen certainly was not cut out for this sort of experiment, which demanded a more or less intellectual notion of painting, a speculative mind he did not possess; he said (exaggerating, of course): "I am like a cow. I paint what I see." While his friends were appraising the austere, calculated art of Cézanne as well as African sculpture, both of which diverted them completely from colour orchestration, Van Dongen remained an ardent colourist who had not exhausted the resources of pure colour and kept aloof from pre-Cubist experiments. We must admit that the problems of space did not haunt him as they did the other Fauves; Van Dongen had supplied simple solutions which satisfied him completely and he felt no need for any fresh speculation on this matter. To him the aim of painting was primarily a quest for beautiful harmonies; his main concern was to express himself forcefully through colour. Thus Van Dongen's Fauvism exceptionally went on beyond 1907, and we might even say that his painting, through all its changes, never really ceased to be Fauve.

Dufy

At the time he was exhibiting at Berthe Weill's, Dufy was also showing six canvases at the Salon des Indépendants, most probably including *Vieilles Maisons sur le bassin à Honfleur* (Old Houses at Honfleur Harbour; Pl. 83) (Private Collection) and *Port du Havre* (Musée des Beaux-Arts, Nantes) dating from 1906, works with a radiant lyricism that did not, however, preclude a concern for artistic organization.

We can get a fairly clear idea of Dufy's artistic output during the summer of 1907, which he spent in Normandy. At Ste. Adresse a new subject appeared, that of "anglers" who, like the subject of "streets decked with flags and bunting" gave rise to several variations.[79] Most remarkable in that series was the artist's determination to carry abbreviation to an extreme: the abbreviation of the composition, now reduced to a cut-out of three or four triangular surfaces separated by lines (one horizontal, plus one, two or three slanting ones) across the whole canvas; an abbreviation of small figures which organize the surface vertically; an abbreviation of colour harmony based only on blues and yellows lightly modulated and heightened by bright orange or red. Never before had Dufy achieved that degree of simplification which enabled him to give his canvases the utmost power of expression. Never before had the artist's inner vision reached the point where the subject became merely an excuse for the painting; the reference to physical reality seems to become increasingly tenuous. Dufy's artistic imagination took an abstract turn. This tendency had shown itself as early as 1906 in the series of "streets decked with flags and bunting", but now Dufy went further. In his new pictures he no longer needed the underpinning of reality, nor its inspiration; he needed it only to provide a subject—the work itself could take shape in the studio. He had no need for any communion with nature.

Dufy had three entries at the Salon d'Automne. One of them can probably be identified as the *Quatorze Juillet au Havre* (Fourteenth of July at Le Havre), dating from 1907, a companion piece to the canvas in the Musée National d'Art Moderne painted in 1906. The second item may be identified as *Le Jardin d'hiver* (The Winter Garden) (Private Collection, Neuilly-sur-Seine) in which the artist strove predominantly to give the picture a serene structure. The same spirit is found in *Le Vestibule aux vitraux* (Vestibule with Stained-Glass Windows) which shows another view of the same winter garden: here the organization of persistently repeated orthogonal lines gives the impression of a rather cold severity. Dufy, as we can see, attached great importance to composition, to the organization of the surface, and gives it an altogether characteristic geometrical look. Perhaps it owed something to Cézanne's teaching, although we must remember that it was actually done before the Salon d'Automne of 1907.

Dufy travelled to Marseilles and Martigues in the fall. Several known canvases of the old port of Notre-Dame-de-la-Garde must have been painted at

119. Friesz *Le travail à l'automne*, 1907-1908.

120. Vlaminck *Baigneuses*, 1907.

121. Derain *Baigneuses*, 1907.

122. Dufy *Pêcheurs à Sainte-Adresse*, 1907.

123.   Braque *La calanque*, 1907.

124.   Braque *Femme assise se coiffant*, 1907.

125. Friesz *Portrait de Fernand Fleuret*, 1907.

126. Friesz *La Ciotat*, 1907.

that time. Although their abstract tendency is as great as that of the series of "anglers", they nevertheless have rhythmic variations which reveal a more complex geometrical treatment. But this did not prevent the colour from being as fresh as in the earlier coloured works. This group of canvases based on the old port of Marseilles again shows how little the subject mattered to Dufy: what mattered were the thousands of artistic possibilities it offered his imagination. The artist had evolved considerably since painting the 1904 (Pl. 23) and 1905 versions of the pier of the Casino at Ste. Adresse, which differed due to changes in the light. From now on Dufy replaced this changing exterior element, the light, by another changing element, but this time an inner one, the pictorial vision of a creative artist. Dufy did not cease to be a Fauve painter—only the character of his writing changed—a Fauve who had found out that there was as much lyrical quality in the straight line as in the curve. Some of the works painted at the same time in the Marseilles region, like *Joueurs de boules à L'Estaque* (Bowls Players at L'Estaque) (Robert Lebel Collection, Paris), *Barques aux Martigues* (Boats at Martigues) (Private Collection, France), and *La Terrasse sur la plage* (Terrace on the Beach) (Musée d'Art Moderne de la Ville de Paris), show a very obvious determination to abstract reality; the forms are stripped of their outline, their volume and matter are drained, as if "disobjectivized". This was not a simple elliptical idiom, this was a true system of signs, but easily decipherable signs, legible hieroglyphics.

Back in Paris, Dufy found that Cézanne was in favour with his friends, which was far from uncongenial to him; however, Cézanne's austere teaching did not let him forget Gauguin's more joyful lesson. In this context he painted *Jeanne dans les fleurs* (Jeanne among Flowers; Pl. 129) (Musée des Beaux-Arts, Le Havre), prepared in earlier canvases of flower still lifes, including above all *Fleurs dans un vase* (Flowers in a Vase) (Perls Galleries, New York), with a relaxed rhythm and deep colouring. Highly calculated, the former picture is all measurement and thought, yet wholly pervaded by the most ardent lyricism.

The "ports of Marseilles" series no doubt ended early in 1908 with *Bateaux au port* (Boats in Port) (Nathan Cummings Collection), pre-Cubist, with a geometrical manner and a treatment of space that expressed the demands of the picture rather than an inner emotion; lyricism was in retreat before a certain hedonism. Thus Dufy's Fauve venture was interrupted for a time, but not terminated, for he came back to it in other guises.

Friesz

The Fauvism of Friesz did not reach its climax until the summer of 1907 at La Ciotat. Until then the artist had not been attracted by the South, as if he had been afraid that in that seductive setting his paint-brush might run riot. At the beginning of the year he let his friend Braque leave for L'Estaque while he completed a series of landscapes he had begun in the autumn of 1906 at Honfleur, on the Côte de Grâce.

At the Salon des Indépendants he exhibited five canvases of this group, which consisted of about ten. It is impossible to ascertain which of them were hung at the Salon—perhaps *Automne à Honfleur* (Autumn at Honfleur; Pl. 105) (Musée de Peinture et de Sculpture, Grenoble) or the very similar version in the Musée d'Art Moderne de la Ville de Paris; perhaps *Arbres à Honfleur* (Trees at Honfleur; Pl. 96) (Musée National d'Art Moderne, Paris) mistakenly called *L'Estaque*.[80] The works in this series are akin to the versions of the "ports of Antwerp". Friesz's position had now become clear: the picture was no longer an objective rendering of a specific point in time; it was the lyrical expression of the "shock" felt through contemplating nature; the attempt at description has completely disappeared; the drawing, although it has not yet achieved the bold simplification soon to be seen in the landscapes of La Ciotat, nevertheless already shows a far more abbreviating character than before; light as a naturalist feature is absent, to make way for an arrangement of coloured areas that become its equivalent. In the case of Friesz, all this was

237

combined with a desire to structure the picture, to arrange forms harmoniously, so much so that we might speak of the "Côte de Grâce" series as composed landscapes in the classical sense.

In the summer Friesz joined Braque at La Ciotat. This was the artist's first visit to the South; in spite of all that has been said on the subject, there had been none before this. His first southern works appeared at the Salon d'Automne of that year; no southern landscape had been exhibited anywhere before that date. This, we think, is enough to rule out any supposed stay in Provence before July 1907, notably in 1905 as has often been claimed. One witness is of some interest—the poet Fernand Fleuret, who knew Friesz around 1905 and often visited him in his studio in place Dauphine (where the painter stayed until the end of 1907). Fleuret refers to canvases Friesz brought back from Normandy, but never mentions a single southern work.[81]

Of all the works executed at La Ciotat, Friesz chose five canvases for the Salon d'Automne, some of which can perhaps be identified. He exhibited one of the five versions of the Bec-de-l'Aigle, the famous rock of La Ciotat. We think that the series began with a study called Paysage fauve aux arbres (Fauve Landscape with Trees) (Private Collection, Switzerland),[82] treated in a style reminiscent of Divisionism because of the broken-up brush-strokes, but fundamentally far too free in its interpretation to be truly Divisionist. It is interesting to note that, in the southern light, the first form of expression he adopted was one inspired by Divisionism. Thus Friesz repeated, three years later, the experience of Matisse and Derain. The second version may have been Le Bec-de-l'Aigle (Pl. 108) (Private Collection, New York), which seems to have an unbalanced composition and to give the impression of a sort of swarm of limp figures; we feel as if the artist had suddenly been too timid to grasp the exuberance of southern nature, unable to select, to leave anything out, even for the sake of conveying this luxuriant growth more adequately.

The three other versions, which retain the left part of the canvas in the American collection, are more assertive; although they have much in common, they differ from each other on a number of points, which helps us to establish their chronology. Friesz continued his quest for a rhythmic harmony of line and colour, and he achieved this superbly in the canvas (Pl. 97) of the Pierre Lévy Collection in Troyes—one of the finest landscapes of Fauve painting—after careful stylization and synthesis, after a series of choices and omissions. We can see, for instance, that Friesz abandoned the angular rhythm of the lower form on the right (the terrace of a house?), a real rhythmic dissonance, for the sake of an unidentifiable curved form, perfectly integrated into a complex of essentially curved forms; the coloured areas also seem more than simplified. For the colours, Friesz chose a harmony based on kindred (yellow-orange-red) rather than on complementary tones. This, we know, was due to the teaching of Gauguin.

While the left-hand section of the picture in the Werner E. Josten Collection became the starting-point for three canvases, the right side of the picture in its turn inspired a work called La Terrasse à La Ciotat (Terrace at La Ciotat), one of the rare works by Friesz to recall Divisionism.

Other pictures that may have been shown at the Salon d'Automne were La Calanque à La Ciotat (Creek at La Ciotat) (Unknown Collection),[83] undoubtedly the first of Friesz's landscapes to have figures, a genre he was to develop considerably[84] and Baigneuses, La Ciotat (Women Bathing, La Ciotat; Pl. 130) (Musée du Petit Palais, Geneva), a work dating from 1907 and not 1905 (the date actually given on the canvas), with echoes of Gauguin, Cézanne, Ingres, Puvis de Chavannes and perhaps even Daumier.

A picture contemporaneous with these, La Ciotat (Pl. 126) (Musée National d'Art Moderne, Paris) is striking because of the freedom with which Friesz used the accentuation of the elliptical method to break away from literal translation, so that the landscape is almost an abstract image.

In September Friesz and Braque were at L'Estaque, where they had an opportunity to study the same

127. Vlaminck *Paysage à Chatou*, 1907.

landscape; but with very different results. In the *La Terrasse à L'Estaque* (Terrace at L'Estaque) Friesz continued in the spirit of his works at La Ciotat: the same Dionysian spirit, the same generous arabesques, the same poetic treatment of space. By contrast, Braque's picture, *L'Estaque vue depuis l'hôtel Mistral* (L'Estaque Seen from the Mistral Hotel), carefully worked out, carefully structured, carefully modelled, can already be regarded as a pre-Cubist work, like some of Dufy's Marseilles canvases. This is accounted for by the fact that Friesz completed his work on the spot, at L'Estaque, on the crest of the Fauve wave, whereas Braque finished his in his Paris studio, in the autumn and winter, when renewed contact with Cézanne's painting and his interest in African art had raised fresh questions.

Cézanne's art very soon came to represent to Friesz everything that had to be reconquered: weight of form, discipline of composition, modulation of the painted space, subjection of colour to the economy of the picture. All this appeared in the *Portrait de Fernand Fleuret* (Portrait of Fernand Fleuret; Pl. 125) (Musée National d'Art Moderne, Paris), which retains some Fauve features, but related in such a way that the actual artistic system used ceased to be Fauve.

Friesz ended the year 1907 with two compositions, *Les Moissonneurs* (The Reapers) (now lost) and *Le Travail à l'automne* (Autumn Work; Pl. 119) (Nasjonalgalleriet, Oslo), which illustrate his new ideas. In the second picture he again used the landscape of the Côte de Grâce into which he inserted large figures representing the various tasks of autumn, and tried to make this combination as harmonious as possible. The colour here has lost its brilliance and preponderance to become only one feature among others equally essential for the general equilibrium of form and the unity of the picture. "Colour", Friesz said, "ceased to be the master of the picture, and under volume and light the drawing was reborn; colour remained a savoury adjunct."

It is an exaggeration to say that Friesz "laid the foundations of Cubism", as André Salmon has claimed,[85] but it would be wrong not to acknowledge that he participated, like Derain, Dufy and Braque, in the formulation of a new pictorial idiom that broke completely with Fauvism and ultimately led to Cubism.

Braque

Back in Paris in February, Braque exhibited six canvases at the Salon des Indépendants, at least one of which belonged to the "ports of Antwerp" series. The others were views of L'Estaque painted in the previous year, perhaps *L'Olivier* (The Olive Tree) (Musée d'Art Moderne de la Ville de Paris). From that time on Braque, who saw very little of his Le Havre friends, was held in high esteem by the other Fauves; Matisse, Derain and Vlaminck asked to make his acquaintance in order to congratulate him.

At the beginning of the summer he went to stay at La Ciotat, where he painted landscapes (at least fifteen) which were very different from those of L'Estaque. Their composition was much more supple; curves predominated. Straight lines were rarely introduced; to avoid them, Braque avoided houses and harbour works and chose rolling hills and sinuous trees with rounded foliage—even the horizon line has a strong bend. The colours, transposed and saturated, explode here in contrasting flat patterns creating planes, there in small dynamic brush-strokes that demolish the surface. Which way were Braque's experiments going? We think that he started off in a style fairly close to that of his earlier works, which we can see in, for instance, *Le Port de La Ciotat* (The Port of La Ciotat; Pl. 95) (Private Collection, New York), and came to do such works as *La Petite Baie à La Ciotat* (Small Bay at La Ciotat; Pl. 109) (Musée National d'Art Moderne, Paris) (or *La Ciotat* (Pl. 98)[86]—that is, he strove to use an increasingly simplified vocabulary, spare both in line and colour, and an increasingly arbitrary idiom. Of course, Braque's experiments did not differ from those of the other Fauves, who, in varying degrees, sought to "rid themselves of objective things", as Derain said; and,

128. Dufy *Pêcheurs à la ligne, coup de vent,* 1907.

like them, Braque was, as it were, led to abstract works, such as *La Calanque* (The Creek; Pl. 123) (Private Collection, Paris), comparable to *La Ciotat* (Pl. 126) (Musée National d'Art Moderne, Paris), the landscape Friesz was painting at precisely the same time, which is just as "disobjectivized".

In September, before returning to Paris, Braque, accompanied by Friesz, spent some time at L'Estaque. Here the last sparks of Braque's Fauvism were extinguished. As Braque's two stays at L'Estaque were separated by only a two-month interval (winter of 1906-7 and late summer 1907), these two very different periods have often been confused. The style of the second can be seen clearly in *Paysage à L'Estaque* (Landscape at L'Estaque; Pl. 111) (Jean Salomon Collection, Geneva) which bears the date 1907; we can see a new quality which comes from the overall forceful structure due to the thick contour lines and the strong, clear organization of successive planes in the manner of Cézanne. However, the concern with—already geometrical—structure did not prevent Braque's picture from being lively thanks to the blazing chromatism and a still sensuous lyricism. Then, however, we come to a more deliberate, more meditated work in the landscape of *L'Estaque vue depuis l'hôtel Mistral*, in which Braque accentuated the geometrical experiments. Here figurative data have replaced emotion so that the picture breaks free from the Fauve system and already belongs among the new experiments of the end of the year. The picture was undoubtedly completed in the artist's Paris studio during the fall, which explains the echoes of Cézanne in it. Before finishing it, Braque had seen many of Cézanne's works exhibited in Paris in October and frankly acknowledged that he was struck by them. "I had been impressed by Cézanne, by his pictures...; I felt that there was something very private in his painting."

At the Salon d'Automne, in which he took part for the first time, Braque exhibited a single painting, *Rochers rouges* (Red Rocks), which cannot be identified. Why only one? Was it due to the artist's reluctance to show his work in public? Or should we believe Apollinaire's statement that "almost his entire submission was rejected"?[87] We do know for certain that all of Braque's work was rejected at the Salon d'Automne of 1908; but for 1907 we have only Apollinaire's account of a similar rebuff, which is difficult to understand. Why should Braque be singled out for such peculiar treatment when none of the other Fauves were rejected?

For a time Braque abandoned landscape to devote himself to human figures. At the end of the year, faced with a crisis which we might describe as anxiety about plasticity, he chose the human figure or, more precisely the nude, as if the human body, a complex of volumes, could help him more than any other subject to express his new artistic aims. *Femme assise se coiffant* (Woman Seated, Dressing her Hair; Pl. 124) (Private Collection, Paris),[88] painted in November or December, perhaps after some studies made in the South, undoubtedly completed the output of 1907 and confirmed the trend heralded by his last landscapes of L'Estaque. The main point here was the impression of solidity Braque wanted to convey in painting. The nude was only a means, but an excellent one, of introducing a volumetric form into a space where light played a part. The exaggerated bend of the back, its violent treatment with red and green hatchings setting off the deep groove of the spine, all add force to the volume. But far from seeking a naturalist rendering of the model, Braque primarily created a lyrical hymn to the female body. This woman, seated inaccurately on her chair, with inaccurate relief, is like a transposed image of the plastic beauty of the female body. "I could never show a woman in all her natural beauty," said Braque at about that time, "I haven't the skill. Nobody has. So I had to create a new kind of beauty, a beauty I see in terms of volume, line, mass, weight, and through that beauty I interpret my subjective impression. Nature is simply an excuse for a decorative composition, plus feeling." This *Femme assise* has not ceased entirely to be a Fauve work precisely because of the feeling Braque conveyed through art, but by giving preference to the "decorative composition" the work, we feel, is tilting towards

129. Dufy *Jeanne dans les fleurs*, 1907.

becomes an ellipse or a cylinder or a circle. This manner has been regarded as a way of embroidering, but we see it as a rare, plausible and true rendering of a number of immaterial features. Yes, there are round men and square men. These are views of heads, shoulders, arms and joints that seem to come straight out of Euclid's immortal book."

It was not only indirectly, by way of Rouveyre, that Matisse became acquainted with Golberg's ideas. It is certain that Matisse and Marquet themselves visited Golberg while he was under treatment in the sanatorium. It would be surprising if Golberg and Matisse had not talked about the problem of expression through line at a time when the former was writing a book on the subject and the latter allocated it a primordial place in his painting. But even if Matisse listened avidly to Golberg's arguments, they would not have been as helpful to him as the figurative examples found in Ingres, Gauguin and in Islamic art. How much credence should we give to Rouveyre when he says that the text of Matisse's *Notes d'un peintre* "was written by Golberg in close collaboration with Matisse"?[89] We have seen how closely Matisse's text "fits" his artistic output of 1906 and 1907 so that it is difficult to believe that a third person (and a theoretician at that!) had played a more important role than the artist's own logic. Things might be different in the case of Derain; he had always liked theorizing and would have taken more kindly to Golberg's ideas which Matisse passed on. This may have been one of the reasons why Derain began to treat form geometrically.

Thus, from 1907 on the Fauve system ceased to exist as a collective and coherent system of expression; it survived only as interpreted and adapted by some painters.

Conclusion   Fauvism—an assessment

In this study we have chosen to exclude painters whom some critics who are too fond of superficial appearances, and some dealers who stand to gain from this confusion, have carelessly called Fauve. We hope that the reader now understands clearly that Fauvism is something very specific and limited; that it is not an elastic concept that can be applied to any painter who uses pure colours.

It is true that a number of painters revolved round the Fauves—studio colleagues or friends—who knew of their experiments, were interested in them, shared in them to some extent, and who exhibited side by side with the Fauves. But their relationship with the Fauves seems incomplete and superficial so that we can only speak of temporary, occasional, or marginal Fauves.

This, as we have seen, was the case of Valtat and Seyssaud. It also applied to several others.

Camoin has often been included in the Fauve group because he was a pupil of Moreau and associated with the Fauves, but he was a pupil of Moreau's for only a few weeks, and the only Fauve he knew well was Marquet. His admiration for both Monet and Cézanne, whom he had met, clearly suggests that he was seeking to reconcile a certain kind of Impressionism with a concern for structured form. Camoin rarely gets away from a naturalist feeling for light, a traditional approach to the use of perspective treating of space; his friendship with Marquet, a Fauve who flirted with Impressionism, did not threaten to change his views. Although he liked to use colour transposition with a feeling for chromatic harmony learnt from

Manet, whom he also consulted as a friend, he never subjected his drawing to daring and arbitrary distortions, for he had little leaning towards lyricism.

Manguin, a pupil of Moreau in 1894, was friendly with several Fauves. If Fauvism could be defined simply as the use of pure colour, Manguin would be one of its foremost exponents, for he used the most fantastic and arbitrary tones of the highest saturation. But this was a passing phase. To him colour then became the driving principle of the picture which was organized according to its demands; the direct apposition of contrasting areas of colour led to a figurative treatment of space which conveyed the lyrical feeling nature evoked in the painter. This certainly places Manguin very close to the Fauves. However, he parted company with them when he refused to use one of the essential terms of the Fauve vocabulary—simplification. Manguin's style, in fact, is often descriptive, overloaded, without abbreviation. His art is in some ways reminiscent of that of his former teacher, Moreau. Although he was close to Matisse and Marquet, he did not adopt his friends' manner of paring down form to make it more expressive.

Another pupil of Moreau's and friend of the Fauves, Jean Puy, was denounced along with some of the Fauves in *L'Illustration* of 1 November 1905, although he had nothing in common with them except the use of a palette of pure tones which did not, however, deter him from a close study of real light. He admired Cézanne, "correct in values" he thought. He certainly did not see Cézanne in the same way that the Fauves did since he believed that Cézanne had "put Impressionism back on a logical traditional course".[90] In the name of Cézanne, the Fauves invented colour-space; in the name of Cézanne, Puy remained faithful to light-space.

Reserved by nature, Chabaud knew the Fauves only through their works. He did not start to paint his major canvases until 1907: night views of Montmartre, music-hall and brothel scenes, in dull, moving, not very arbitrary colours. His artistic vocabulary had a great deal in common with the Fauves', especially Van Dongen's, but his line and colour reached a degree of dramatization that created a gulf between him and Fauvism and brought him closer to Expressionism. Incidentally, he was a friend of Seyssaud with whom he must have felt he had a lot in common.

Marinot, who was also a solitary character, did not associate with the Fauves, but knew their works through the exhibitions at the Salons d'Indépendants and d'Automne, in which he himself also participated. His Fauvism was only skin-deep. He modelled his forms with pure colour, subordinating them to a preliminary drawing and the structural demands of the picture. Marinot's colour contrasts and saturation never created figurative space that would be, like the Fauves', the equivalent of real space; he remained faithful to a fundamentally illusionist concept in this regard. He did not like either the fantasy or the frenzied accents characteristic of Fauve idiom. His angular drawing, his strict colour-plane ratios, became so accentuated that Vauxcelles dubbed his work, before Braque's, "a game of coloured cubes".[91] The important place Marinot assigned to geometrical design suggests that he knew Golberg's comments on Rouveyre's drawing. He certainly played a more important part in 1907-8, the phase that ended in Cubism, than during the Fauve period.

Other names could be cited; less well known today, they were mentioned by some of the commentators of the time who attacked their palette (their only link with Fauvism): A.-M. Le Beau, G. Bouche, R. Piot and L. Lehmann.

The further we move away from the narrow circle of the real Fauves, the more clearly we see that Fauvism was greatly misunderstood, that only its surface feature was discerned—heightened tones. However, there was one exception: R. Delaunay, who very quickly realized the profound lessons of Fauvism.

We must make it clear that by refusing the description of "Fauve" to the painters we have cited we do not, of course, mean that they were inferior to the Fauves. We are not judging their art by Fauve criteria. To say a painter was Fauve and another was not in no way constitutes a judgment on their value as painters, for value is not measured by the degree of Fauvism we can see in their works. To be Fauve is not itself a claim to glory.

The unity and cohesion of the Fauve movement was ensured mainly by the faithfulness of its creators to an invariable logic which is not found in the sporadic participants or fringe followers. This was what Matisse called "expression" and what we often call expressiveness, that is, the degree of intensity attained by the pictorial idiom in relation to the relatively simple means it uses. In a first phase, this quest for expressiveness prompted the Fauves to consider Neo-Impressionism, which struck them as the sole contemporary figurative system that excluded both literary and anecdotal symbolism, that did not seek the unusual or the bizarre, but was predominantly concerned with artistic problems, especially those relating to expression through colour. But the Fauves soon realized that Divisionism had not divested itself of some of the sequels of Impressionist naturalism, notably its concept of illusionist space; that the elimination of the continuous line deprived the painter of an important means of expression; that it was, at heart, no more than a system of fixed harmony that imprisoned the painter in a complicated and constraining grammatical structure which weakened, even inhibited, the expressive, poetic and lyrical potential of the picture. The quest for an ever more expressive idiom compelled the Fauves to resort to what Derain called "deliberate disharmonies", that is, free and arbitrary transposition. This led the Fauves, in a second phase, to a reappraisal of Gauguin's art which they had at first rejected because of its literary and exotic aspect. It was at that point that the painting became transformed into a pictorial statement, the statement of the painter. The expressiveness of the Fauve picture increased as the constituents of physical reality—light, matter, depth, local colour—were transformed into pure figurative values independent of data outside the artist and solely dependent on his own special needs. In a third phase, the Fauves became aware of the need to treat line as they had treated colour, to simplify it, to purify it, to distort it, to endow it with the maximum force of transposition so as to increase expressiveness. At that point they turned to Islamic, Asiatic and African art, which provided interesting ideas. In a final phase, that same logic led the Fauves to paint abstract pictures, since they thought that the essential thing in a work of art was the relation of the subject to the object and not the object itself. But this they rejected, which accounts for the fact that they soon found themselves in an impasse.

No other figurative movement has ever been so short-lived as Fauvism; there were several reasons for this which we have already mentioned but which we feel we must now discuss more fully.

To begin with, the Fauves grew frightened of their own excesses, for there is no doubt that Fauvism was a frenzied, an inevitably frenzied form of painting since it is the brain-child of the imagination and achieved in a feverish state. After a wild period when each painter vied to outdo the others, to go even further, the Fauves realized that it was impossible to go beyond a certain level of demented extravagance, particularly in heightening colour; most of them mentioned how exhausting they found it constantly to restimulate their enthusiasm and passion, and spoke of the thanklessness of colour orchestration and a sort of onanism of the chromatic idiom. Camille Mauclair rightly said in 1906: "It is now impossible for three quarters of these exhibitors to go any further in the amorphism of the figures and the crudeness of the colours, and this will be obvious next year."[92] Indeed, in 1907 we can see the Fauves refusing to go into the full paroxysm of lyricism; only a few still adhered to the Dionysian intoxication—or perhaps it was pure hedonism. Although they realized fully that to contain the lyrical spirit meant running the risk of demolishing the living force of the painting, they all finally agreed to discipline the spontaneity of their impulse, to bring reasoning into the creative act, to face the age-old anxiety about plasticity. At that crisis point they came upon Oriental and Far Eastern art, the art of Cézanne and Africa, which taught them corrective methods if not alternative solutions. It is an incontestable fact that the Fauves rejected the excesses of fantasy and lyricism. It is possible that, consciously or unconsciously, they followed certain imperatives of the predominant artistic ideology with which they were faced and that they never intended to stray too far from the French pictorial tradition, especially the precepts of common sense and measure often invoked by the critics of the time.

Other restraints played a part. What mattered most to the Fauve painter was expressing that invitation to dream contained in every scene of nature, to convey the feeling of things, his relationship with them or their relationship with each other. He did not think it worthwhile to paint the object, even if it was the cause of the sensation, the feeling, the dream that enveloped the artist. The Fauve painter did not see the act of painting as a reproduction of nature but as the expression of his inner self. Thus it was logical that the object underwent arbitrary distortions which were regarded as the justification or the vehicle for the artist's feeling. We have seen that transposition was at first confined to the colour of the object and not the space; subsequently it was applied to the drawing of the object, whether it was a design of arabesques, which bespeaks the artist's intimate impulses, or whether form was treated geometrically to be purified and rendered more expressive, that is, to be more in keeping with the author's dream. Thus we have transpositions, distortions, paring down, ellipses, all operations that finally lead to a sort of "de-realizing", a distortion of form that makes the picture difficult to recognize. Matisse very rightly remarked that "all art is at some moments abstract in itself, when it is basic expression stripped of all anecdote."[93] Logically, the Fauve painting should have become an abstract representation conveying a lyrical feeling in its pure state without reference to the object. This was what Derain envisaged after he had become aware of the basic contradiction within Fauvism: wanting to dissociate oneself from "objective things" yet at the same time never ceasing to refer to them. To avoid the risk of becoming "the slave of stupid things" he dreamed (but never went beyond dreaming) of a type of composition that would simply be a "grouping of forms in light and simultaneously harmonizing them with the material at one's disposal". All the Fauves grew more or less aware of that logic, that inevitablity of abstraction; some of them, especially Derain, for a time came close to a form of pictorial expression in which we can discern something of abstract art. But none of them decided to choose that inevitable course; they all rejected it as if it were taboo. Thus Matisse's course was clear: admittedly, he rejected the spontaneous reaction to the model, but he did not want a simple organization of signs on the surface either. Here again we must remember that the conventional idea of reference to nature was part of the artistic ideology that still reigned supreme in the era of the Fauves. It was generally agreed that the painter could not do without nature and that it had to be reproduced in the picture; even Gauguin had shared this view only a short time before although stating explicitly that art was an abstraction. As early as 1905, as we have seen, the critics accused Matisse of being too much of a theorist, of applying a system, of painting "noumena of pictures" and of getting too far away from nature. Derain himself admitted it: "We painted with theories, ideas; that was the abstract,"[94] and he was not proud of it. Fundamentally, the Fauves contented themselves with weakening the representative function of the picture, at most a dislocation of the image. Yet this had a considerable impact and was a challenge to the petrified image left by the Renaissance.

We might think that the acceptance of a truly abstract idiom, completely freed from any reference to the object, would have been a more satisfactory solution than painting forms—admittedly purified and geometricized (sometimes amounting to no more than a banal stylization)—but not liberated from the servitude of representation. To assert the exclusive rights of subjectivity, the Fauves would have had to accept the elimination of the object. By not doing so, they encouraged the restoration of the object, which was precisely what happened with the advent of Cubism. Cubism actually ran the same risks of abstraction, which it too rejected just as the Fauves had done.

The problem of abstraction was realized particularly well by the Fauves because to them the precise organization of the painted surface was fundamental. The Fauve picture obviously cannot be interpreted by referring to reality; it is an arbitrary space in which coloured forms of a certain size are distributed, in a calculated relationship to each other, with the aim of creating a certain impression. Colour here played a new part: its traditional function of rendering the local tone disappeared; from now on colour referred only to itself.

Thus the question of reference to reality was allocated a secondary place among pictorial problems. By eroding allusions to reality on the one hand, by diminishing the physical reality and, on the other, by giving precedence to plastic expression, the Fauve picture paved the way for a new course in which sensations and emotions would be expressed by a system of signs independent of nature. "I went from objects to the sign," Matisse said.

The Fauve substitution of the figurative statement for the illusionist painting that had animated all of the naturalism of the nineteenth century had far-reaching consequences. If the painted image no longer coincided with the model it was because the Fauve artist no longer saw nature as a coherent whole before it was put into the picture; he no longer saw the world as a form of order and henceforth strove to create another by means of figurative signs. In this way Fauvism illustrated the possibility of multiplying the humanist dimension of a work of art. This was clearly perceived by Louis Grodecki, who, partially referring to Fauvism, discussed what was "essential" for modern art: "If a work of art does not belong to the realm of pure visibility, if it is a reality in itself and not a reflection of nature, a thing and not an image, the experience of art cannot be separated from the whole of our mental and physical life."[95]

Finally, we must agree that one of the chief merits of Fauvism lay in making abstract painting possible, in preparing the ground for painters who would be able to accept abstraction. We must remember that Kandinsky regarded none other than Matisse as an initiator in this field, and that Delaunay came to abstract art after a Fauve experiment which was in other respects more important than his pseudo-Cubist attempts. Beyond its own system, Fauvism initiated the quest for a fundamentally new figurative idiom which would affect the whole of Europe.

We must admit that Fauvism met with little understanding in France; this is proved by the swift coming of Cubism, its opposite, even if we can consider that it was in some measure derived from it.[96] By contrast, it was much better understood in Germany, where some of the Fauve painters exhibited. In 1907 Matisse exhibited at the Secession in Berlin, at the invitation of Hans Purrmann, a young Bavarian painter who got in touch with him in Paris and urged him to open an academy. In 1908 Van Dongen, invited by Pechstein, and Marquet exhibited with Matisse; in 1909 Vlaminck exhibited alone. Matisse made trips to Germany: he stayed in Bavaria during the summer of 1908, and in Berlin a few months later, where Cassirer seems to have devoted a one-man show to him. The painters who founded the *Brücke* in Dresden in 1905 first consulted the art of van Gogh and Gauguin; it was on the basis of these examples that Kirchner, in 1906, published a manifesto which, with inevitable logic, had some links with Fauve art. From 1907 onward the development of German Expressionist painting can probably be explained in part by the direct contact some of the German painters had with French artists. In that year Pechstein met Van Dongen in Paris, and perhaps Matisse too; Franz Marc was also in Paris.

Fauve art probably affected the founders of the New Association of Artists in Munich and the *Blaue Reiter*, for although it is not certain that they met the Fauve painters themselves, it is certain that they saw their works. Kandinsky made frequent visits to Paris; he lived in Sèvres in 1906 and 1907. He exhibited regularly at the Salon d'Automne from 1904 to 1907, even became a shareholder and in 1905 was on the jury. Jawlensky travelled and worked in France in 1905, 1906 and 1907. He exhibited at the Salon d'Automne in 1905 and 1906. Paula Modersohn-Becker came to Paris regularly from 1900 on; she was there for the important Salons of 1905, 1906 and 1907 (we know that she was deeply influenced by the Gauguin retrospective at the Salon d'Automne of 1906). There are similarities between the art of Kandinsky and Jawlensky and that of the Fauves. Kandinsky's case is particularly strange: his painting evolved in stages that followed, with a certain time lag, the phases in the evolution of Fauvism. As he had little interest in Impressionism, Kandinsky explored Neo-Impressionist art from 1902 until about 1907, using it as the Fauves had, that is, assimilating the Divisionist achievements and then overtaking them and creating an original style. At Murnau, in the landscapes painted in 1908 and 1909, he showed that he was greatly influenced by Fauvism, although we cannot speak of imitation. But it is noteworthy that Kandinsky accepted the logical consequences of his figurative system by totally eliminating all reference to the object. He went where the Fauves had refused to go.

The Fauves did not affect only Germany. Their influence can be seen in the work of the group of Belgian painters among whom Rik Wouters, especially, revealed that he had looked at Matisse's œuvre (Matisse and Marquet exhibited in Brussels in 1906; in 1907 it was the turn of Vlaminck, Derain and Friesz; Marquet exhibited in Liège in 1908). It is also evident in the work of some artists in Holland (where Van Dongen was well known), like Sluyters and perhaps Mondrian, in the work of the Russian avant-garde painters (almost all the Fauves exhibited in

Moscow, in Odessa and in Kiev in 1908 and 1909), in the paintings of the Hungarian Czobel, who worked in Paris from 1905 to 1908, who certainly associated with the Fauves, exhibited regularly with them and returned to his country in 1908 and perhaps also in the works of some of the Italian Futurists.

We cannot really say that Fauvism disappeared completely in France after 1907; it continued and was transformed in the hands of some of its authors, like Matisse, Van Dongen and Dufy, who, at given moments, preserved variations of some of the formulas of the Fauvism of 1905-7. Some painters who belonged to the Fauves' generation, though not Fauves themselves, nevertheless drew on Fauvism throughout almost their entire careers by giving colour a predominant role in figurative expression; this was the case of Bonnard, Léger, Robert and Sonia Delaunay, Kupka and La Fresnaye.

Then Fauvism was somewhat forgotten when Cubism, abstract painting and Surrealism were in the forefront of the art scene; the museums did not rush to buy Fauve works and there were hardly any exhibitions devoted to Fauve painters. Things looked up for the Fauves from the time of the retrospective exhibitions of the Galerie Bing in 1927 and of the *Gazette des Beaux-Arts* in 1934. These brought a kind of revival of colour lyricism, which inspired some artists of the generation between the two world wars, like Walch and Desnoyer, some of the generation of the Second World War like Estève, Bazaine, Gischia, Lapicque, Pignon and Singier, and finally some of the post-war generation who, during the 1950s, created the trend of lyrical abstract art, like Messagier, Soulages, Riopelle, De Staël and O. Debré.

So many years have passed and yet there are still painters who find the art of the Fauves inspiring; Fauvism seems to have been a vital force in contemporary painting, and Matisse certainly did not exaggerate when he said: "Fauve painting isn't everything, but it is the foundation of everything."[97]

Notes

1 JEAN-CLAUDE LEBENSZTEJN, "Sol", *Scolies*, Paris, P.U.F., 1 (1971, pp. 95-122; 2 (1972), pp. 89-124.

2 The word "Fauve" was used by Vauxcelles in his review of the Salon d'Automne of 1905 published in the supplement of *Gil Blas* of 17 October 1905, p. 2.

3 LEBENSZTEJN, *op. cit.*

4 ANDRÉ DERAIN, *Lettres à Vlaminck*, Paris, 1955, pp. 121, 132, 133.

5 Told by FRANCIS JOURDAIN, "Né en 76, souvenirs", Paris, 1951, p. 159.

6 ANDRÉ BILLY, *La Littérature française contemporaine*, Paris, 1928, p. 5.

7 Letter published, together with Gide's lecture, in *La Grande Revue*, 10 December 1910, p. 454.

8 JULES DE GAULTIER, "De Kant à Nietzsche", *Le Mercure de France*, January 1900, p. 104.

9 DERAIN *op. cit.*, p. 168.

10 FERNAND LÉGER, *Fonctions de la peinture*, Paris, 1965, p. 15.

11 Mentioned in MAURICE DENIS, *Théories*, Paris, 1920, p. 179.

12 Told by CLAUDE ROGER-MARX, *R. Seyssaud*, Paris, 1958, p. 3.

13 CHARLES MORICE, "Enquête sur les tendances actuelles des arts plastiques", *Le Mercure de France*; Signac's reply: 1 September 1905, pp. 79-80.

14 Quoted by Verhaeren in the preface to the Catalogue of the Cross exhibition, Galerie Druet, 1905.

15 Written by Friesz at the time of Denis's death, found among his papers.

16 PIERRE FRANCASTEL, *Peinture et société, naissance et destruction d'un espace plastique*, Paris, 1965, p. 143.

17 For Moreau, see PIERRE-LOUIS MATHIEU, *Gustave Moreau*, Paris, 1976.

18 FRANCIS EDWIN HYSLOP, *Henri Evenepoel à Paris. Lettres choisies 1892-1899*, Brussels, 1976.

19 ANDRÉ MASSON, "Conversation avec Matisse", *Critique*, May 1974, p. 395.

20 All Matisse's writings and sayings are collected in MATISSE, *Ecrits et propos sur l'art*. Text, notes and index compiled by D. FOURCADE, Paris, 1972.

21 This has been confirmed by Marguerite Duthuit.

22 It was prepared by Jean-Claude Martinet, nephew of Marcelle Marquet.

23 This is what Marcelle Marquet told us; the canvases are scattered in private collections.

24 FERNANDE OLIVIER, *Picasso et ses amis*, Paris, 1933, pp. 107-8.

25 The catalogue raisonné of Derain's work has been compiled by Michel Kellermann.

26 After Derain's death, Vlaminck published the letters his friend had written to him (DERAIN, *op. cit.*). Unfortunately, many letters were not dated by their author, and when filing them Vlaminck made several demonstrable mistakes, for instance in mixing up the letters sent to Collioure in 1905 and those written to Cassis in 1907. Critics have not taken these errors into account which has led to some faulty judgements.

27 *Album de dessins de Derain*, Cabinet des dessins, Musée National d'Art Moderne, dated by Bernard Dorival from the spring of 1903 to the fall of 1905.

28 Signac's canvas was exhibited at the Salon des Indépendants in 1895. Did Derain see it a few years later? He could have seen a study in 1902.

29 Notably: *Tournant dangereux*, Paris, 1929; *Portraits avant décès*, Paris, 1943.

30 MARCEL SAUVAGE, *Vlaminck, sa vie et son message*, Paris-Geneva, 1956. Paul Pétridès compiled the catalogue raisonné of the paintings.

31 Signed "FLAMENC"; exhibition, Paris, 1956, No. 3.

32 LOUIS CHAUMEIL, *Van Dongen, l'homme et l'artiste; la vie et l'œuvre*, Geneva, 1967.

33 MAURICE LAFFAILLE, *Raoul Dufy, Catalogue raisonné de l'œuvre peint*, vol. I, Foreword by Maurice Laffaille, Preface by Marcelle Berr de Turique, Geneva, 1972.

34 We have found many interesting thoughts in Friesz's—as yet unpublished—notes which Mme Friesz allowed us to consult: some of his sayings have been published in: MAXIMILIAN GAUTHIER, *Othon Friesz*, Geneva, 1957.

35 The catalogue raisonné of Braque's painting by Nicole Mangin, in the process of publication (publ. Maeght), does not yet cover the Fauve period.

36 His presence at Perpignan is documented by a letter sent to the Under-Secretary of the Beaux-Arts.

37 ANDRÉ GIDE, "Promenade au Salon d'Automne", *Gazette des Beaux-Arts*, December 1905.

38 On this subject, see MARCEL GIRY, "Le curieux achat fait à Derain et à Vlaminck au Salon des Indépendants de 1905 ou deux tableaux retrouvés", *L'Œil*, September 1976.

39 See DERAIN, *op. cit.* Two letters are dated: one of 28 July (pp. 154-7), the other of 5 August (pp. 157-60); we think that two other undated letters must be earlier (pp. 147-8 and pp. 161-3), although Vlaminck filed one of them after the letter of 5 August.

40 Signed and dated lower left 06; Exhibition, Paris, Galerie Charpentier, 1955, No. 2; Sale, Sotheby, London, 24 April 1968; present collection unknown.

41 Quoted in DORA VALLIER, *Jacques Villon, œuvres de 1897 à 1956*, Paris, n. d., p. 42.

42 PAUL JAMOT, "Le Salon d'Automne", *Gazette des Beaux-Arts*, 1906, vol. II, p. 456.

43 Letter from Derain to the President of the Royal Academy, 15 May 1953, published in RONALD ALLEY, Tate Gallery Catalogue, *The Foreign Paintings, Drawings and Sculpture*, London, 1959, pp. 64-5, No. 6030.

44 PIERRE LÉVY, *Des artistes et un collectionneur*, Paris, 1976, p. 124.

45 For a fuller study of this picture, see MARCEL GIRY, "Une composition de Derain: *La danse*", *Bulletin de la Société de l'Histoire de l'Art Français*, 1978.

46 Other examples of this gesture could be seen at the Musée des Monuments Français, notably on a bas-relief of St. Sernin of Toulouse and on a capital from Nazareth.

47 One might add that Derain was also influenced by Delacroix, from whom he took the attitude of the black servant in the *Women of Algiers* for his figure on the right.

48 DERAIN, *op. cit.*, pp. 146-7.

49 VLAMINCK, *Portraits avant décès*, Paris, 1943, p. 52.

50 VLAMINCK, *Tournant dangereux*, Paris, 1929, p. 94.

51 CHAUMELL, *op. cit.*, p. 101.

52 Colour reproduction: JEAN MÉLAS KYRIAZI, *Van Dongen et le fauvisme*, Lausanne, 1971, p. 90.

53 LAFFAILLE, *op. cit.*, No. 192: Exhibition, Saint-Germain-en-Laye, 1967, No. 92.

54 LAFAILLE, *op. cit.*, No. 123; Exhibition, Paris, Galerie Charpentier, 1962, No. 51.

55 Reproduction: GAUTHIER, *op. cit.*, Pl. 11.

56 Letter from Friesz to André Salmon, 3 July 1922.

57 LOUIS VAUXCELLES, "Le Salon des Indépendants", *Gil Blas*, 20 March 1907. ERNST C. OPPLER quoted this neglected source before we did, in: *Fauvism Re-examined*, New York, 1976.

58 Quoted by CHARLES CHASSÉ, *Les Fauves et leur temps*, Paris, 1963, p. 163.

59 DERAIN, *op. cit.*, pp. 152-3. This letter was wrongly dated 1905 by Vlaminck.

60 *Ibid.*, pp. 149-50. Another letter wrongly dated 1905 by Vlaminck.

61 Letter from Matisse to FÉLIX FÉNÉON, 21 August 1907, quoted in the catalogue of the Matisse exhibition, Paris, 1970, p. 53.

62 The parallel between the nude by Matisse and that by Braque is not based solely on the plastic problems it posed; it rests also on the attitude of the figure seen almost completely from the back whereas the head is almost full-face. This sort of movement, as we have seen, appeared for the first time in Derain's *La danse*.

63 GUILLAUME APOLLINAIRE, "Henri Matisse", *La Phalange*, No. 2, 15-18 December 1907.

64 PAUL JAMOT, "Exposition de tableaux d'Albert Marquet", *Chronique des arts et de la curiosité*, 23 February 1907, pp. 51-2.

65 PIERRE HEPP, "Exposition de tableaux à la Galerie Eugène Blot", *Chronique des arts et de la curiosité*, 9 November 1907, pp. 322-3.

66 Exhibition, Paris, Galerie Schmit, 1973, No. 31.

67 VAUXCELLES, *op. cit.*

68 Exhibition, New York, The Museum of Modern Art, 1976, No. 31.

69 OPPLER, *op. cit.*, p. 289.

70 DERAIN, *op. cit.*, pp. 152-3 for the first letter, pp. 149-50 for the second.

71 Reproduction: GEORGES HILAIRE, *Derain*, Geneva, 1959, Pl. 53.

72 Reproduction: *ibid.*, Pl. 69.

73 GERTRUDE STEIN, *Autobiographie d'Alice Toklas*, Paris, 1934, p. 25; for English ed. see Bibliography.

74 Exhibition, Paris, Galerie Schmit, 1977, No. 76, colour reproduction.

75 Exhibition, Paris, Orangerie des Tuileries, 1967, No. 159.

76 PIERRE HEPP, "Exposition de tableaux chez B. Weill", *Chronique des arts et de la curiosité*, 16 November 1907, p. 332.

77 Exhibition, Paris, Galerie Schmit, 1978, No. 59, colour reproduction.

78 MÉLAS KYRIAZI, *op. cit.*, p. 92.

79 For the catalogue of Dufy's work, see LAFFAILLE, *op. cit.*

80 See MARCEL GIRY, "A propos d'un tableau d'Othon Friesz au Musée National d'Art Moderne", *La Revue du Louvre et des Musées de France*, 1970, No. 3.

81 FERNAND FLEURET, "Petits mélanges sur un grand peintre", *Friesz, œuvres 1901-1927*, Paris, 1928.

82 Exhibition, New York, The Museum of Modern Art, 1976, No. 45.

83 Reproduction: GAUTHIER, *op. cit.*, Pl. 26.

84 See MARCEL GIRY, "Le paysage à figures chez Othon Friesz (1907-12)", *Gazette des Beaux-Arts*, January 1967.

85 ANDRÉ SALMON, *Othon Friesz*, Paris, 1920, p. 12.

86 Exhibition, Braque, Munich, 1963, No. 8.

87 GUILLAUME APOLLINAIRE, "Le Salon d'Automne, Georges Braque", *Je dis tout*, 19 October 1907.

88 There is a version in the Jacques Helft Collection, Buenos Aires.

89 ANDRÉ ROUVEYRE, "Souvenir de mon commerce dans la contagion de Mécislas Golberg", *Le Mercure de France*, 15 April 1922.

90 CHARLES MORICE, *op. cit.*, J. Puy's reply: 15 August 1905, pp. 554-5.

91 LOUIS VAUXCELLES, "Le Salon d'Automne", *Gil Blas*, 30 September 1908.

92 CAMILLE MAUCLAIR, *Trois Crises de l'art actuel*, Paris, 1906, p. 310.

93 MATISSE, *op. cit.*, p. 252.

94 P. LÉVY, *op. cit.*, p. 80.

95 LOUIS GRODECKI, "Berenson, Woelfflin et la critique de l'art moderne", *Critique*, July-August 1954, p. 67.

96 See MARCEL GIRY, "Le style géométrique dans la peinture en 1907", *Travaux IV. Le cubisme*, C.I.E.R.E.C., University of St. Etienne, 1973.

97 MATISSE, *op. cit.*, p. 55.

Bibliography

Memoirs, Correspondence, Interviews

APOLLINAIRE, GUILLAUME, *Chroniques d'art (1902-1918)*, compiled with preface and notes by L. C. Breunig, Paris, Gallimard, 1960.
— *Le Flâneur des deux rives*, Paris, N.R.F., 1928.
BILLY, ANDRÉ, *L'Epoque 1900*, Paris, Tallandier, 1951.
— *L'Epoque contemporaine*, Paris, Tallandier, 1956.
BLANCHE, JACQUES-EMILE, *Essais et portraits*, Paris, Dorbon-aîné, 1912.
— *Propos de peintre. Deuxième série. Dates.* Paris, Emile-Paul Frères, 1921.
CARCO, FRANCIS, *De Montmartre au Quartier latin*, Paris, Albin Michel, 1927.
— *L'Ami des peintres. Souvenirs*, Geneva, Editions du Milieu du Monde, 1944.
CARRIÈRE, EUGÈNE, *Ecrits et lettres choisies*, Paris, Mercure de France, 1907.
CHIPP, HERSCHELL B., contributions by SELZ, PETER and TAYLOR, JOSHUA C., *Theories of Modern Art. A Source Book by Artists and Critics*, Berkeley and Los Angeles, University of California Press, 1968.
COURTHION, PIERRE, *Montmartre, Geneva, Skira, 1956.*
— *Paris des temps nouveaux*, Geneva, Skira, 1957.
CRESPELLE, JEAN-PAUL, *Montmartre vivant*, Paris, Hachette, 1964.
DECAUDIN MICHEL, «Apollinaire et les peintres en 1906 d'après quelques notes inédites», *Gazette des Beaux-Arts*, February 1970.
DENIS, MAURICE, *Théories (1890-1910). Du symbolisme et de Gauguin vers un nouvel ordre classique*, Paris, Rouart et Watelin, 1920.
— *Journal*, vol. I, *1884-1904*, vol. II, *1905-1920*, Paris, La Colombe, Editions du Vieux Colombier, 1957.
DERAIN, ANDRÉ, *Lettres à Vlaminck*, Paris, Flammarion, 1955.
DORGELÈS, ROLAND, *Au beau temps de la Butte*, Paris, 1949.
EVENEPOEL, HENRI, "Gustave Moreau et ses élèves. Lettres d'Henri Evenepoel à son père", *Mercure de France*, I (XV), 1, 1923.
— *Lettres à mon père*, Paris, Albin Michel.
— see HYSLOP.
FEGDAL, CHARLES, *Ateliers d'artistes*, Paris, Stock, 1925 (chap. III: Marquet; chap. IV: Van Dongen).
FELS, FLORENT, *Propos d'artistes*, Paris, La Renaissance du Livre, 1925 (notably on Derain, Friesz, Matisse, Vlaminck).
GAUSS, CHARLES EDWARD, *The Aesthetic Theories of French Artists from Realism to Surrealism*, Baltimore and London. The Johns Hopkins Press, 1973, pp. 53-78.

GIDE, ANDRÉ, *Journal 1889-1939*, Paris, Gallimard, Bibliothèque de la Pléiade, 1951.
GOLBERG, MÉCISLAS, "Axiomes et dilemmes", *La Plume*, 15 March 1904.
— *La Morale des lignes*, Paris, A. Messein, 1908.
GUENNE, JACQUES, *Portraits d'artistes. Bosshard, Favory, Gromaire, Guérin, Kisling, Lhote, Matisse, Simon-Lévy, Vlaminck*, Paris, Marcel Seheur. 1927.
HEPP, PIERRE, "Sur le choix des maîtres", *L'Occident*, December 1905. pp. 263-5.
HERBERT, ROBERT L. and EUGENIA, W., "Artists and anarchism. Unpublished letters of Pissaro, Signac and others", *The Burlington Magazine*, November and December 1960.
HERBERT, EUGENIA W., *The Artist and Social Reform: France and Belgium 1885-1898*, New Haven, Yale University Press, 1961.
HYSLOP, FRANCIS E., *Henri Evenepoel à Paris. Lettres choisies 1892-1899*, with an introduction and notes, Brussels, La Renaissance du Livre, 1976.
JOURDAIN, FRANCIS, *Né en 1876, souvenirs*, Paris, Editions du Pavillon, 1951.
— *Sans remords ni rancune*, Paris, Corréa, 1953.
JOURDAIN, FRANTZ, *L'Atelier Chantorel, mœurs d'artistes*, Paris, Charpentier et Fasquelle, 1893.
KAHNWEILER, DANIEL-HENRY, *Mes galeries et mes peintres. Entretiens avec Francis Crémieux*, Paris, Gallimard, 1961.
LÉVY, PIERRE, *Des artistes et un collectionneur*, Paris, Flammarion, 1976.
LHOTE, ANDRÉ, *De la palette à l'écritoire*, Paris, Corréa, 1946.
MATISSE, HENRI, "Notes d'un peintre", *La Grande Revue*, 25 December 1908, pp. 731-45.
MAUCLAIR, CAMILLE, *Trois Crises de l'art actuel*, Paris, Fasquelle 1906.
MOORE, GEORGE, *Confessions of a Young Man*, London, Sonnenschein & Co., 1888, rev. ed., Harmondsworth, Penguin Books, 1939.
MORICE, CHARLES, "Enquête sur les tendances actuelles des arts plastiques", *Le Mercure de France*, 1 August 1905 (pp. 346-59); 15 August 1905 (pp. 538-55); 1 September 1905 (pp. 61-85). On the fourth question: "Quel état faites-vous de Cézanne?" see VENTURI, LIONELLO, *Cézanne*, Paris, 1936, vol. I, pp. 370, No. 107.
NOCHLIN, LINDA, *Impressionism and Post-Impressionism, 1874-1904. Sources and Documents*, Englewood Cliffs (New Jersey), Prentice-Hall, 1966.
OLIVIER, FERNANDE, *Picasso et ses amis*, Paris, Stock, 1933 and 1973.
OZENFANT, AMÉDÉE, *Mémoires 1886-1962*, foreword by Katia Granoff, introduction by Raymond Cogniat. Paris, Seghers. 1968.
REDON, ARÏ, and BACOU, ROSELINE, *Lettres de Gauguin, Gide, Huys-*

mans, Jammes, Mallarmé. Verhaeren à Odilon Redon, introduced by A. Redon, texts and notes by R. Bacou, Paris, José Corti, 1960.

REDON, ODILON, Lettres d'Odilon Redon 1878-1916, published by the family with a preface by Marius-Ary Leblond. Paris and Brussels, Van Oest & Cie, 1923.

— A soi-même, Journal (1867-1915). Notes sur la vie, l'art et les artistes, Paris, José Corti, 1961.

ROUAULT, GEORGES, Souvenirs intimes, Paris, E. Frapier, 1927.

ROUVEYRE, ANDRÉ, "Souvenirs de mon commerce: dans la contagion de Mécislas Golberg", Mercure de France, 15 April 1922, pp. 297-323.

SALMON, ANDRÉ, Propos d'atelier, Paris, Crès, 1922.

— Souvenirs sans fin, vol. I, 1903-1908, Paris, Gallimard, 1955.

STEIN, GERTRUDE, Autobiography of Alice B. Toklas, London, John Lane, 1933.

VALLOTTON, FÉLIX, Documents pour une biographie et pour l'histoire d'une œuvre, Vol. II, 1900-1914, selection and notes by Gilbert Guisan and Doris Jakubec, Lausanne-Paris, La Bibliothèque des Arts, 1974.

VANDERPYL, FRITZ R., Peintres de mon époque, Paris, Stock, 1931.

VENTURI, LIONELLO, Les Archives de l'impressionnisme, 2 vols., Paris-New York, Durand-Ruel, 1939.

VLAMINCK, MAURICE, Tournant dangereux, Paris, Stock, 1929.

— Portraits avant décès, Paris, Flammarion, 1943.

— Paysages et personnages, Paris, Flammarion, 1953.

VOLLARD, AMBROISE, Souvenirs d'un marchand de tableaux, Paris Albin Michel, 1937 and 1948; new edition with illustrations and notes by Simone Lamblin, Paris, Albin Michel et Libraires Associés, Club des Libraires de France, 1957.

— En écoutant Cézanne, Degas, Renoir, Paris, Grasset, 1938.

WARNOD, ANDRÉ, Ceux de la Butte, Paris, Julliard, 1947.

— Les Peintres, mes amis, Paris, Les Heures Claires, 1965.

— Visages de Paris, Paris, Firmin-Didot, 1930.

WARNOD, JEANINE, Le Bateau-Lavoir 1892-1914, Paris, Presses de la Connaissance, 1975.

WEILL, BERTHE, Pan! dans l'œil! ou trente ans dans les coulisses de la peinture contemporaine 1900-1930, Paris, Lipschutz, 1933.

Studies Including the Fauves

APOLLONIO, UMBRO, Fauves et Cubistes, Paris, Flammarion, 1959.

ARGAN, GIULIO CARLO, L'arte moderna 1770-1970, Florence, Sansoni, 1970.

BEERLI, CONRAD-ANDRÉ, "Couleur et société", Mélanges d'histoire économique et sociale en hommage au professeur Antony Babel, vol. II, Geneva, 1963, pp. 625-79.

BOWNESS, ALAN, Modern European Art, London, Thames and Hudson, 1972.

BRION, MARCEL, La Peinture moderne de l'impressionnisme à l'art abstrait, Paris, Gründ, 1957.

CASSOU, JEAN, Panorama des arts plastiques contemporains, Paris, Gallimard, 1960.

CASSOU, JEAN, LANGUI, EMILE, and PEVSNER, NIKOLAUS, Les Sources du XXe siècle, Paris, Editions des Deux Mondes, 1961.

CHASTEL, ANDRÉ, "Au seuil du XXe siècle. Seurat et Gauguin", Art de France, II, 1962, pp. 297-305.

CLARK, KENNETH, Landscape into Art, Harmondsworth, Penguin Books, 1956.

COGNIAT, RAYMOND, Histoire de la peinture, 2 vols, Paris, Nathan, 1955.

COQUIOT, GEORGES, Cubistes, Futuristes, Passéistes. Essai sur la jeune peinture, Paris, Ollendorf, 1914 and 1923.

CRESPELLE, JEAN-PAUL, Les Maîtres de la belle époque, Paris, Hachette, 1966.

DELEVOY, ROBERT L., Dimensions du XXe siècle, 1900-1945, Geneva, Skira, 1965.

DENVIR, B., Fauvism and Expressionism, London, Thames and Hudson, 1975.

DIEHL, GASTON, La Peinture moderne dans le monde, Paris, Flammarion, n.d.

DORIVAL, BERNARD, La Peinture française, Paris, Larousse, "Arts, Styles et Techniques", 1942.

— Les Etapes de la peinture française, vol. II: Le Fauvisme et le cubisme, 1905-1911, Paris, Gallimard, 1944.

— Les Peintres du vingtième siècle, Nabis, Fauves, Cubistes, Paris, Tisné, 1957.

— "L'art de la Brücke et le fauvisme", Art de France, I, 1961, pp. 381-5.

D'UCKERMANN, PIERRE, L'Art dans la vie moderne, Paris, Flammarion, 1937.

ESCHOLIER, RAYMOND, La Peinture française, XXe siècle, Paris, Floury, 1937.

FELS, FLORENT, L'Art vivant de 1900 à nos jours, 2 vols., Geneva, Cailler, 1950.

— Le Roman de l'art vivant de Claude Monet à Bernard Buffet, Paris, Fayard, 1959.

FOCILLON, HENRI, La Peinture aux XIXe et XXe siècles. Du réalisme à nos jours, Paris, H. Laurens, 1928.

FONTAINAS, ANDRÉ and VAUXCELLES, LOUIS, Histoire générale de l'art français de la Révolution à nos jours, Paris, Librairie de France, 1922.

FRANCASTEL, PIERRE, Histoire de la peinture française. Du classicisme au cubisme, Paris, Gonthier-Médiations, 1955.

— Peinture et société, naissance et destruction d'un espace plastique. De la Renaissance au cubisme, Paris, Gallimard, 1965.

FRANCASTEL, GALIENNE and PIERRE, Le Portrait, cinquante siècles d'humanisme en peinture, Paris, Hachette, 1969.

GENAILLE, ROBERT, La Peinture contemporaine, Paris, Nathan, 1955.

GIRY, MARCEL, La Peinture à Paris en 1905, Ph. D. thesis, Université de Strasbourg, 1967 (typewritten).

— "Le Salon d'Automne de 1905", L'Information d'Histoire de l'Art, January-February 1968, pp. 16-25.

— "Le Salon des Indépendants de 1905", L'Information d'Histoire de l'Art, May-June 1970, pp. 110-14.

GLEIZES, ALBERT, Art et religion. Art et science. Art et production, Chambéry, Editions Présence, 1970.

GOLDING, JOHN, Le Cubisme, Paris, Juillard, 1963.

GOLDWATER, R. J., Primitivism in Modern Painting, New York-London, Harper, 1938; New York, Vintage Books, 1967.

GRODECKI, LOUIS, "Berenson, Wölfflin et la critique de l'art moderne", Critique, 86-87, July-August 1954, pp. 657-75.

HAFTMANN, WERNER, Malerei im 20. Jahrhundert, Munich, Prestel, 1954.

— Painting in the 20th Century, New York, Praeger, 1960.

HAMMACHER, A. M., "The changing values of light-space-form between 1876 and 1890", Studies in Western Art, vol. IV: Problems of the Nineteenth and Twentieth Centuries, Princeton, New Jersey, Meiss, 1963, pp. 104-10.

HAMILTON, GEORGE HEARD, *Painting and Sculpture in Europe, 1880 to 1940*, Baltimore, Penguin, 1967.

HOOG, MICHEL, "La peinture et la gravure. Fauvisme et expressionnisme", *Histoire de l'art. Du réalisme à nos jours*, Encyclopédie de la Pléiade, vol. IV, Paris, N.R.F., 1969, pp. 526-612.

— "Les *Demoiselles d'Avignon* et la peinture à Paris en 1907-1908", *Gazette des Beaux-Arts*, October 1973, pp. 209-16.

HUYGHE, RENÉ, *Histoire de l'art contemporain: la peinture*, published under the direction of René Huyghe with the collaboration of several authors; Supplement to *L'Amour de l'art*, Paris, 1933.

— *La Peinture française. Les contemporains*, Paris, Tisné, Bibliothèque Française des Arts, 1939 and 1949.

HUYGHE, RENÉ and RUDEL, JEAN, *L'Art et le monde moderne*, 2 vols., Paris, Larousse, 1970.

JALARD, MICHEL-CLAUDE, *Le Post-impressionnisme*, Lausanne, Rencontre, 1966.

JOURDAIN, FRANTZ and REY, ROBERT, *Le Salon d'Automne*, Paris, Les Arts et le Livre, 1926.

LADENDORF, H. "L'Age d'or retrouvé par la peinture du XXe siècle sur la côte de la Méditerranée", *La Méditerranée de 1919 à 1939*, Publications of the Faculté des Lettres et Sciences Humaines de Nice, 1st quarter 1969.

LAPAUZE, HENRY, *Le Palais des Beaux-Arts de la Ville de Paris*, Paris, Lucien Laveur, 1910.

LHOTE, ANDRÉ, *Traité du paysage*, Paris, Floury, 1948.

— *Traité de la figure*, Paris, Floury, 1950.

MAUCLAIR, CAMILLE, *L'Art indépendant français sous la Troisième République*, Paris, La Renaissance du Livre, 1919.

— *Les Etats de la peinture française de 1850 à 1920*, Paris, Payot, 1921.

— *Le Théâtre, le cirque, le music-hall et les peintres du XVIe siècle à nos jours*, Paris, Flammarion, 1926.

MAYBON, DANIEL and SCHURR, GÉRALD, *Carnet des arts*, Paris, Editions des Intérêts Privés, 1970.

MEYERSON, IGNACE, *Problèmes de la couleur*, Report and discussions of the Centre de Recherches de Psychologie comparative held in Paris on 18, 19 and 20 May 1954, collected by Ignace Meyerson. Bibliothèque Générale de l'Ecole Pratique des Hautes Etudes, Paris, S.E.V.P.E.N., 1957.

MOULIN, RAYMONDE, *Le Marché de la peinture en France*, Paris, Editions de Minuit, 1967.

MULLER, JOSEPH-EMILE, *La Peinture moderne de Manet à Mondrian*, Paris, Hazan, 1960.

— *L'Art moderne*, Paris, Librairie Générale Française, 1963.

MULLER, JOSEPH-EMILE and ELGAR, FRANCK, *A Century of Modern Painting*, London, Thames and Hudson, 1972.

PUY, MICHEL, *Le Dernier Etat de la peinture. Les successeurs des Impressionnistes*, Paris, Union Française d'Edition, 1910.

— *L'Effort des peintres modernes*, Paris, Albert Messein, 1933.

RAYNAL, MAURICE, *Anthologie de la peinture en France de 1906 à nos jours*, Paris, Editions Montaigne, 1927.

RAYNAL, MAURICE, READ, HERBERT and LEYMARIE, JEAN, *Histoire de la peinture moderne. De Baudelaire à Bonnard. Naissance d'une vision nouvelle*, Geneva, Skira, 1949.

RAYNAL, MAURICE, RUDLINGER, ARNOLD, BOLLIGER, HANS, LASSAIGNE, JACQUES, SCHMIDT, GEORG, *Histoire de la peinture moderne. Matisse, Munch, Rouault, Fauvisme et expressionnisme*, Geneva, Skira, 1950.

RAYNAL, MAURICE, LASSAIGNE, JACQUES, SCHMALENBACH WERNER,

RAYNAL, MAURICE, *Peinture moderne*, Geneva, Skira, 1966.

READ, Sir HERBERT E., *A Concise History of Modern Painting*, London, Thames and Hudson, 1959.

RICHARDSON, EDGAR PRESTON, *The Way of Western Art, 1776-1914*, Cambridge, Harvard University Press, 1939.

ROGER-MARX, CLAUDE/, "Le mouvement dans le paysage de Corot à nos jours", *Arts*, 22 February 1952.

RUDEL, JEAN, see HUYGHE, RENÉ.

RUDLINGER, ARNOLD, BOLLIGER, HANS, *Histoire de la peinture moderne. De Picasso au surréalisme*, Geneva, Skira, 1950.

SALMON, ANDRÉ, *La jeune peinture française*, Paris, Albert Messein, 1912.

— *L'Art vivant*, Paris, Crès, 1920.

SAUNIER, CHARLES, *La Peinture au XXe siècle. Anthologie d'art français*, Paris, Larousse, n.d. (c. 1911).

SCHAPIRO, MEYER, "The reaction against Impressionism in the 1880's: its nature and causes", *Studies in Western Art: Problems of the 19th and 20th centuries*, Princeton, Millard Meiss, 1963.

SCHATTUCK, R., *The Origins of the Avant-Garde in France 1885 to the World War*, New York, Anchor Books, Doubleday, 1961.

SCHMIDT, GEORG, *Petite Histoire de la peinture moderne de Daumier à Chagall*, Neuchâtel, Griffon, n.d.

SOTRIFFER, KRISTIAN, *Modern Graphics. Expressionism and Fauvism*, New York-Toronto, McGraw-Hill, 1972.

VALLIER, DORA, *Histoire de la peinture 1870-1940. Les mouvements d'avant-garde*, Brussels, Editions de la Connaissance, 1963.

VENTURI, LIONELLO, *La Peinture contemporaine*, Milan, Ulrico Hoepli, 1948.

WILLET, JOHN, *L'Expressionnisme dans les arts 1900-1968*, Paris, Hachette, "L'Univers des connaissances", 1970.

ZERVOS, CHRISTIAN, "Un demi-siècle d'art en France. Notes sur le renouvellement esthétique de notre époque", *Cahiers d'art*, 1955, p. 9.

Studies Devoted to Fauvism

BAZIN, GERMAIN, see HUYGHE, RENÉ.

BURGESS, GELETT, "The Wild Men of Paris", *The Architectural Record*, New York, vol. 27, May 1910, pp. 400-14.

CHASSÉ, CHARLES, *Les Fauves et leur temps*, Lausanne-Paris, Bibliothèque des Arts, 1963.

— "L'histoire du fauvisme revue et corrigée", *Connaissance des arts*, October 1962, pp. 54-9.

CHASTEL, ANDRÉ, "Le fauvisme ou l'été chaud de la peinture", *Le Monde*, 21 August 1959.

COWART, WILLIAM JOHN, *Ecoliers to Fauves: Matisse, Marquet and Manguin Drawings: 1890-1906*, Ph. D. thesis, Johns Hopkins University, Baltimore, 1972.

CRESPELLE, JEAN-PAUL, *Les Fauves*, Neuchâtel, Ides et Calendes, 1962.

DIEHL, GASTON, *Les Fauves. Œuvres de Braque, Derain, Dufy, Friesz, Marquet, Matisse, Van Dongen, Vlaminck*, Paris, Editions du Chêne, 1943 and 1948.

— *Les Fauves*, Paris, Nouvelles Editions Françaises, 1971.

DORIVAL, BERNARD, "Fauves: The Wild Beasts Tamed", *Art News Annual* (New York), 1952-3, pp. 98-129, 174-6.

DORRA, HENRI, "The Wild Beasts. Fauvism and its Affinities at the Museum of Modern Art", *Art Journal*, College Art Association of America, fall 1976, XXXVI/1, pp. 50-4.

DUTHUIT, GEORGES, "Le fauvisme", *Cahiers d'art*, 1929 (Nos 5, 6, 10), 1930 (No. 3), 1931 (No. 2). Reprinted in DUTHUIT G., *Représentation et présence. Premiers écrits et travaux*, Paris, Flammarion, 1974, pp. 195-231.

— *Les Fauves*, with a bibliography by Bernard Karpel, Geneva, Trois Collines, 1949.

ELDERFIELD, JOHN, *The Wild Beasts. Fauvism and its Affinities*, New York, The Museum of Modern Art, 1976.

GIRY, MARCEL, "Le style géométrique dans la peinture vers 1907", *Travaux IV. Le cubisme*, Centre Interdisciplinaire d'Etudes et de Recherches sur l'Expression Contemporaine, Université de Saint-Etienne, 1973, pp. 29-34.

HOOG, MICHEL, "La Direction des Beaux-Arts et les Fauves, 1903-1905", *Arts de France*, III, 1963, pp. 363-6.

— "Fauves", *Album No. 7 de la Collection Pierre Lévy*, Paris, Mourlot, 1972; reprinted in LÉVY, PIERRE, *Des artistes et un collectionneur*, Paris, 1976, pp. 294-305.

HUYGHE, RENÉ, "Le fauvisme: le réveil des traditions", *L'Amour de l'art*, No. 7, July 1933, pp. 153-6 (text reprinted in the following).

HUYGHE, RENÉ and BAZIN, GERMAIN, "Le fauvisme. Les coloristes (chap. IV); "Le fauvisme. Les peintres pathétiques" (chap. V); "Le fauvisme. Le réveil des traditions" (chap. VI), *Histoire de l'art contemporain*, Paris, Félix Alcan, 1935.

JEDLICKA, GOTTHARD, *Der Fauvismus*, Zurich, Büchergilde Gutenberg, 1961.

LASSUS, JEAN (de), "Les Fauves", *L'Amour de l'art*, No. 6, June 1927, pp. 209-11.

LEBENSZTEJN, JEAN-CLAUDE, "Sol", *Scolies, Cahiers de Recherches de l'Ecole Normale Supérieure*, Paris, P.U.F., 1 (1971), pp. 95-122; 2 (1972), pp. 89-114.

LEYMARIE, JEAN, *Le Fauvisme*, Geneva, Skira, 1959.

— "Il fauvismo: la fase preparatoria", "La formazione del movimento", "La piena maturità" (L'espressionismo e il fauvismo), *L'Arte moderna*, 3 vols., Milan, Fratelli Fabbri, 1967-1968-1969, pp. 201-320.

MARUSSI, G., *I Fauves*, Venice, 1950.

MULLER, JOSEPH-EMILE, *Le Fauvisme*, Paris, Hazan, Bibliothèque Aldine des Arts, 1956.

— *Le Fauvisme*, Paris, Hazan, 1967.

NEGRI, RENATA, *Matisse e i Fauves*, Milan, Fratelli Fabbri, 1969.

OPPLER, ELLEN CHARLOTTE, *Fauvism Reexamined*, Ph. D. thesis, Columbia University, New York, 1969; New York and London, Garland Publishing, 1976.

OZENFANT, AMÉDÉE, see VAUVRECY.

PUY, MICHEL, "Les Fauves", *La Phalange*, 15 November 1907, pp. 450-9; reprinted in *L'Effort des peintres modernes*, Paris, Messein, 1933, pp. 61-78.

SALMON, ANDRÉ, "Les Fauves et le fauvisme", *L'Art vivant*, 1 May 1927, pp. 321-4.

— *Le fauvisme* (24 plates), Paris, Somogy, 1956.

SUTTON, DENYS, "Aspects of the Venice Biennale: The Fauves", *The Burlington Magazine*, September 1950, pp. 263-5.

VAUVRECY (pseudonym of OZENFANT, AMÉDÉE), "Les Fauves, 1900-1907", *L'Esprit nouveau*, No. 16, pp. 1871-2.

VAUXCELLES, LOUIS, "Les Fauves, à propos de l'exposition de la Gazette des Beaux-Arts", *Gazette des Beaux-Arts*, December 1934, pp. 273-82.

— *Le Fauvisme*, Geneva, Cailler, 1958.

WATTENMAKER, RICHARD J., "The Fauves", exhibition catalogue *The Fauves*, Art Gallery of Ontario, Toronto, 1975.

WHITFIELD, S., "Fauvism", *Concepts of Modern Art*, by T. Richardson and N. Stangos, Harmondsworth, Penguin, 1974.

ZERVOS, CHRISTIAN, *Histoire de l'art contemporain. Le fauvisme*, Cahiers d'Art, 1933, pp. 113-38.

Collective and One-Man Exhibitions of the Period

See: GORDON, DONALD E., *Modern Art Exhibitions 1900-1916, Selected Catalogue Documentation*, 2 vols., Munich, Prestel-Verlag, 1974.

Collective Exhibitions Devoted to the Fauves since 1926

BASLE, June-July 1966, Galerie Beyeler, *Autour de l'impressionnisme*.

— 1969, Galerie Beyeler, *Die Fauves*.

BERNE, 29 April - 29 May 1950, Kunsthalle, *Die Fauves und die Zeitgenossen*. Preface by A. Rudlinger.

BESANÇON, August-September 1964, Musée des Beaux-Arts, *Valtat et ses amis, Albert André, Charles Camoin, Henri Manguin, Jean Puy*. Preface by G. Besson.

— July-October 1965, Musée des Beaux-Arts, *Collection George et Adèle Besson*. Preface by J. Vergnet-Ruiz.

BORDEAUX, 1966, Galerie des Beaux-Arts, *La Peinture française dans les collections américaines*.

CHARLEROI, November 1967 - January 1968, Palais des Beaux-Arts, *Autour du fauvisme. Valtat et ses amis*. Texts by R.Rousseau and G. Peillex.

COLMAR, 27 June - 20 September 1964, Musée d'Unterlinden, *Fenêtre ouverte sur une collection privée* (Pierre Lévy, Troyes). Text by A. Dunoyer de Segonzac.

GENEVA, 1969, Galerie du Théâtre, *Peintres français*.

— 1973, Musée d'Art et d'Histoire, *L'Art du XXᵉ siècle*.

HAMBURG, 25 May - 10 July 1966, Kunstverein, *Matisse und seine Freunde. Les Fauves*.

LAUSANNE, 1964, Palais de Beaulieu, *Chefs-d'œuvres des collections suisses de Manet à Picasso*.

LONDON, 16 November - 21 December 1978, The Lefevre Gallery, *Les Fauves*. Preface by D. Sutton.

MALINES, 14 September-16 November 1969, Cultureel Centrum Burgmeester Antoon Spinoy, *Fauvisme in de Europese Kunst*. Preface by J. Leymarie, Em. Langui and D. Van Daele.

MARSEILLES, 26 June - 1 September 1962, Musée Cantini, *Gustave Moreau et ses élèves*. Preface by J. Cassou.

MUNICH, see PARIS, 1966.

NEW YORK, 1941, Marie Harriman Gallery, *Les Fauves*. Preface by R. Lebel.

— 8 October 1952 - 4 January 1953, The Museum of Modern Art, *Les Fauves*. Preface by J. Rewald.

— 1970, The Museum of Modern Art, *Four Americans in Paris. The Collections of Gertrude Stein and her family*.

— 13 November - 23 December 1970, Sidney Janis Gallery, *Les Fauves*. Text by G. Duthuit and R. Lebel.

— 26 March - 1 June 1976, The Museum of Modern Art, *The Wild Beasts. Fauvism and its Affinities*.

OSAKA, 15 November-8 December 1974, Galeries Seibu Takatsuki, *Les Fauves*. Text and catalogue by F. Daulte.

PARIS, 1926, Grand Palais, *Trente Ans d'art indépendant*.
— 15 - 30 April 1927, Galerie Bing, *Les Fauves, 1904 à 1908* (Dufy, Friesz, Derain, Matisse, Marquet, Vlaminck, Manguin, Braque, Czobel, Camoin, Puy). Preface by W. George (reprinted in *L'Art vivant*, No. 54, 15 March 1927, pp. 206-8).
— December 1933 - January 1934, Les Expositions de "Beaux-Arts et de la Gazette des Beaux-Arts", *Seurat et ses amis. La suite de l'impressionnisme*. Preface by P. Signac.
— November-December 1934, Exposition de la Gazette des Beaux-Arts, *Les Fauves. L'atelier de Gustave Moreau*. Preface by L. Vauxcelles, catalogue by R. Cogniat.
— 1935, Petit Palais, *Les Chefs-d'œuvre du Musée de Grenoble*. Preface by J. Robiquet, catalogue by G. Barnaud.
— June-October 1937, Petit Palais, *Les Maîtres de l'art indépendant 1895-1937*. Preface by R. Escholier.
— 13 June - 11 July 1942, Galerie de France, *Les Fauves. Peintures de 1903 à 1908*.
— 14 January-15 February 1947, Galerie de France, *L'Influence de Cézanne. Œuvres de 1903 à 1914*.
— June-September 1951, Musée National d'Art Moderne, *Le fauvisme*. Preface by J. Cassou, catalogue by G. Vienne.
— 7-29 November 1952, Galerie Nina Dausset, *Symbolistes. Divisionnistes, Fauves. Hommage à Gustave Moreau*.
— 1952, Musée des Arts Décoratifs, *Cinquante Ans de peinture française dans les collections particulières de Cézanne à Matisse*.
— November 1960-January 1961, Musée National d'Art Moderne, *Les Sources du XXᵉ siècle. Les Arts en Europe de 1884 à 1914*. Introduction and text by J. Cassou, texts by G. C. Argan and N. Pevsner, catalogue by J. Cassou and A. Châtelet.
— 7 March-31 May 1962, Galerie Charpentier, *Les Fauves*. Preface by R. Nacenta.
— November 1963, Galerie Romanet, *Deux Cents aquarelles et dessins de Renoir à Picasso*. Text by A. Romanet.
— December 1964 - February 1965, Musée du Louvre, *Collection George et Adèle Besson*. Preface by J. Cassou.
— 12 October - 6 November 1965, Galerie de Paris, *La Cage aux Fauves du Salon d'Automne 1905*. Preface by J. Cassou, text by P. Cabanne.
— 1965, Galerie M. Knoedler & Cie, *Quarante Tableaux d'une collection privée* (Pierre Lévy, Troyes). Text by W. George.
— September 1965-January 1966, Musée du Louvre, *Chefs-d'œuvre de la peinture française dans les musées de Leningrad et de Moscou*.
— 15 January - 6 March 1966, Musée National d'Art Moderne, *Le Fauvisme français et les débuts de l'expressionnisme allemand*; MUNICH, Haus der Kunst, 26 March - 15 May 1966. Prefaces by B. Dorival and L. Reidemeister, catalogues by M. Hoog.
— 1966, Orangerie des Tuileries, *Collection Jean Walter-Paul Guillaume*.
— 1966, Musée Galliéra, *60 Maîtres de Montmartre à Montparnasse, de Renoir à Chagall* (Modern Art Foundation Oscar Ghez, Geneva). Catalogue by O. Ghez, F. Daulte and E. Gribaudo.
— 1966, La Palette Bleue, Romanet-Rive Gauche, *Cent Dessins et aquarelles de Renoir à Picasso*.
— June 1967, La Palette Bleue, Romanet-Rive Gauche, *Fauves et Cubistes*.
— 1967, Orangerie des Tuileries, *Chefs-d'œuvres des collections suisses de Manet à Picasso*. Texts by J. Chatelain, F. Daulte, H. Adhémar, catalogue by F. Daulte.
— 7 May - 7 June 1969, Galerie Schmit, *Cent Ans de peinture française*.

— 26 May - 27 July 1970, Musée National d'Art Moderne, *L'Expressionnisme européen*. Texts by J. Leymarie, P. Vogt and L. J. F. Wijsenbeck.
— May-November 1971, Musée Delacroix, *Delacroix et le fauvisme*.
— 1973, Galerie Schmit, *Tableaux de maîtres français, 1900-1955*. Text by J. Bouret.
— February-April 1974, Grand Palais, *Jean Paulhan à travers ses peintres*.
— 22 November 1974 - 20 January 1975, Musée National d'Art Moderne, *Dessins du Musée National d'Art Moderne 1890-1945*. Texts by D. Bozo and P. Georgel.
— 1974, Caisse Nationale des Monuments Historiques et des Sites, *La Collection Germaine Henry-Robert Thomas, peintures, sculptures et objets d'art, XIXᵉ-XXᵉ siècles*.
— 1975, Musée Jacquemart-André, *Le Bateau-Lavoir, berceau de l'art moderne*. Texts by R. Huyghe and J. Warnod.
— 1976, Musée d'Art Moderne de la Ville de Paris, *La Donation Germaine Henry-Robert Thomas, peintures, sculptures et objets d'art*.
— 11 May - 25 June 1977, Galerie Schmit, *Choix d'un amateur*.
— 21 February - 20 May 1978, Musée d'Art Moderne de la Ville de Paris, *La Collection Thyssen-Bornemisza. Tableaux modernes*.
— 16 February - 16 April 1978, Orangerie des Tuileries, *Donation Pierre Lévy*. Introduction by M. Hoog.
— 10 May-30 June 1978, Galerie Schmit, *Aspects de la peinture française, XIXᵉ-XXᵉ siècles*.
RENNES, April-May 1952, Musée des Beaux-Arts, *Le Fauvisme*.
SAINT-GERMAIN-EN-LAYE, February-March 1967, *Chefs-d'œuvre des collections privées*.
SAINT-TROPEZ, 1 July - 16 September 1978, Musée de l'Annonciade, *D'un espace à l'autre: la fenêtre. Œuvres du XXᵉ siècle*. Texts by A. Mousseigne, A. M. Lecoq, P. Georgel, P. Schneider, D. Milhau, J. Vovelle, J. M. Royer.
STRASBOURG, 1963, Château des Rohan, *La Grande Aventure de l'art du XXᵉ siècle*. Introduction by H. Haug.
TORONTO, 11 April - 11 May 1975, Art Gallery of Ontario, *The Fauves*. Text by R. J. Wattenmaker.
TROYES, 6 - 28 November 1976, Hôtel de Ville, *A la découverte de la collection Pierre Lévy*.
— 18 June - 29 August 1977, Hôtel de Ville, *Donation Pierre Lévy, Deuxième exposition*.
TURIN, February-April 1964, Galleria Civica d'Arte Moderna, *80 pittori da Renoir a Kisling* (Modern Art Foundation Oscar Ghez, Geneva). Texts by F. Daulte and O. Ghez.
VENICE, 1950, XXV Biennale, *I Fauves*. Preface by R. Longhi.

Monographs

BRAQUE

BONJEAN, JACQUES, "L'époque fauve de Braque", *Les Beaux-Arts*, 18 February 1938, p. 4.
BRAQUE, *Cahiers de Georges Braque, 1917-1947*, Paris, Maeght, n.d. (1948).

— *Le Jour et la nuit. Cahiers de Georges Braque, 1917-1952*, Paris, Gallimard, N.R.F., 1952.

— "Pensées et réflexions sur la peinture", *Nord-Sud*, December 1917, pp. 3-5.

— (exhibition), Paris, Galerie Daniel-Henry Kahnweiler, 9-28 November 1908. Preface by G. Apollinaire.

— (exhibition), New York, The Museum of Modern Art in collaboration with The Cleveland Museum of Art, 1939. Preface by J. Cassou, text and catalogue by H. R. Hope, bibliography by H. B. Muller. New York, Simon & Schuster, 1939.

— (exhibition), Basle, Kunsthalle, 1960. Texts by A. Rüdlinger, P. Volboudt and C. Einstein.

— (exhibition), Munich, Haus der Kunst, 1963. Catalogue by D. Cooper.

— (exhibition), Paris, Musée du Louvre, from 26 May 1965, *Présentation de la donation Braque.* Catalogue by the technical services of the Création Artistique.

— (exhibition), Paris, Orangerie des Tuileries. October 1973-January 1974. Text by J. Leymarie ("L'espace et la matière"), catalogue by M. Richet and N. Pouillon. Paris, Editions des Musées Nationaux, 1973.

BRUNET, CHRISTIAN, *Braque et l'espace*, Paris, Klincksieck 1971.

CAHIERS D'ART, special number: "Georges Braque", 1933, Nos. 1-2, pp. 1-86.

CARRA, MASSIMO, see DESCARGUES, PIERRE.

COGNIAT, RAYMOND, *Braque*, Paris, Flammarion, 1970.

COOPER, DOUGLAS, *Braque*, London, L. Drummond, 1948.

DESCARGUES, PIERRE (introduction) and CARRA, MASSIMO (catalogue), *Tout l'œuvre peint de Braque, 1908-1929*, Paris, Flammarion, 1973.

EINSTEIN, CARL, *Georges Braque*, Paris, Chroniques du Jour, 1934.

FUMET, STANISLAS, LIMBOUR GEORGES, RIBEMONT-DESSAIGNES, GEORGES, "Braque", *Le Point,* October 1953.

FUMET, STANISLAS, *Braque*, Paris, Maeght, 1965.

GIEURE, MAURICE, *Georges Braque*, Paris, Tisné, 1956.

HOPE, HENRY R., *Georges Braque*, New York, The Museum of Modern Art, 1949.

ISARLOV, GEORGES, *Georges Braque*, Paris, José Corti, 1932 (with a catalogue of works from 1905 to 1929, unfortunately not illustrated).

LEYMARIE, JEAN, *Braque*, Geneva, Skira, 1961.

MANGIN, NICOLE, *Catalogue raisonné de l'œuvre de Braque*, Paris, Maeght (5 vols. published, the last of which doesn't go back beyond 1916).

MULLINS, EDWIN, *Braque*, London, Thames and Hudson, 1968.

PAULHAN, JEAN, *Braque le Patron*, Geneva-Paris, Trois Collines, 1946.

— "Vie imagée de G. Braque", *Arts*, 15 February and 22 February 1952.

PLEYNET, MARCELIN, "Georges Braque et les écrans truqués", *Art Press*, December 1973-January 1974, pp. 6-9.

POUILLON, NADINE, *Braque*, Paris, Nouvelles Editions Françaises, Le Musée personnel, 1970.

— see RICHET, MICHÈLE.

RICHARDSON, JOHN, *Georges Braque*, London, Penguin, 1959; Paris, Bibliothèque des Arts, 1961.

RICHET, MICHÈLE and POUILLON, NADINE, "G. Braque à l'Orangerie des Tuileries", *La Revue du Louvre et des Musées de France*, 1973, Nos 4-5, pp. 319-22.

RUSSELL, JOHN, *Georges Braque*, London, Phaidon, 1959.

VALLIER, DORA, "Braque, la peinture et nous. Propos de l'artiste", *Cahiers d'Art*, No. 1, October 1954, pp 13-24.

DERAIN

BASSANI, EZIO, "La maschera bianca di Vlaminck e di Derain", *Critica d'Arte*, Florence, No. 133.

DERAIN, ANDRÉ, *Lettres à Vlaminck*, Paris, Flammarion, 1955.

— "Propos sur l'art", *Prisme des arts,* November 1956, pp. 2-6.

— (exhibition), Paris, Musée National d'Art Moderne, 11 December 1954-30 January 1955. Catalogue by G. Vienne, text by J. Cassou.

— (exhibition), Paris, Galerie Charpentier, 1955, *Cinquante Tableaux importants de Derain.* Texts by R. Nacenta and G. Hilaire.

— (exhibition), London, Wildenstein Gallery, 1957. Catalogue by D. Sutton.

— (exhibition), Geneva, Musée de l'Athénée, 1959.

— (exhibition), Marseilles, Musée Cantini, 1964.

— (exhibition), London, Hayward Gallery, January-March 1973, *The Impressionists in London*, organized by The Arts Council of Great Britain. Introduction by A. Bowness, catalogue by A. Callen (5 pictures by Derain exhibited).

— (exhibition), Albi, Musée Toulouse-Lautrec, June-September 1974, *Derain connu et méconnu.* Preface by Cl. Roger-Marx, text by G. Diehl.

— (exhibition), Paris, Galerie Schmit, 12 May - 20 June 1976. Preface by J. Bouret.

— (exhibition), Paris, Grand Palais, 11 February - 11 April 1977. Texts by G. Apollinaire, A. Breton and A. Giacometti, catalogue by I. Monod Fontaine.

DIEHL, GASTON, *Derain*, Paris, Flammarion, n.d.

DORIVAL, BERNARD, "Un album de Derain au Musée National d'Art Moderne", *La Revue du Louvre et des Musées de France*, 1969, Nos 4-5, pp. 257-68.

— "Un chef-d'œuvre fauve de Derain au Musée National d'Art Moderne", *La Revue du Louvre et des Musées de France*, 1967, Nos 4-5, pp. 283-8.

FAURE, ELIE, *André Derain*, Paris, Crès, 1926.

GIRY, MARCEL, "Le curieux achat fait à Derain et à Vlaminck au Salon des Indépendants de 1905 ou deux tableaux retrouvés", *L'Œil*, September 1976.

— "Une composition de Derain: *La danse*", *A travers l'art français (Hommage à René Jullian)*, Archives de l'art français published by La Société de l'Histoire de l'Art Français, Paris, De Nobele, 1976, pp. 443-7.

HAYOT, MONELLE, "André Derain: une cote qui devrait monter", *L'Œil*, March 1973, pp. 38-41.

HILAIRE, GEORGES, *Derain*, Geneva, Cailler, 1959.

HOOG, MICHEL, *"Les deux péniches* de Derain, Musée National d'Art Moderne", *La Revue du Louvre et des Musées de France*, 1972, No. 3, pp. 212-16.

KAHNWEILER, DANIEL-HENRY, *André Derain*, Leipzig, Klinkhardt und Biermann, 1920.

KELLERMANN, MICHEL, *Catalogue raisonné de l'œuvre de Derain* (in preparation).

LÉVY, PIERRE (Madame), "Propos d'André Derain", *Prisme des arts,* November 1956, pp. 2-6.

LEYMARIE, JEAN, *Derain ou le retour à l'ontologie*, Geneva, Skira, 1948.

PAPAZOFF, GEORGES, *Derain mon copain*, Paris, Valmont, SNEV, 1960.

SALMON, ANDRÉ, *André Derain*, Paris, N.R.F., 1924.

— *André Derain*, Paris, Chroniques du Jour, 1929.

SUTTON, DENYS, *André Derain*, London, Phaidon, 1959.

VAUGHAN, MALCOLM, *Derain*, New York, Hyperion, 1941.
ZERVOS, CHRISTIAN, "Histoire de l'art contemporain, André Derain", *Cahiers d'Art*, 1938, pp. 173-84.

DUFY

BERR DE TURIQUE, MARCELLE, *Raoul Dufy*, Paris, Floury, 1930.
— "Collection Pierre Lévy: Raoul Dufy", *Album No. 4*, Paris, Mourlot, 1969; reproduced in LÉVY, PIERRE, *Des artistes et un collectionneur*, Paris, Flammarion, 1976, pp. 267-87.
BRION, MARCEL, *Raoul Dufy*, London, Phaidon, 1959.
CAMO, PIERRE, *Raoul Dufy l'enchanteur*, Lausanne, Marguerat, 1947.
CASSOU, JEAN, *Raoul Dufy, poète et artisan*, Geneva, Skira, 1946.
COGNIAT, RAYMOND, *Raoul Dufy*, Paris, Flammarion, 1967.
COURTHION, PIERRE, *Raoul Dufy*, Paris, Chroniques du Jour, 1928.
— *Raoul Dufy*, Geneva, Cailler, 1951.
— *Dufy*, with an introduction and notes. London, The Faber Gallery, 1954.
DAULTE, FRANÇOIS, "Marquet et Dufy devant les mêmes motifs". *Connaissance des Arts*, November 1957, pp. 86-93.
DEMETZ, DANIÈLE, "Le legs de Madame Raoul Dufy au plus grand nombre de musées français", *La Revue du Louvre et des Musées de France*, 1968, No. 6, pp. 399-402.
DESLANDRES, MADELEINE, *Dufy et le fauvisme*, thesis, Université de Paris-Sorbonne, 1969 (typed).
DORIVAL, BERNARD, "Les *Affiches à Trouville* de Raoul Dufy", *La Revue des arts*, 1957, No. 5, pp. 225-8.
— "Le legs de Mme Raoul Dufy au Musée National d'Art Moderne", *La Revue du Louvre et des Musées de France*, 1963, Nos 4-5, pp. 209-21.
DUFY (exhibition), Paris, Galerie Berthe Weill, October 1906.
— (exhibition), Geneva, Musée d'Art et d'Histoire, 1952.
— (exhibition), Paris, Musée National d'Art Moderne, 1953. Preface by J. Cassou, catalogue by B. Dorival.
— (exhibition), Honfleur, Musée de la Ville; Marseilles, Musée Cantini, 1954, *Hommage à Raoul Dufy*.
— (exhibition), Lyons, Musée des Beaux-Arts, 1957. Text by R. Jullian *(Les tentations de Dufy)*.
— (exhibition), Le Havre, Musée-Maison de la Culture, 1963, *70 œuvres léguées au Musée du Havre par Madame Dufy*. Text by R. Arnould.
— (exhibition), Paris, Palais du Louvre, Galerie Mollien, 1963. *Donations Dufy*. Text by B. Dorival.
— (exhibition), Lille, Palais des Beaux-Arts; Colmar, Musée d'Unterlinden; Chambéry, Musée des Beaux-Arts, 1964, Text by P. Quoniam, catalogue by G. Viatte.
— (exhibition), Tokyo, National Museum of Western Art, 1967; Kyoto, National Museum of Modern Art, 1968. Preface by B. Dorival.
— (exhibition), Hamburg, Kunstverein; Essen, Museum Folkwang, 1967-8. Texts by H. Platte, M. Berr de Turique and A. Robert.
— (exhibition), Bordeaux, Galerie des Beaux-Arts, 1970. Texts by R. Huyghe, J. Lassaigne and R. Cogniat, catalogue by G. Martin-Méry.
— (exhibition), Munich, Haus der Kunst, 1973. Preface by B. Dorival.
— (exhibition), Paris, Grand Palais (Salon d'Automne), 1973, *Hommage à Raoul Dufy*. Texts by B. Dorival and H. Gaffié.

— (exhibition), Monte Carlo, Sporting Club d'Hiver, 1974. Text by H. Gaffié.
— (exhibition), London, Wildenstein Gallery, October 1975. Preface by H. Gaffié.
— (exhibition), Paris, Musée d'Art Moderne de la Ville de Paris, 1976, *Œuvres de R. Dufy, peintures, aquarelles, dessins. Collections de la Ville de Paris*. Texts by J. Lassaigne, catalogue by A. Abdul Hak.
GAUTHIER, MAXIMILIEN, *Raoul Dufy*, Paris, Les Gémeaux, 1949.
LAFFAILLE, MAURICE, *Raoul Dufy, catalogue raisonné de l'œuvre peint*, vol. 1. Foreword by M. Laffaille, preface by M. Berr de Turique, biography by B. Dorival, Geneva, Editions Motte, 1972.
LASSAIGNE, JACQUES, *Dufy*, Geneva, Skira, 1954.
MARTIN-MÉRY, GILBERTE, "Hommage à Raoul Dufy" (on the occasion of the exhibition in Bordeaux, 1970), *La Revue du Louvre et des Musées de France*, 1970, Nos 4-5, pp. 305-8.
POUILLON, CHRISTIAN and NADINE, see WERNER, ALFRED.
RENÉ-JEAN, *Raoul Dufy*, Paris, Crès, Les artistes nouveaux, 1931.
ROGER-MARX, CLAUDE, *Raoul Dufy*, Paris, Hazan, Aldine des Arts, 1950.
THIRION, JACQUES, "Le legs Matisse et Dufy", *Art de France*, IV, 1964, pp. 364-8.
VINCENT, MADELEINE, "Trois œuvres de R. Dufy au Musée des Beaux-Arts de Lyon", *Bulletin des Musées Lyonnais*, 1958, No. 3.
WERNER, ALFRED, POUILLON, CHRISTIAN and NADINE, *Raoul Dufy*, Paris, Nouvelles Editions Françaises, 1970.
ZERVOS, CHRISTIAN, "Raoul Dufy", *Cahiers d'Art*, 1928.

FRIESZ

BRIELLE, ROGER, *Othon Friesz*, Paris, Crès, Les artistes nouveaux, 1930.
FLEURET, FERNAND, VILDRAC, CHARLES and SALMON, ANDRÉ, *Othon Friesz, œuvres 1901-1927*, Paris, Chroniques du Jour, Les Ecrivains Réunis, 1928.
FRIESZ (exhibition), Paris, Galerie Berthe Weill, 12 May-10 June 1905, *Peintures, pastels par Bouche, Dufrenoy, Fornerod, Friesz, Minartz*.
— (exhibition), Le Havre, 5-11 September 1906, *Vues d'Anvers*.
— (exhibition), Paris, Galerie Druet, November 1907. Preface by F. Fleuret.
— (exhibition), Paris, Galerie Charpentier, 1950, *Rétrospective Othon Friesz*. Preface by M. Gauthier, text by Ch. Vildrac.
— (exhibition), Geneva, Galerie Motte, October 1950, *Othon Friesz l'un des créateurs du fauvisme*. Text by W. George *(Friesz et la tradition vivante de la peinture française)*.
— (exhibition), Paris, Galerie Paul Pétridès, November-December 1950, *Fleurs, fruits, compositions, marines et portraits*.
— (exhibition), Lyons, Musée des Beaux-Arts, October-December 1953. Texts by R. Jullian *(Friesz et la tradition)* and M. Giry *(Friesz et le fauvisme)*.
— (exhibition), Paris, Musée Galliéra, October-November 1959. Preface by R. Héron de Villefosse.
— (exhibition), Honfleur, Grenier à Sel, July-August 1971. Texts by R. Barotte, J. Bouyssou and M. Saelens.
— (exhibition), Paris, Galerie Drouant, 1973.
GAUTHIER, MAXIMILIEN, *Othon Friesz*, Paris, Les Gémeaux, 1949.
— *Othon Friesz*, Geneva, Cailler, 1957.
GIRY, MARCEL, "Le paysage à figures chez Othon Friesz. 1907-1912", *Gazette des Beaux-Arts*, January 1967, pp. 45-57.

— "A propos d'un tableau d'Othon Friesz au Musée National d'Art Moderne", *La Revue du Louvre et des Musées de France*, 1970, No. 3, pp. 168-70.

SALMON, ANDRÉ, *Emile-Othon Friesz*, Paris, Nouvelle Revue Française, 1920.

— see FLEURET, FERNAND.

VILDRAC, CHARLES, see FLEURET, FERNAND.

MARQUET

BESSON, GEORGES, *Marquet*, Paris, Crès, Les Cahiers d'aujourd'hui, 1920 and 1929.

— *Marquet*, Geneva, Skira, Trésors de la peinture française, XXᵉ siècle, 1948.

DAULTE, FRANÇOIS, "Marquet et Dufy devant les mêmes motifs", *Connaissance des Arts*, November 1957, pp. 86-93.

— see MARQUET, MARCELLE.

DORIVAL, BERNARD, "Nouvelles œuvres de Matisse et Marquet au Musée National d'Art Moderne", *La Revue des Arts*, May-June 1957, pp. 115-20.

FOSCA, FRANÇOIS, *A. Marquet*, Paris, N.R.F., Les Peintres nouveaux, 1922.

JAMOT, PAUL, "Exposition de tableaux d'Albert Marquet" (Galerie Druet), *Chronique des arts et de la curiosité*, 23 February 1907, pp. 51-2.

JOURDAIN, FRANCIS, *Marquet*, Paris, Braun, 1948.

— *Marquet*, Paris, Cercle d'art, 1959.

MARQUET, JEAN-CLAUDE, *Catalogue raisonné de l'œuvre de Marquet*, in preparation.

MARQUET, MARCELLE, *Marquet*, Paris, Laffont, 1951; Hazan, 1955.

— *Vie et portrait de Marquet*; DAULTE, FRANÇOIS, *L'œuvre de Marquet*, Lausanne, Spes, La Bibliothèque des Arts, 1953.

— (exhibition), Paris, Galerie Druet, 11-23 February 1907.

— (exhibition), Paris, Musée National d'Art Moderne, October-December 1948. Texts by J. Cassou, G. Besson and Cl. Roger-Marx.

— (exhibition), Vevey, Musée Jenisch, 1953.

— (exhibition), Besançon, Musée des Beaux-Arts, 1955. Text by B. Dorival.

— (exhibition), Albi, Musée Toulouse-Lautrec, 1957. Text by G. Besson.

— (exhibition), Nancy, Musée des Beaux-Arts; Metz, Musée de la Ville, 1959, Text by G. Besson.

— (exhibition), Lyons, Galerie Saint-Georges, 13 April - 4 May 1961. Text by G. Besson.

— (exhibition), Lyons, Musée des Beaux-Arts, 1962. Text by R. Jullian *(Marquet peintre de l'eau)*.

— (exhibition), Hamburg, Kunstverein, November 1964 - January 1965. Introduction by H. Platte.

— (exhibition), Paris, Galerie Bernheim Jeune, 27 April - 13 July 1972. Text by Ch. Kunstler.

— (exhibition), Bordeaux, Galerie des Beaux-Arts, 9 May-7 September 1975; Paris, Orangerie des Tuileries, 24 October 1975-5 January 1976. Text by J. Cassou, M. Sembat and M. Marquet.

SANDOZ, MARC, "Il y a dix ans... Albert Marquet", *Le Jardin des Arts*, June 1957.

TERRASSE, CHARLES, *Albert Marquet*, Paris, Crès, L'art d'aujourd'hui, 1929.

— *Albert Marquet*. Paris. Albert Morancé, n.d., taken from the preceding work.

MATISSE

ALLEMAND, MAURICE, "Musée d'Art et d'Industrie de Saint-Etienne. Récentes acquisitions", *La Revue du Louvre et des Musées de France*, 1967, No. 2, pp. 115-24.

APOLLINAIRE, GUILLAUME, "Henri Matisse", *La Phalange*, No. 2, 15-18 December 1907; reprinted in MATISSE, *Ecrits et propos sur l'art*, Paris, Hermann, 1972.

BARR, ALFRED H., Jr., *Matisse, his Art and his Public*, New York, The Museum of Modern Art, 1951 (contains a basic bibliography).

BESSON, GEORGES, *Matisse*, Paris, Braun, Les Maîtres, 1943.

CRITIQUE, *Henri Matisse*. Texts by A. Masson, J. Cl. Lebensztejn, Y. A. Bois, D. Fourcade and P. Schneider, Paris, May 1974.

DIEHL, GASTON (ed.), *Les Problèmes de la peinture*, Lyons, Editions Confluences, 1945, pp. 237-40.

— *Henri Matisse*. Notes by HUMBERT, AGNÈS. Paris, Tisné, 1954.

— *Matisse*, Paris, Nouvelles Editions Françaises, 1970.

DORIVAL, BERNARD, "Nouvelles œuvres de Matisse et Marquet au Musée National d'Art Moderne", *La Revue des arts*, May-June 1957, pp. 115-20.

DUTHUIT, GEORGES, *Matisse, période fauve*, Paris, Hazan, Petite encyclopédie de l'art, 1956.

ESCHOLIER, RAYMOND, *Henri Matisse, 68 reproductions*, Paris, Floury, 1937.

— *Matisse, ce vivant*, Paris, Fayard, 1956.

FERMIGIER, ANDRÉ, "Matisse et son double", *Revue de l'art*, No. 12, 1971, pp. 100-7.

FLAM, JACK D., "Matisse's *Backs* and the development of his painting", *Art Journal*, summer 1971, XXX/4, pp. 352-61.

— *Matisse on Art*, London, Phaidon, 1973.

FRY, ROGER, *Henri Matisse*, New York, E. Weyhe, Chroniques du Jour, 1930.

GIRAUDY, DANIÈLE, "Correspondance Henri Matisse-Charles Camoin", *Revue de l'art*, No. 12, 1971, pp. 7-34.

GIRY, MARCEL, "Matisse et la naissance du fauvisme", *Gazette des Beaux-Arts*, May-June 1970, pp. 331-44.

GUICHARD-MEILI, JEAN, *Henri Matisse, son œuvre, son univers*, Paris, Hazan, 1967.

JACOBUS, JOHN, *Henri Matisse*, Paris, Cercle d'Art, 1974.

LASSAIGNE, JACQUES, *Matisse*, Geneva, Skira, 1959.

LE POINT, texts by G. Besson, R. Cogniat, R. Huyghe, J. Puy and J. Romains; *Notes d'un peintre sur son dessin* by Matisse. Souillac, No. XXI, July 1939.

MARCHIORI, GIUSEPPE, *Matisse*, Paris, La Bibliothèque des Arts, 1970.

MATISSE, HENRI, "Notes d'un peintre", *La Grande Revue*, 25 December 1908, pp. 731-45.

— *Ecrits et propos sur l'art*. Text, notes and index by D. Fourcade. Paris, Hermann, Collection Savoir, 1972.

— "Autres propos de Henri Matisse", introduced by D. Fourcade, *Macula 1*, 1976, pp. 92-115.

— (exhibition), Paris, Galerie Vollard, June 1904. Preface by R. Marx.

— (exhibition), Paris, Musée National d'Art Moderne, 28 July-13 November 1956, *Rétrospective H. Matisse*. Preface by J. Cassou, catalogue by G. Vienne.

— (exhibition), Saint-Paul-de-Vence, Fondation Maeght, 1969, *A la rencontre de Matisse*. Text by L. Aragon, catalogue by N. S. Mangin.

— (exhibition), Paris, Grand Palais, April-September 1970, *Exposition*

du centenaire. Text by P. Schneider, catalogue by the latter and T. Préaud.
— (exhibition), Marseilles, Musée Cantini, June-September 1974, *130 dessins de Matisse.* Text by Matisse.
— (exhibition), Paris, Musée National d'Art Moderne, 29 May-7 September 1975, *Dessins et sculpture.* Preface by P. Hulten, introduction by D. Bozo, text by D. Fourcade *("Je crois qu'en dessin j'ai pu dire quelque chose").*
NEGRI, RENATA, *Matisse e i Fauves*, Milan, Fratelli Fabbri, 1969.
PLEYNET, MARCELIN, "Le système de Matisse", *L'Enseignement de la peinture, essais*, Paris, Seuil, 1971, pp. 25-98.
PURRMANN, HANS, "Aus der Werkstatt Henri Matisse", *Kunst und Künstler* (Berlin), February 1922, pp. 167-76.
ROSENTHAL, LÉON, "Exposition de tableaux de H. Matisse", *Chronique des arts et de la curiosité*, 24 March 1906.
RUSSELL, JOHN, *The World of Matisse 1869-1964*, New York, Time-Life Books, 1969.
— "Matisse-en-France", *L'Œil*, April 1970, pp. 17-25.
SCHNEIDER, PIERRE, "L'exposition H. Matisse aux Galeries Nationales du Grand Palais", *La Revue du Louvre et des Musées de France*, 1970, No. 2, pp. 87-96.
SELZ, JEAN, *Matisse*, Paris, Flammarion, n.d.
SEMBAT, MARCEL, *Henri Matisse*, Paris, Nouvelle Revue Française, 1920.
TRAPP, FRANK ANDERSON, *The Paintings of Henri Matisse: Origins and Early Development (1890-1917)*, Ph. D. thesis, Harvard University, Cambridge, Mass., 1951.
XXᵉ SIÈCLE, *Hommage à Henri Matisse*, special number, 1970. Texts by J. Cassou, P. Courthion, J. L. Ferrier, T. Guichard-Meili, G. Jedlicka, H. Read, G. Rouault, S. Lazzarro, Y. Taillandier and A. Verdet.
ZERVOS, CHRISTIAN, "Notes sur la formation et le développement de l'œuvre de H. Matisse", *Cahiers d'Art*, Nos 5-6, 1931, pp. 229-316.
— "Histoire de l'art contemporain, Henri Matisse", *Cahiers d'Art*, 1938, pp. 147-72.

VAN DONGEN

BAZIN, GERMAIN, "Van Dongen", with a bibliographical note and bibliography by G. Bazin and Ch. Sterling, *L'Amour de l'art*, May 1933.
CHAUMEIL, LOUIS, "Van Dongen et le fauvisme", *Art de France*, I, 1961, pp. 386-9.
— *Van Dongen, l'homme et l'artiste, la vie et l'œuvre*, Geneva, Cailler, 1967.
DES COURIÈRES, EDMOND, *Van Dongen*, Paris, Floury, 1925.
DIEHL, GASTON, *Van Dongen*, Paris, Flammarion, 1968.
ERTEL, K. F., "Kees van Dongen anlässlich seines 90. Geburtstages", *Kunst*, vol. 65 (1966-7), pp. 567-70.
FIERENS, PAUL, *Van Dongen, l'homme et l'œuvre*, Paris, Les Ecrivains Réunis, 1929.
GUILLEMOT, MAURICE, "Exposition K. van Dongen" (Galerie Druet), *L'art et les artistes*, 1905, 2nd semester, p. 91.
HOOG, MICHEL, "Repères pour Van Dongen", *La Revue de l'art*, 1971, 12, pp. 93-7.
LOUP, FRANÇOISE, *L'Influence de Paris sur Kees Van Dongen*, thesis, Université de Paris-Sorbonne, 1971 (typed).
MARX, ROGER, " Exposition de peintures et dessins de R. Carré,

Delannoy, E. Torent, C. Van Dongen" (Galerie Berthe Weill), 16 January-15 February 1905, *Chronique des arts et de la curiosité*, 28 January 1905, p. 26.
MÉLAS, KYRIAZI JEAN, *Van Dongen et le fauvisme*, Lausanne-Paris, La Bibliothèque des Arts, 1971.
PARINAUD, ANDRÉ, "Riscoperta di Van Dongen", *Arti*, vol. 17 (1967), No. 10, pp. 13-17.
STERLING, CHARLES, see BAZIN, GERMAIN.
VAN DONGEN, KEES, *Van Dongen raconte ici la vie de Rembrandt et parle à ce propos de la Hollande, des femmes et de l'art*, Paris, Flammarion, 1927.
— (exhibition), Paris, Galerie Vollard, 15-25 November 1904. Preface by F. Fénéon (reproduced in FÉNÉON FÉLIX, *Au-delà de l'impressionnisme*, Paris, Hermann, 1966, pp. 150-1).
— (exhibition), Paris, Galerie E. Druet, 23 October - 11 November 1905.
— (exhibition), Paris, Galerie Bernheim Jeune, 25 November - 8 December 1908. Preface by M. A. Leblond.
— (exhibition), Paris, Galerie Charpentier, 1949, *Œuvres de 1890 à 1948.* Preface by A. Siegfried.
— (exhibition), Nice, Galerie des Ponchettes, 1959. Foreword by J. Thirion, texts by J. Cocteau and L. Chaumeil.
— (exhibition), Lyons, Musée des Beaux-Arts, 1964. Text by R. Déroudille *(Kees Van Dongen chroniqueur des années folles).*
— (exhibition), Paris, Musée National d'Art Moderne, 13 October - 26 November 1967; Rotterdam, Museum Boymans-van Beunigen, 8 December 1967-28 January 1968. Preface by B. Dorival.
— (exhibition), Marseilles, Musée Cantini, June-September 1969, *Hommage à Van Dongen.* Foreword by Ch. Wentinck, catalogue by D. Giraudy.
— (exhibition), Paris, Grand Palais (Salon d'Automne), 31 October - 27 November 1972. Text by J. Mélas Kyriazi.
WENTINCK, CHARLES, "Van Dongen, avant-propos", Revue *Marseille*, 1969, No. 78, pp. 41-4 (same text as in the catalogue of the exhibition in Marseilles, 1969).

VLAMINCK

BAZIN, GERMAIN, "Maurice de Vlaminck", with "Notices", *L'Amour de l'art*, June 1933, pp. 133-6.
BOUDAILLE, GEORGES, *Vlaminck*, Paris, Le Musée personnel, 1968.
CABANNE, PIERRE, *Vlaminck, paysages*, Paris, Hazan, Petite encyclopédie de l'art, 1966.
CARCO, FRANCIS, *Vlaminck*, Paris, N.R.F., Les Peintres français nouveaux, 1920.
CRESPELLE, JEAN-PAUL, *Vlaminck, fauve de la peinture*, Paris, Gallimard, 1958.
DUHAMEL, GEORGES, *Maurice de Vlaminck*, Paris, Les Ecrivains réunis, 1927.
FELS, FLORENT, *Vlaminck*, Paris, Marcel Seheur, 1928.
GENEVOIX, MAURICE, *Vlaminck*, Paris, Flammarion, 1954 and 1967.
GIRY, MARCEL, "Le curieux achat fait à Derain et à Vlaminck au Salon des Indépendants de 1905 ou deux tableaux retrouvés", *L'Œil*, September 1976.
JOLINON, JOSEPH, "La rencontre de Vlaminck avec Derain", *L'Art vivant*, No. 158, March 1932, p. 121.
KAHNWEILER, DANIEL-HENRY, *Maurice de Vlaminck*, Leipzig, Klinkhardt und Biermann, 1920.

MAC ORLAN, PIERRE, *Vlaminck, peintures 1900-1945*, Paris, Editions du Chêne, 1945.

PERLS, KLAUS G., *Vlaminck*, New York, Harper, 1941.

PETRIDÈS, PAUL, *Catalogue raisonné de l'œuvre de Vlaminck*, in preparation.

REY, ROBERT, *Maurice de Vlaminck*, Paris, Flammarion, 1955.

ROGER-MARX, CLAUDE, "Vlaminck ou le Fauve intégral", *Le Jardin des Arts*, April 1956, pp. 350-4.

SAUVAGE, MARCEL, *Vlaminck, sa vie et son message*, Geneva, Cailler, 1956.

SELZ, JEAN, *Vlaminck*, Paris, Flammarion, n.d. (1962).

VLAMINCK, MAURICE, *Tournant dangereux*, Paris, Stock, 1929.

— *Portraits avant décès*, Paris, Flammarion, 1943.

— *Paysages et personnages*, Paris, Flammarion, 1953.

— (exhibition), Paris, Petit Palais, 1933.

— (exhibition), Paris, Galerie Charpentier, 1956. Text by Cl. Roger-Marx.

— (exhibition), Berne, Kunstmuseum, 1961. Preface by H. Wagner.

— (exhibition), New York, Perls Galleries, 1968, *Vlaminck, his Fauve period, 1903-1907*. Text by J. Rewald.

WERTH, LÉON, *Vlaminck, vingt et une reproductions*, Paris, Bernheim-Jeune, 1925.

Index

List of Illustrations

270

273

Photo Credits

The author and publishers wish to thank all those who have supplied photographs for this book. The numbers refer to the plate numbers.

Amsterdam, Stedelijk Museum, Gemeente Musea Collection, 28, 77
Bagnols-sur-Cèze, Musée de Bagnols-sur-Cèze 17, 101 (Photo Lauros-Giraudon, Paris)
Baltimore, Baltimore Museum of Art 117
Basle, Galerie Ernst Beyeler 75
Besançon, Musée des Beaux-Arts 14 (Photo Studio Meusy, Besançon)
Bordeaux, Musée des Beaux-Arts 13, 20, 47
Buffalo, N.Y., Albright-Knox Art Gallery, Gift of Seymour H. Knox 12
Cambridge, Mass., Fogg Art Museum, Harvard University, Grenville L. Winthrop Bequest 43
Copenhagen, Statens Museum for Kunst 100 (Photo Hans Petersen, Copenhagen)
Geneva, Musée du Petit Palais 60, 74, 102, 130
— Jean Salomon Collection 111
Grenoble, Musée de Peinture et de Sculpture 46, 70 (Photo IFOT, Grenoble), 105
Houston, Texas, The Museum of Fine Arts, Gift of the *Houston Post* 55 (Photo Hickey & Robertson, Houston), 66, John A. and Audrey Jones Beck Collection 86 (Photo A. Mewbourn, Bellaire)
Le Havre, Musée des Beaux-Arts 37, 129 (Mme Raoul Dufy Bequest, 1962)
Leningrad, Hermitage 11, 56
Liège, Cabinet des Estampes, 89 (Photo Bockiau)
London, Tate Gallery 34

Lugano, Thyssen-Bornemisza Collection 85 (Photo Brunel, Lugano)
Lyons, Musée des Beaux-Arts 36
Merion, Pa., The Barnes Foundation 69
Montreuil-sous-Bois, Town Hall 42 (Photo Philippe Deleporte)
Moscow, Pushkin Museum of Fine Arts 56
New York, The Museum of Modern Art 121 (William S. Paley and Abby Aldrich Rockefeller Funds), 128
Nice, Musée des Beaux-Arts Jules Chéret 88 (Mme Raoul Dufy Bequest, 1962)
— Musée Matisse 4 (Photo M. Bérard, Nice)
Oslo, Nasjonalgalleriet 119 (Photo O. Vaering, Oslo)
Paris, Galerie Schmit 120
— Musée d'Art Moderne de la Ville de Paris 26, 58, 87 (Photo Bulloz, Paris)
— Musée Guimet 114, 115 (Photos Réunions des Musées nationaux, Paris)
— Musée Gustave Moreau 3 (Photo Bulloz, Paris)
— Musée du Louvre, Cabinet des Dessins 2 (Photo Réunion des Musées nationaux, Paris)
— Musée National d'Art Moderne, Centre Georges Pompidou 25, 39, 40, 72, 99 (Photos Réunion des Musées nationaux, Paris), 23, 53, 67, 78, 96, 106, 109, 125, 126
Pau, Musée des Beaux-Arts 24 (Photo M. L. Pérony, Pau)
St. Tropez, Musée de l'Annonciade 48 (Photos Réunion des Musées nationaux, Paris), 80
Troyes, Musée d'Art Moderne Pierre Lévy 45, 57, 112 (Photos André Godin, Troyes), 63, 97
Washington, National Gallery of Art, Chester Dale Collection 76
Private Collections 1, 5, 6, 7, 8, 9, 10, 15, 16, 18, 19, 21, 22, 29, 30, 31, 32, 33, 35, 38, 41, 44, 49, 50, 51, 52, 54, 59, 61, 62, 64, 65, 66, 68, 73, 79, 81, 82, 83, 84, 90, 91, 92, 93, 94, 95, 98, 102, 104, 107, 108, 110, 113, 116, 118, 122, 123, 124, 127

This book was printed in August 1982 by Paul Attinger,
Neuchâtel
The photolithographs were done by Cooperativa Lavoratori
Grafici, Verona (colour) and Atesa-Argraf SA, Geneva (black
and white)
The binding is the work of Mayer & Soutter, Renens
Production: André Rosselet and Marcel Berger

Produced in Switzerland